Twilight of the

Twilight of the Idols

*Hollywood and the Human Sciences
in 1920s America*

———

Mark Lynn Anderson

UNIVERSITY OF CALIFORNIA PRESS
Berkeley   Los Angeles   London

University of California Press, one of the most distinguished university presses in the United States, enriches lives around the world by advancing scholarship in the humanities, social sciences, and natural sciences. Its activities are supported by the UC Press Foundation and by philanthropic contributions from individuals and institutions. For more information, visit www.ucpress.edu.

University of California Press
Berkeley and Los Angeles, California

University of California Press, Ltd.
London, England

Library of Congress Cataloging-in-Publication Data

Anderson, Mark Lynn, 1960–
    Twilight of the idols : Hollywood and the human sciences in 1920s America / Mark Lynn Anderson.
        p.   cm.
    Includes bibliographical references and index.
    ISBN 978-0-520-23711-7 (cloth) — ISBN 978-0-520-26708-4 (pbk.)
    1. Motion pictures—Social aspects—United States.   2. Popular culture—United States.   3. Motion picture industry—United States—History—20th century.   4. Motion picture actors and actresses—United States.   5. Celebrities—United States.   I. Title.
    PN1995.9.S6A58 2011
    384'.80973—dc22

                                                                    2010040841

Manufactured in the United States of America

20   19   18   17   16   15   14   13   12   11
10   9   8   7   6   5   4   3   2   1

This book is printed on Cascades Enviro 100, a 100% post consumer waste, recycled, de-inked fiber. FSC recycled certified and processed chlorine free. It is acid free, Ecologo certified, and manufactured by BioGas energy.

For Alice
Wherever you are . . .

Denunciation of the misleading seduction of "consumer society" was initially the deed of elites gripped by terror at the twin contemporary figures of popular experimentation with new forms of contemporary life: Emma Bovary and the International Workingmen's Association. Obviously, this terror took the form of paternal solicitude for poor people whose fragile brains were incapable of mastering such multiplicity. In other words, the capacity to reinvent lives was transformed into an inability to judge situations.

—JACQUES RANCIÈRE, "THE MISADVENTURES OF CRITICAL THOUGHT"

CONTENTS

ILLUSTRATIONS

ACKNOWLEDGMENTS

Every author knows that books have no real beginnings or endings. It is impossible for me to say exactly where or when *Twilight of the Idols* took shape, but its first incarnation as a manuscript was as a doctoral thesis I wrote at the University of Rochester. Thus, my first thanks go to a wonderful dissertation committee, each of whom pushed me to think about mass media and personality in new ways. Lisa Cartwright, who chaired the committee, never let me forget about the astonishing everydayness of science or the real possibilities of popular scientific practices. Whenever I strayed too far from my earlier training in continental philosophy, D. N. Rodowick always found some way to remind me of its importance, helping me to thoughtfully pose new questions about history, power, and representation. Finally, Douglas Crimp taught me that it is both possible and necessary to do lucid critical work on sexual identity without forfeiting the real complexities and pleasures of lived sexuality. My first writing on what ultimately became the subject of that dissertation began in one of his seminars, a thoroughly life-changing experience for me. Thank you, Douglas.

At the University of Rochester, I was blessed to be amongst an incredible cohort of film studies graduate students, all of whom shaped my thinking about the cinema and its histories in one way or another. This group initially began with Mark Betz, Heather Hendershot, Amanda Howell, and Bethany Ogden, but later included Mark Berrettini, Kelly Hankin, Amy Herzog, Daniel Humphrey, and Joe Wlodarz. As a student of silent cinema, I was more than fortunate to be at the University Rochester were I was able to study with both Jan-Christopher Horak and Paolo Cherchi-Usai, two of the world's premier film archivists and both, in their different ways, important historians of the silent era.

Rochester, NY, is also home to the George Eastman House where much of the initial research for this book was conducted. My thanks to a wonderful staff of librarians there, including Becky Simmons and Rachel Stuhlman, but also Tracey Lemon. In the Motion Picture Department at George Eastman House, Ed Stratmann's assistance was (and remains) always invaluable, while Carol Radovich helped me locate important print and paper materials, just as Nancy Kauffman has done more recently. During my days at Eastman House, I benefited from the keen insight, good humor, and wonderful companionship of archivist Christel Schmidt. I also conducted extensive research at the Library of Congress where, on occasions now too numerous to recall, the legendary Rosemary Hanes and Madeline Matz made my life far better by making my work so much easier. While researching at the Library of Congress, my gracious hosts at the Blue Hotel in West Virginia, Sherryrobin and Charles Boland, always provided me with exceptional accommodations and with the pleasantest of company. Imagine waking to a breakfast of crawfish étouffée with fried green tomatoes. Every cultural historian should be so lucky.

Additionally, I visited several other archives while working on this book, including the Chicago Historical Society in Chicago, IL, and the Margaret Herrick Library, at the Academy of Motion Picture Arts and Sciences in Los Angeles, CA, where Barbara Hall's expertise and generous advice has led me to new ways of thinking about film history and about the purpose of collections. My gratitude also goes to the many interlibrary loan librarians and staff members at the various institutions where I have taught while working on the manuscript. As a former clerk in the interlibrary departments of more than one federal medical library, I feel a particular solidarity with these often underappreciated but dedicated workers. In chronological order, I want to thank the interlibrary loan staffs of Rush Rhees Library at the University of Rochester, the Warren Hunting Smith Library at Hobart and William Smith Colleges, the S. E. Wimberley Library at the Florida Atlantic University, and Hillman Library at the University of Pittsburgh. My gratitude is also fondly extended to Mary Ann Clark at the New York State Appellate Court Law Library in Rochester, NY, as well as to the library staff of the old Margaret Woodbury Strong Museum, also in Rochester. Finally, I want to acknowledge the work of Bruce Long and Marilyn Slater, two independent researchers who have aided scores of Hollywood historians by generously making accessible online their vast collections of materials related to, respectively, the William Desmond Taylor murder of 1922 and the life and work of actress Mabel Normand.

My work on *Twilight of the Idols* has benefited from the many colleagues and friends who have shared their critical insights with me at several professional conferences over the last fifteen years, including the annual meetings of the Society for Cinema and Media Studies and the bi-annual international congresses on

Women and the Silent Screen. These generous friends include Michael Aronson, Constance Balides, Mark Garrett Cooper, Mary Desjardins, Kathryn Fuller-Seeley, Jane Gaines, Lee Grieveson, Amelie Hastie, Sumiko Higashi, Jennifer Horne, Catherine Jurca, Charlie Keil, Jon Lewis, Denise McKenna, Adrienne McLean, Paul Moore, Anne Morey, Sara Ross, Nic Sammond, Shelley Stamp, Jacqueline Najuma Stewart, and Haidee Wasson. My colleagues in the Film Studies Program at the University of Pittsburgh have also been important for continually providing me with challenging new ways of thinking about the cinema and its past. I have the unbelievable good fortune to share my daily professional grind with the likes of Nancy Condee, Jane Feuer, Lucy Fischer, Randall Halle, Marcia Landy, Adam Lowenstein, Colin McCabe, Neepa Majumdar, Daniel Morgan, and Vladimir Padunov.

I want to single out my colleague and friend Eric Smoodin for special thanks. More than anyone else, Eric is responsible for my choosing to become a historian of the American cinema. I did not know it at the time, but my life changed forever when, almost by chance, I walked into his office in the Department of Literature at American University way back in the fall of 1986. Eric has been important to me in innumerable ways throughout my studies and professional career (not the least of which was his introducing me to the late Richard deCordova, another inspirational figure for me). While Eric remains a dear friend and mentor, he is also my ideal of a film historian.

Actually, it was Eric who took on this book project when he was still an editor at the University of California Press, but it has been Mary Francis who has seen *Twilight of the Idols* through to completion. I cannot imagine having a more wise, supportive and caring book editor, and I am deeply grateful for her understanding and patience, particularly while my life has taken so many unforeseen personal and professional turns over the years (mostly good ones). Part of Chapter 1 appeared as "Shooting Star: Understanding Wallace Reid and His Public," in *Headline Hollywood: A Century of Film Scandal*, edited by Adrienne L. McLean and David A. Cook (Rutgers University Press, 2001). A shorter version of Chapter 5 was published as "Reading Mabel Normand's Library" in *Film History* 18:2 (2006).

Finally, this book would have been impossible without Lynn Arner. There is not an argument or idea in this book that has not been shaped in profound ways by our many long conversations about cultural politics, institutional power, mass organization, the disruptive possibilities of pleasure, political economy, historiography, and the vicissitudes of struggle. While the words are mine, whatever is of value in these pages is also the result of Lynn's passionate dedication to intellectual work that is socially meaningful and politically useful. She is the Marx to my Engels, the Burns to my Allen. Only death shall tear us asunder.

Introduction

Inarguably one of the most important and influential essays written about mass culture during the last century, Walter Benjamin's "The Work of Art in the Age of Its Technological Reproducibility," is itself one of the most reproduced, translated, and widely circulated works of cultural criticism ever published. *Twilight of the Idols*, like so many other books, is an implicit engagement with several of the insights in Benjamin's essay, an engagement, in this case, that takes seriously his claims that mass culture was making possible new types of cultural authority and new forms of knowledge that could only be understood as particular instances of reception. Such instances could no longer be the prerogative of the traditional critic or connoisseur, but were now controlled by the masses whose spontaneous yet coordinated responses to cultural works constituted radically new forms of diversified expertise. As is well known, Benjamin considered the technological basis of the motion picture as well as the industrial basis of the cinematic institution to be the most progressive manifestations of this social transformation. "It is in the technology of film, as of sports, that everyone who witnesses these performances does so as a quasi-expert."[1] However, Benjamin's view of the Hollywood film industry was similar to those held by many European intellectuals, seeing America's dominance in the world film market as the exploitation of these new conditions for increasing the profits and furthering the power of an elite capitalist class. Despite the progressive potential of a few Hollywood motion pictures—the films of Charles Chaplin, for example—Benjamin saw Hollywood as more or less concomitant with fascism in its mystification of a few exceptional individuals as personalities worthy of popular devotion. In other words, the Hollywood star system was, for Benjamin, little more than a cult of personalities.

Nevertheless, "The Work of Art in the Age of Its Technological Reproducibility" makes the film actor and the new technological conditions under which actors must perform the most sustained example of the types of expertise that were coming to be realized in mass reception. Describing both the temporal and spatial distances of the film audience from the actor's performance, a performance that is, nevertheless, viewed up close, as well as the mechanical mounting of that performance through editing, Benjamin discusses at length the actor's alienation from himself as image. It is the image only, and not the living actor, that now appears before the public. Because the film audience responds to a mechanically recorded performance its members assume a newly critical attitude toward that performance by identifying with the recording device, the camera/projector. Benjamin also describes this critical reception of motion pictures by the masses in mechanical terms ("a collective ratio") and he sees the audience as subjecting the actor's performance to a series of segmental optical tests, what we might now call screen tests. Given that some of these filmed actors were also widely known international movie stars whose images and voices were further duplicated and dispersed in newspapers, magazines, and on radio broadcasts—across those emergent mass media that so deeply interested Benjamin—it is somewhat surprising how emphatically he derided the star system as incapable of any revolutionary potential. "Not only does the cult of the movie star which [film capital] fosters preserve that magic of the personality which has long been no more than the putrid magic of its own commodity character, but its counterpart, the cult of the audience reinforces the corruption by which fascism is seeking to supplant the class consciousness of the masses."[2] Rather than treating the movie star as a commodity form itself, Benjamin views the film star as an epiphenomenal distortion of motion picture capital, an ideological effect leading to both commodity fetishism and audience reification. While such a position is understandable within the context of rapidly spreading fascism and in light of Benjamin's embrace of Dziga Vertov's anti-Hollywood militancy, I have always been dissatisfied with such a summary dismissal of the star system as holding any historical potential for progressive social transformation. *Twilight of the Idols* grew from that dissatisfaction. If, by the mid-1930s, the star system "may have long been no more than putrid magic," it is not at all clear to me that it always was so or that it remains so in every instance. With this book I contend that the early Hollywood star system functioned, like so many other early twentieth-century cultural institutions in the process of formation and like the cinema itself, as a means for the masses to take "an interest in understanding themselves and therefore their class consciousness."[3] By a certain point, definitely by the First World War, the star system had become so inextricable from the American cinema that it, in turn, would become one of the chief sites for the studios to fully wrest control of the cinema away from a mass audience. Because the industrial and financial powers represented by the American studio system successfully narrowed the cultural context of motion pictures to principally issues of entertainment and consumption, in part through managing the discourse on personality, Benjamin and other cultural critics mistakenly identified the star system as inherently reactionary.

In this book I examine the Hollywood star system of the 1920s as an important site for theorizing the historical construction and eventual containment of a mass audience. My aim is to demonstrate the cinema's participation in the popularization of a set of knowledge categories about deviance and identity, a popularization that was made possible, in part, by transformations of film stardom after the First World War and by Hollywood's historical and discursive relations to the modern human sciences: psychology, sociology, and anthropology. The film star of the 1920s, either through dramatic roles in modern photoplays or through public scandal, often embodied new popular scientific conceptions of personality and personality disorders. Furthermore, these new understandings of personality transformed the star system itself, in that they made the star both an object of a new rhetoric of interpretation based on the organic development of subjectivity and a new site for social intervention and industrial regulation. Thus, rather than seeing the film star as registering or reflecting emerging notions of abnormality, this project maintains that certain media personalities were productive of knowledge about deviance and disease, and that the audiences of film stars in the 1920s became both students of the deviant personality and potentially susceptible to the star's presumed destructive influences.

Drawing on historical resources such as fan magazines and trade journals, as well as newspapers and tabloids, *Twilight of the Idols* describes how Hollywood's promotion of individual stars (Mabel Normand, Wallace Reid, and Rudolph Valentino) was responsive to a growing popular interest in abnormal personalities and deviant behavior, an interest that was not simply the paranoid imaginings of the era's many conservative social reformers. The most convincing evidence for a widespread interest in deviant personalities is the amount and type of coverage that the nation's newspapers and tabloids devoted to sex, drug, and crime scandals involving both prominent celebrities and those whose celebrity was the result of their deviance. Furthermore, these celebrity scandals notwithstanding, star publicity of the postwar period sought to speak a more modern discourse about personality by reference to contemporary psychological and sociological theories of human development. Thus, this book draws on works of psychology and of social science, not so much to uphold a distinction between the original (scientific theory) and its quotation (publicity), but to chart out the logics of a larger cultural construction of the deviant personality and to demonstrate and explain the cinema's contributing role.

Even though I discuss women celebrities here, much of my study concerns the personalities of male film stars of the period. The rationale for such a focus is that it was principally the dynamics of male deviance as an object of both public fascination and scientific inquiry that produced a specific transformation of the star-audience relation in this historical period. It was also during this period that deviance came to be understood more and more as a developmental phenomenon; males were often assumed to have a more complex trajectory of psychological and social development as a result of the demands of (masculine) public life. For these reasons, male deviance posed an important set of problems for a public institution such as the cinema. While there were certainly female stars who were considered deviant, or who performed deviance in different ways, women's relation to deviance was constructed differently and often understood in the literature on deviance within the more circumscribed sphere of the domestic. Hollywood's continual acknowledgment of its own social effects in this period, together with its attempts to educate its audiences about public life and social conditions, meant that male deviance, as an abnormality of psychological adjustment and socialization, had to be negotiated within a system of mass communications whose star system was thought to be as emotionally affective as it was educational. In other words, the film industry had to attend to and represent its own role in the creation or prevention of social problems.

Because I consider the ways in which the star system participated in transformations of modern understandings of personality and deviance, this project is in dialogue with current work in film studies (especially, of course, work on film stars and the star system), American cultural history, and queer theory. While each chapter is organized around specific media personalities, I am not centrally interested in producing studies of individual stars. I write about particular celebrities only in order to demonstrate the cinema's historical relations to other institutions and to specify as clearly as possible those discourses that spoke about particular types of identities that Hollywood movie stars of the period often exemplified through the ways they appeared before the public. Thus, *Twilight of the Idols* is not principally a book about male film stars or even masculinity, though gender definition counts throughout this study as a crucial context for mass cultural address and popular reception. In many ways, this study is more interested in contestations over gender and radical gender transience at particular sites of receptions where the gendering of audiences remained crucially indeterminate and, therefore, became an impetus for regulatory concerns. Such contestations over gender definition cannot be divorced from considerations of sexuality, social class, race, and ethnicity. During the period covered by this study, the matinée idol was a prominent mass cultural figure commanding the attention of millions. He seemingly lived his life in public view, and he was available for projects far beyond the scrutiny of traditional authorities. The new possibilities of the matinée idol were quickly curtailed through trivializing his cultural significance as merely a symptom of a cult mentality. *Twilight of the Idols* refuses this trivialization and seeks a return to those unaccountable possibilities. As film historian Lea Jacobs has recently shown, the early twentieth century saw the emergence of a set of critical discourses on taste that eventually cast the romantic dramas of the early 1920s, that place where the matinée idol most commonly made his on-screen appearance, as overly sentimental, old-fashioned, and unsophisticated, attributions clearly not innocent of gender, racial, and sexual connotations. Jacobs convincingly demonstrates how those romantic dramas that were built around the single male star in the early 1920s were soon eclipsed in the latter part of the decade by Hollywood's promotion of the romantic star duo; how, for example, Rudolph Valentino comes to be replaced as a star attraction by Greta Garbo and John Gilbert as a star couple.[4] It is more than likely that the attacks on sentimentality discussed by Jacobs played a key role in disciplining a mass audience to see the conflicted passion of the heterosexual couple as the key dramatic issue worthy of their interest, investment, and aesthetic education.[5]

Important contributions to the study of stars have also been made in separate studies by Richard deCordova and Janet Staiger. They have sought to ground the study of film stars within analyses of the star system as both an economic and a semiotic system. In their work, the star is understood in terms of her or his historical conditions of existence within the institutional practices of the cinema.[6] For deCordova and Staiger, the star system emerged in the 1910s out of a particular industrial refinement of the picture personality (an actor's performed identity over a series of films), one that grafted onto that personality a publicity discourse about the real life of the particular performer. The revelations of the personal life of the film performer established a continuous circuit of consumption and a new model of spectatorship where every film appearance of a particular star and every mention of the star within a publicity discourse promised to add something new to the viewer's knowledge of and pleasure in that star's identity.

Staiger and deCordova seek to account for the historical appearance of the star within the parameters of the cinema as an institution. My study extends their work by analyzing some of the ways in which the appearance and development of the film star related to larger transformations of knowledge and subjectivity. I pose questions about the roles that film stars and the star system played within the broader cultural field of modernity outside of the cinema. Along these lines, deCordova ends his study by considering competing historical models of continuity and discontinuity to explain the star scandals of the early 1920s. Rather than settling on an account that views the scandals as a rupture or crisis within the system, he suggests, via Michel Foucault, that the scandals conformed to a more encompassing modern project: "The star system continually set us out on an investigation, an investigation that is, both in its methods (eliciting confessions and unveiling secrets) and in its promised result (revealing the sexual as the ultimate, ulterior truth of the player's identity), closely tied to the construction and deployment of sexuality in modern times."[7] Taking deCordova's suggestion as my starting point, I seek to demonstrate that the star system as it developed after the First World War not only resembled those strategies of power described by Foucault in *The History of Sexuality* and elsewhere—the confession, the case history, the life sciences—but that it was an integral participant in the elaboration of personal identity and psychological health during the early twentieth century.

Previous approaches to early film stars have often failed to provide any sustained analysis of the political importance of film stardom for changes in U.S. society and the entrenchment of a hegemonic mass culture.[8] This is partially explained by the predominance of the institutional paradigm of film history that grew out of apparatus theory in the 1970s, where the cinema's ideological work could be understood in terms of an autonomous system of filmic signification. Cultural studies, though, is one area where stardom has been analyzed within its larger social context. The work of Richard Dyer,[9] in particular, has led to an understanding of stars as unstable cultural texts that either embody or enact specific sets of social tensions or contradictions. As a film scholar, Dyer adopts a broader framework of cultural analysis that addresses the diverse and divergent reception contexts for celebrity personalities. For Dyer and others, the star-as-text functions to reproduce, resist, or unmask contradictions within dominant social ideologies for historically situated audiences. Drawing on the earlier work of Edgar Morin,[10] Dyer sees stars as composites of contradictory qualities that relate to societal instabilities at specific historical moments. The combination of innocence and sexuality of Marilyn Monroe, for example, can be related to conflicts between normative morality and discourses on feminine sexuality within 1950s patriarchy.[11] Because the star persona is an intertextual construct whose identity is informed by ideological contradiction, the star as a complex social sign is a potential site for oppositional readings, especially by marginalized social and cultural groups. Such an approach has produced some important analyses of individual stars and of the uses different audiences make of particular stars.[12] However, a difficulty immediately arises in determining to what extent the meanings that might be produced by marginalized audiences are, in fact, in any way oppositional. As media scholar Judith Mayne has cautioned, "it has been crucial to contest readings that would posit a wholly successful system of control and manipulation as the essence of mass culture, but all too frequently what is left out of the 'leaks' is the complex way in which subversion and the status quo are not necessarily opposed, but rather constantly enmeshed with each other."[13] Mayne points to the need to interrogate the incoherencies and contradictions of cultural texts (such as stars) from a position that is skeptical about the easy decidability of their effects. Furthermore, she suggests that such incoherencies are often definitive of the normative work of many cultural products.

In *Twilight of the Idols*, I propose that the star scandals of the early 1920s and the resulting "crisis" of the star system, as well as the subsequent transformations of the Hollywood film star, worked to reiterate and consolidate a set of new hegemonic categories of social deviance and psychological abnormality. It is important to note that these new categories were themselves often understood in terms of incoherence and disintegration, and I examine the ways that these notions of deviance and abnormality were articulated in the American cinema of the 1920s. By analyzing the various interrelations between star discourses and theories of human development and personality, I wish to situate the deviant silent film star within a broader context of cultural practices in order to demonstrate the star system's integration with other modern systems of knowledge production. In this way, I seek to contribute to ongoing discussions about mass culture and spectatorship by reading star culture as part of a broader cultural transformation that was significantly influenced by the historical emergence of the human sciences as a mode of popular understanding. For while the human sciences were certainly important for the industrial and governmental regulation of film through censorship boards, audience studies, and reform movements, they also provided a framework and a point of reference for film audiences to interpret motion picture stories and the stars who appeared in them. Furthermore, these "new" forms of knowledge about personality and development, as they were taken up by the mass media, gave audiences important new ways to understand their own relationship to film celebrities and the industry. How that self-understanding finally related to the definition of a mass audience in the 1920s is a story that *Twilight of the Idols* seeks to tell.

Twilight of the Idols also takes up and expands deCordova's argument that sexuality might be the ultimate "truth" of the star's identity, and that sexual identity, in large measure, accounts for our fascination with the star. I argue here that sexuality powerfully determined the ways in which star discourses operated and the ways in which particular star identities were able to appear within the mass media. I do not assume, however, that discourses about sexuality during the late silent period worked to reveal to audiences a fixed, autonomous, and private identity that was in some way perceived as the "true" personality behind the more "public" layers of a performer's identity. If the rhetorical gestures of sensational journalism and tabloid exposé supported such a model of identity, that model needs to be further contextualized within the interpretive strategies that were available to cinema audiences through popularized ideas of public life and mental health, as well as through their own social experiences. I seek to show that the

Hollywood star as deviant personality, particularly the male star, was produced and popularly received within the field of sexuality (as conceived through the scientific and institutional discourses of the period) primarily through his or her shifting relations to others. One of the implications of my argument is that audiences of the Hollywood film star in the late silent period were encouraged to understand the star's identity as a product of discernible social and psychological relations, relations in which those audiences themselves played an active part. This mutuality of the star-audience relationship is evinced in reformers' concerns about the influence of certain stars on susceptible audience members and the possible dissipative effects of stardom on the lives of the stars themselves. Such ideas about the social effects of motion picture personalities had relevance because they were coextensive with a logic of star promotion and publicity that emphatically deployed scientific models of personal development and social behavior to explain cinema stars' personalities and their popular appeal.

One of the assumptions of this historical project is that the very notion of personality was being contested within mass culture at this time. It has been assumed by many cultural historians that although there were many versions of "the psychological" recognizable in American culture during the 1920s, personality was always more or less equated with individuality and "the psychological" always represented some model of subjective depth. For example, in an essay on the popularization of psychology, cultural historian Joel Pfister works from the assumption that "by the 1920s a divide was often in place between movements of 'personal' and 'political' emancipation." He concludes "that the psychological was glamorized successfully as a value, an identity, and a performance of self in large part because it was connected to related writing of the self during the 1910s and 1920s."[14] Not surprisingly, the majority of the texts that Pfister uses to locate this "writing of the self" are taken from middle-class culture: Floyd Dell and Max Eastman of the bohemian socialist publication *The Masses*, the plays of Eugene O'Neill, and society magazines such as *Vanity Fair*. While these texts circulated at all levels of society, there is no reason to assume that their respective representations of personality were always received as validating the forms of middle-class individualism and subjectivity that they seemingly promoted. This study begins with the assumption that the political and the personal were not necessarily becoming mutually exclusive at all levels of American society during the 1910s and 1920s. It was only after a period of discounting and pathologizing alternative understandings and appropriations of personality that the modern ego gained widespread popular recognition.

Besides accounting for these emerging and conflicting conceptions of personal identity and their communication to a mass audience, my central concern is to investigate the kinds of complications in the status of knowledge about film stars that resulted from the popularization of the human sciences, especially as that knowledge devolved toward questions of sexual definition. In this respect, my work draws on queer theory and recent contributions to the history of sexuality, particularly the work of Eve Kosofsky Sedgwick. In *Epistemology of the Closet*, Sedgwick argues that a series of epistemological contradictions around sexual definition (what she refers to as "homo/heterosexual definition") have been crucial to almost every Western political and cultural project of the twentieth century. One of the central contradictions of sexual definition that Sedgewick identifies is the repetitive coincidence of minoritizing and universalizing discourses. Minoritizing discourses produce the homosexual as a distinct identity, one that is isolatable from the rest of the population, while universalizing discourses assume "that apparently heterosexual persons and object choices are strongly marked by same-sex influences and desires, and vice-versa for apparently homosexual ones."[15] What is important for Sedgwick is not the dominance of either one of these types of discourses at a particular moment, but the ways that they are simultaneously mobilized to structure the conditions of modern knowledge and experience.

The intractable but productive contradictions that exist between the minoritizing and universalizing discourses of sexual definition, which for Sedgwick constitute the crucial twentieth-century trope of the closet, bear a striking resemblance to the theorization of the film star by Morin, Dyer, and others. The star's simultaneous accessibility and distance, his or her combination of ordinary and extraordinary qualities, would seem to suggest that the film star is a particularly rich site for analyzing the operations of the closet. I argue here that the star culture of the late silent period raised specific problems of sexual definition through the promotion of certain stars. The male film star as deviant personality was particularly salient in revealing the erotic basis of an identity that was held in place by the unpredictable contingencies of one's knowledge about his past and his present relations to others. I seek to use the deviant star, then, to think about the way star culture both participated in and accommodated itself to popular scientific ideas about personality, developmental processes, and modern society. More specifically, I hope to challenge the notion that the ideological category of deviance worked only to marginalize, stigmatize, or simply erase groups of individuals within mass culture.[16] Instead, my project investigates how deviance functioned as an important interpretive category for film audiences in a particular historical period.

Chapter 1 provides an overview of the star scandals of the early 1920s, situating those scandals in the context of the public discussion about the health of the film industry and the need for government regulation and censorship. I pay particular attention to the stardom of Wallace Reid and his death from drug addiction in 1923. The publicity around Reid's addiction was important for the way it problematized the idea of normative masculinity. Reid embodied many of the social contradictions of narcotic use, and his death helped transform popular notions about the identity of the addict and the causes of addiction. I briefly consider Reid's stardom in relation to that of Douglas Fairbanks. Fairbanks and Reid emerged as important film stars at approximately the same time (1914–1919), and both were promoted by the film industry as typifying the ideals of the new (white) American male. On the one hand, Fairbanks continues to be discussed as playing an important role in the consolidation of new cultural standards of physical and mental health for men through his athleticism, his pragmatic optimism, and his rational leisure.[17] On the other hand, little attention has been paid to the way Reid's stardom, especially his posthumous stardom in the 1920s, helped define new ideas about masculine vulnerability, disease, and the dangers of undisciplined consumption.

In Chapter 2, I look at the trial of Leopold and Loeb, two young and wealthy men convicted in the summer of 1924 of murdering their fourteen-year-old neighbor. The trial took place during a transitional period between the construction of star criminals in the early 1920s and the proliferation of criminal stars at the decade's end (Al Capone, "Legs" Diamond, for example), making it an important moment in the development of different types of celebrity discourses.[18] I argue that, by 1924, the cinema and the Hollywood scandals had already played an important role in constructing a mass audience for the trial of Leopold and Loeb. The celebrity status of the two young murderers depended, in part, on a new conception of the media personality that was made possible by the previous Hollywood star scandals as well as by the deployment of psychoanalysis by the film industry to teach audiences how to read and understand unconscious motivations. In this chapter I read the Leopold and Loeb trial as having registered specific tensions that were developing around star-fan relations; these tensions resulted from the way that the discourses of criminality, entertainment, psychoanalysis, and male homosexuality informed one another at that particular historical moment. Furthermore, the trial and the publicity surrounding it marked a crucial moment for a particular ideological linking of homosexuality and criminality.

Chapters 3 and 4 are both organized around the mass reception of Rudolph Valentino. Valentino's stardom has taken on critical importance for theories of female spectatorship and for analyses of historical film audiences, primarily through the work of Miriam Hansen and Gaylyn Studlar. These scholars have been attentive to how issues of gender, sexuality, and ethnicity complicated Valentino's star image to provide audiences with alternative images of masculinity and gender relations. In Chapter 3, I take up Hansen's analysis of Valentino's masochism. For Hansen, the instability of Valentino's gaze supports an alternative regime of vision and desire for the female spectator. By approaching Valentino as a model of male deviance, I contextualize the so-called ambivalence of Valentino's erotic identity within a larger social conflict between divergent and competing popular notions of sexual identity. This conflict over the meaning of male sexual deviance resulted from differences between the visibility of the male invert in urban working-class culture—an identity appreciably different from our contemporary recognition of the homosexual—and middle-class ideas about gender, sexual identity, and object choice. The historical clash of these divergent conceptions of sexuality helps to explain how theories of sexual pathology played a significant part in Valentino's popular reception. I explore how the gender-transitive aspects of Valentino's star persona were intimately tied to a struggle over the meaning of male deviance and that the primary terms of that struggle were social class and ethnicity.

Studlar has situated the Valentino phenomenon within the rise of the "cult of the body" and the growing popularity of ethnic dance in the 1910s.[19] In Chapter 4, I continue this consideration of the star's relation to dance, but I shift the emphasis away from considerations of high-art ballet and middle-class dance culture. Instead, I inquire into Valentino's stardom in the context of a set of social concerns about race, ethnicity, and urban dance halls in the 1920s. I look at the ways cultural conceptions of ethnicity and race were involved in Valentino's deviant stardom and his association with exotic dancing. Richard Dyer has written about "whiteness" as a specific system of cultural discourses and practices that continues to play an important role in the creation and reception of films and film stars.[20] His work also suggests that "blackness," as a corollary system of signification and values grounded in racial difference, is similarly, though not isomorphically, implicated in the production of Hollywood film stars.[21] In this chapter, I isolate some of those sociological discourses within mass culture that figured blackness as a destructive social and sexual force which threatened to obliterate ethnic and racial distinctions altogether within the cultural hybridity of the metropolis. By performing various exotic ethnicities in his films, Valentino's Italian identity took on a fluidity that, while glamorous, was quite threatening to emerging notions of public health, social development, and the commodity form in consumer capitalism. I consider Valentino's stardom and sexuality in relation to these ideas about ethnicity, the modern city, and social disintegration, and I conclude that the imagined negating power of blackness, which helped underwrite public policies of racial segregation, played an important role in the different receptions of Valentino and in the construction of his audience.

Since the popular discourses on deviance that are evident within the mass media of the 1920s figured personality both as developmental and as socially relational, and since film stars of the period often performed deviant identities in a variety of ways, the audience's relation to the picture personality became an important area for scientific study and social intervention. Perhaps the most well-known result of this interest in star-audience relations was the publication of the Payne Fund studies in 1933, the culmination of more than six years of empirical research on the influence that motion pictures have children and young adults, investigations designed and conducted by various university educators and social scientists.

One of the main goals of the Payne Fund studies was to measure the effects of the cinema on audiences (particularly child and adolescent audiences) in terms of motion pictures' contribution to two general types of abnormality: sexual promiscuity and criminal delinquency. While not exclusively linked to gender identities, the former tended to be viewed as a greater risk for women, the latter for men. Yet sexual deviance in men, in the form of homosexual desire, was also a recurring if understated (or usually unremarked) concern of these studies, especially with respect to star worship. I argue here that the models of spectatorship and the specific constructions of gender differences that were employed in many of the Payne studies were made possible by specific tensions that developed within the star system and around cinema audiences' relation to Hollywood stars after 1919. These tensions resulted from a commingling of the discourses of deviance with entertainment practices, the particular way they informed one another at that historical moment, and the way modern conceptions of personality were articulated within the popular media in general and the star system in particular.

In Chapter 5, I discuss the scandal that engulfed Mabel Normand after the murder of Hollywood director William Desmond Taylor. While the scandal was ostensibly about the actress' intimate relations with the slain director, the deeper issues concerned Normand's status as an intellectual movie star interested in questions of psychology and philosophy. The attenuation of her career in the mid-1920s illustrates how the rapid implementation of regulatory discourses during the period was making mass cultural products such as stars subject to various forms of verification and institutional certification. Normand's fading stardom is significant since it provided an effective means of imposing upon the troubled star system a truth functionality that stigmatized individuals (both film stars and members of their publics) who misuse the mass media in claiming for themselves lives, identities, and desires that were unavailable to sanctioned authentication or that ultimately failed when subjected to independent scrutiny. The rather startling success of this particular regulatory project which found Mabel Normand so unworthy of popular adulation suggests that the star system of the early 1920s was more amenable to regulatory control through interrogations of gender and class than through the policing of race, ethnicity, and sexuality. At the end of the chapter, I once again look briefly at the Payne Fund studies and the impact that Hollywood film stardom, especially as it relates to the vicissitudes of deviance, had on these extensive sociological investigations of film audiences and sexual definition. Media historian Garth Jowett has pointed out that the Payne Fund studies, though a very important event in the history of film industry regulation, were not widely read by the public.[22] Yet, because the Payne Fund studies and their findings were often cited in news reports and editorials, they played an important role in shaping popular opinions about film and deviance. Moreover, these studies shared with a mass audience certain presumptions about audience-star relations and spectatorship. The Payne Fund studies did not use the category of the film star as a focus of research, but instead restricted themselves to a content analysis of films. Nevertheless, the rationale and research methods of many of these studies presupposed that the respective identities of the picture personality and the spectator were mutually sustaining ones. Whenever "test subjects" provided evidence of holding this same belief, however, they were seen as susceptible to the suggestive influences of the cinema. Thus, those types of mass cultural receptions that I have shown to have been cultivated by discursive problems of personality and sexual definition (through the intersections of star discourse and the human sciences) have now become definitive of a deviant film audience. I conclude the book by discussing the ways that the Payne Fund studies negotiated a terrain of mass culture where knowledge of socialization and psychological development had already left their mark.

A short explanation is in order about the title of this book. *Twilight of the Idols* is recognizable, of course, as the title of the English translation of *Die Götzen-Dämmerung*, one of the last books published by the German philosopher Friedrich Nietzsche before he became insane in 1889. My use of this title is meant as a brash or even reckless act of appropriation, somewhat in the spirit of the philosopher's own work. However, this book is neither an engagement with Nietzsche's ideas nor an application of his thought. While he was arguably one of the first critics of the emerging human sciences (and perhaps also an early practitioner), and while many of his ideas about psychology resonate with ideas that appear in these pages, at present I have no interest in pursuing these particular relations. Many people in North America during the early part of the twentieth century considered the translated works of Nietzsche quite dangerous, particularly when read by those who were ill prepared to understand his thought or resist its influence. Young people were particularly susceptible, and, during the Jazz Age, the philosopher was sometimes seen as providing youth with a falsely erudite justification for their rejection of convention and embrace of amorality.[23] It is the Nietzsche of the culture wars in 1920s America that the book's title most directly references. Nevertheless, like this book and like the early star system, Nietzsche was deeply interested in questions of pathology. His approach to health was one of curing pathology by seeking to understand degeneracy as an expressly human condition, thereby living through pathology's awfulness so as to avoid the real morbidity of delusion, hypocrisy, and rationalization. I propose that the Hollywood star system offered something similarly dangerous between 1920 and 1926.

The Early Hollywood Scandals and the Death of Wallace Reid

Just after the First World War, the word *junkie* entered into American parlance to describe a population of heroin addicts—a visible and growing population of male derelicts in and around New York City—who supported their drug habit by scouring that city's junkyards in search of scrap metal, which they then sold to junk dealers. As medical historian David Courtwright has noted, the emergence of the term *junkie* at the beginning of the 1920s marked an historical transition in the general demographics of narcotic addiction in the United States. No longer was the typical addict a white, middle-aged, middle- or upper-class rural housewife, whose addiction had begun when her physician administered therapeutic doses of morphine to relieve pain. The new addict was more likely to be a young, white male who decidedly belonged to the urban underclass and whose addiction was more likely to have started when he began sniffing heroin with his friends at cheap dance halls.[1] Yet junkie also rather neatly describes the transformation, in both popular and medical understandings of narcotic addiction, from a notion that morphinism was an organic disorder of the individual that resulted from medical treatment, to the view that narcotic addiction was a type of social disease, an unfortunate by-product of a modern industrial society and thus a pressing public health issue.

It was within the context of such a transformation that the popular film star Wallace Reid died in January 1923 at the age of thirty-one, due to complications resulting from an attempted withdrawal from narcotic addiction. Reid's death is generally considered one of the three most significant scandals of early Hollywood, along with the criminal trials of the film comedian Roscoe "Fatty" Arbuckle in 1921 and 1922 and the sensationalized murder of director William Desmond

Taylor in February 1922. Reid was remarkably handsome and had been a very successful matinée idol from the mid-1910s until his death. Like other popular male stars of the period such as Douglas Fairbanks and Thomas Meighan, Reid typified a rugged, all-American virility that was a compelling version of psychological and physical health for young white men. Often reported to stand at 6′ 3″ and to weigh approximately 190 pounds, Reid was usually portrayed in the fan magazines as a happy and playful giant. He was also represented as somewhat of a dilettante with scattered interests in music, painting, chemistry, automobile racing, book collecting, golf, and a host of other pastimes. A man of many accomplishments, Reid was presumably so full of wonder at the world that he could not be bothered to devote a great amount of time or attention to any single activity.

Although younger than Fairbanks by almost a decade, Reid was part of the same generation of film stars who, like Fairbanks, emerged in the mid-1910s to become public representatives of the newly formed movie colony in southern California. Unlike the newcomer Fairbanks, however, Reid had been working steadily in the film industry since 1910, making over one hundred films as a featured player for the Vitagraph, Universal, and Majestic film companies. When Jesse Lasky signed Reid with his company in June 1915, Reid was already a well-known and established performer, though Reid's popularity rose rapidly after Lasky paired him with Metropolitan Opera star Geraldine Farrar in a couple of prestige pictures directed by Cecil B. DeMille. Reid's masculinity also differed from the "vim, vigor, and vip" of Fairbanks by departing from the latter's insistence upon rational self-discipline. While Fairbanks's healthy manliness resulted from the adoption of a youthful mental attitude which valued carefully planned and regimented physical activities, Reid's boyish charm rested more on a naturally robust physique and a much more spontaneous athleticism. Although his many film performances and even the scandal with which his name is linked are largely forgotten today,[2] in the early 1920s, when it appeared as if the film industry itself was in danger of imminent collapse, Reid's drug addiction was a significant moment in the history of the star system and in the consolidation of Hollywood as a mass cultural institution. Reid's death afforded the film industry its first opportunity to explain how good stars can go wrong. The industry succeeded not only in containing the scandal of Reid's drug use, but in reinterpreting his death as both a private tragedy and a great public sacrifice. In this chapter I outline some of the specific strategies of this coverage, indicate its stages of development during and in the aftermath of the scandal, and draw some conclusions about the ways film audiences were encouraged to understand Reid's stardom and their own relationship to his death. Because the Reid affair had a more or less direct relationship to the continuing threats of external controls over the film industry, it is first necessary to lay out the larger historical and cultural contexts of the early star system and film regulation practices of the period before examining the media's attention to Reid's narcotic addiction.

THE BIRTH OF AN AGENCY

Historical accounts of U.S. film censorship often note that the star scandals of the early 1920s aided in the formation of the Motion Picture Producers and Directors of America (MPPDA), the most important regulatory agency to emerge within the film industry. Film historians are quick to add, however, that the MPPDA's other less publicized functions were to stave off federal antitrust interventions, to maintain the prevailing relations of production within the industry, to arbitrate costly litigious conflicts between distributors and exhibitors, and to control public information about Hollywood business practices. The industry's responses to star scandals are, then, often considered publicity diversions behind which the more important exercise of managerial power was concealed.[3] Nevertheless, part of the MPPDA's implicit public charter was to guarantee the moral quality of the industry's products and its personnel, particularly its stars and leading players. When prominent Republican politician Will Hays accepted the film industry's offer to head the newly formed MPPDA in early 1922, one of his immediate tasks was to reassure the many church groups, women's clubs, and other reform organizations then seeking federal oversight of the industry that the major Hollywood studios were seriously committed to improving the moral quality of their pictures. He was also charged with halting the further creation of any more state or local film censorship boards. Six states already had film censorship boards when Hays took up his post, and thirty-two additional states would consider new film censorship legislation in 1921 and 1922. Hays attempted to placate the moral and educational critics of the industry by appearing to patiently listen to their concerns and by promising stringent internal reforms. With Hays at the helm, the MPPDA successfully defeated new proposals for state censorship boards through extensive organized political action in individual states.[4] At the time he took up his post, Hays was President Harding's postmaster general, and he had served as the chairman of the Republican National Committee during the 1920 convention. Studio executives hoped that his supervision of the film industry through the auspices of the MPPDA would do for Hollywood's beleaguered reputation what the hiring of federal judge Kenesaw Mountain Landis had done for major league baseball two years before.[5]

Because of the number of public scandals involving film personalities in the years 1920–1922, Hays and Hollywood faced a relatively new type of demand for film censorship. Most movie reform efforts of the late 1910s had targeted film content as in need of improvement and had sought some way of censoring the so-called sex picture, as well as films depicting illegal acts or criminal behavior.

In the early 1920s the demand for cleaner pictures was soon joined by the demand for cleaner stars. The identity of the motion-picture performer had become a site for possible regulation and, at least for the year and a half following the arrest of Arbuckle in September 1921, the identity of the performer was one of the principal concerns of censorship efforts outside the film industry. Arbuckle, who had been arrested for the murder and rape of film actress Virginia Rappe, posed a relatively new set of problems for the smooth functioning of the star system, and it took Hays and film industry executives quite some time to develop effective strategies for controlling and avoiding the type of damage to Hollywood's image that had been caused by this and by other early scandals. By the time Reid's drug addiction was publicly revealed at the end of 1922, the industry's ability to manage star scandals had greatly improved.

Meanwhile, in the summer of 1922, U.S. Senator Henry Lee Myers introduced into committee a bill calling for the establishment of film censorship in the District of Columbia and another requesting a federal investigation into the motion picture industry. On the floor of the Senate he argued that film censorship measures were needed since "many of the pictures are pernicious" precisely because of the immorality of "those who pose for them," and he went on to mention Fatty Arbuckle, Virginia Rappe, William Desmond Taylor, and Rudolph Valentino[6] by name. Like many contemporary critics of Hollywood, Senator Myers used the notoriety of a limited number of sensational scandals to question the moral integrity of the entire filmmaking community and to suggest that its members spent their enormous salaries on "riotous living, dissipation, and 'high rolling.' "[7]

Representatives of the industry defended Hollywood by pointing out that the excesses of a few certainly did not mean that such behavior was indicative of the many. Several stars assured the press about the utter normalcy of their everyday lives and the wholesomeness of their habits, while others criticized the newspapers and tabloids for perpetuating false representations of Hollywood as a vice colony and for fueling the fanciful imaginations of fanatical reformers. D. W. Griffith attempted to expose the hypocrisy of the industry's moral critics by asking them, "Shall we attack the banks when a banker gets into the newspaper, or the church when a minister gets into the newspaper?"[8] Such questions may have had a certain amount of rhetorical force, but the comparison of film stars to bankers and ministers did not likely ring true for the vast majority of the filmgoing public. Film stars represented the film industry in ways that bankers or ministers could never represent the banking interests or the churches of America. This was in part explained by the mass public appeal of film stars as compared to the relative invisibility of the financial world and the smallness of the traditional parish. Film stars were widely known and widely admired, and they were sometimes treated not only as the definitive representatives of Hollywood, but, like famous statesmen or athletes, as representatives of the nation itself, especially during the period immediately following the First World War when film actors and actresses had greatly assisted the government in raising money for the war effort by participating in and publicizing the Liberty Loan Campaigns for the U.S. Treasury Department.[9]

Cleaning the Colony

One of the reasons why film stars were generally understood to synecdochically represent Hollywood, and why the early star scandals so seriously called into question the moral standing of the entire film industry, has to do with the way the star system had developed up to that point. During the second half of the 1910s, the publicity given to stars by the industry—and by its allied publications such as fan magazines—had sought to reveal more and more about the private lives of the stars. Not only was each film appearance of the stars of possible interest to the public, but the domestic lives and leisurely pursuits of the stars became an increasingly important part of industry publicity. As Richard de-Cordova has shown, the star system functioned, both economically and ideologically, through the recurring promise of new and more intimate information about a particular film personality with each new film appearance and with each new magazine article about or interview with that performer. This arrangement established an endless circuit of consumption wherein cinema audiences purchased star publicity in order to increase their knowledge about a particular film performer and to enhance their enjoyment of her or his films; likewise, they attended the star's films in order to possibly learn something else about that star's personality through her or his performance of a fictional character.[10] Yet, while each star was an advertisement for his or her next public appearance, every star was simultaneously an advertisement for the film industry as a totality. The lives of the stars, the homes in which they lived, the clothes that they wore, the recreations that each pursued—all worked to portray an image of Hollywood as a closed and intimate community of gifted artists and technicians who had embarked upon a grand experiment in corporate living and social mobility. "Early Hollywood was not the locale of studios," writes cultural historian Lary May, "[but] rather it was an almost mythic place where movie folk spent money on personal expression. This consumption encouraged creativity and freedom, while it served as a mark of success. A shrewd observer of the industry, producer William DeMille, saw that the movie people's 'conspicuous consumption' gave status to an often routine job, and reflected on the 'company that paid you.'"[11] The movie colony, as it was so often called by journalists, was the beautiful idealization of a smooth functioning industrial order where creative talent, drive, and imagination were quickly transformed into gorgeous homes, exotic automobiles, and idyllic lifestyles, the supreme expressions of personality within the new consumer culture.

During the early 1910s, even before the formation of the movie colony in southern California, the film industry had constructed its public face by thoroughly identifying itself with its beautiful stars, but by the early 1920s it was paying a very high price for such intimacy. The early Hollywood scandals had a way of sticking to everything, haunting those who were named in connection with them, and calling into question the social utility of Hollywood itself. Prior to 1920, film stars were stars, first and foremost, because they had appeared in films. While being featured in films might sound more like a necessary rather than a sufficient condition for film stardom, it must be remembered that the first film celebrities were promoted as having their celebrity status discovered or conferred upon them by the companies who featured them in their productions. It has been a part of the received history of the film industry that the star system began around 1909 from an initial "tidal wave of audience love" for particular performers who were regularly featured in pictures but who remained anonymous only because certain powerful production companies refused to reveal their names.[12] In this well-known version of the story, some of the early popular film performers were simply known to exhibitors and to the film-going public as the "Biograph girl" or the "Vitagraph girl" until producers finally began furnishing the names of their players to film exhibitors and to a curious public. Early film stars were, of course, represented as having appreciative audiences and as having vast popular appeal, but their celebrity was something given to them by the industry that placed them before the public. Audience interest and adoration were important, but the public's appreciation was often represented as only a validation of a company's ability both to find star talent and to know or accurately predict just what the public wanted and enjoyed.[13] Whether or not the first film celebrities appeared, in actuality, as the result of an irresistible public demand or whether they were primarily the creation of a producer's publicity, film performers were, from the very beginning, closely associated in the public's mind with company brand names.[14] The idea that the stars emerged "against the interest of the developing industry" was very likely the product of a later historical moment when the star system was in crisis. Instead, it was the seemingly identical interests of the stars and the studios that originally defined the early star system and which would eventually subtend the representation of Hollywood as a progressive corporate community in the late 1910s. After the scandals, star publicity and industry public relations would never again completely overlap or fit together quite so easily. What was this transformation all about?

First of all, there was a subtle change in the representation of the relationship between film stars and their employers. Hays's response to the attacks on Hollywood stars was quite guarded. The day before Myers addressed the Senate about the debauchery of film stars, Hays had addressed one of the most important and respected organizations committed to motion picture reform, the General Federation of Women's Clubs, whose delegates were then assembled in Chautauqua, New York. In his speech to the federation, without ever having to discuss the star scandals directly, Hays employed an ingenious strategy of acknowledging reformers' demands that the industry be accountable for the integrity of its performers. Hays alluded to and dispensed with the problem of immoral stars through the discourse of "cleaning house." He told the delegates, "There is one place and one place only where the evils can be eliminated and the good and great advantages of motion pictures retained . . . and that is at the point where and when pictures are made . . . and it is primarily the duty of the producers to do it."[15] By making the site of proposed reform identical to the site of film production, Hays was able to have it appear that Hollywood, defined here as vaguely as possible, was itself being placed under MPPDA regulatory control. This formulation allowed Hays to also argue that film industry leaders were themselves best suited to the important task of reform since they already possessed the most direct and effective means of control over the house that needed cleaning: the film studios. Not only were film producers capable of effective industrial in-house reform, but, according to Hays, it was their duty.

Interestingly, when it came to furnishing the details of how motion pictures should be cleansed "at their source," Hays almost always understood that source to be the film script or the literary work upon which the script was based. Film performers and other production personnel were never specifically mentioned by Hays as important obstacles to better pictures. A week after his address to the General Federation of Women's Clubs, Hays told members of the National Education Association to judge the success of the industry's reform efforts not by past failures, but by the "pictures now being made by members of the [MPPDA]." Even here though, when talking about purported improvements in selected film stories and in the finished film product itself, Hays was able to equivocate just enough on the word *performances* (closely related to the word *performer*) to insinuate that the off-screen behavior of Hollywood's inhabitants was also being improved and was available to external evaluation. "While asking for your aid and cooperation I would like to ask, too, that you judge us by our actual performances rather than by any promises we make."[16] Thus, Hays often had the appearance of making the studios themselves seem entirely capable of and accountable for improvements in both the moral quality of motion pictures and the personal conduct of the players who appeared in them. Of course, studios simply passed this responsibility onto the performers themselves by making the terms of their employment void if, by their involvement in a public controversy, their reputations became compromised. Morality clauses were introduced into actor's contracts on a regular basis in 1922.

It is generally thought that Hays had seriously underestimated the resolve of those groups that, in 1922, were concerned about the personal conduct of film performers. At the end of the year, Hays, while continuing the industry's ban on distribution contracts for Arbuckle's previous films, reinstated the now infamous actor's right to pursue employment in the motion picture industry. This decision was met by loud and angry protests from those very reformers who continued to advocate for the regulation of film stars. The MPPDA's relations with several reform and educational groups were sorely compromised, groups to whom the MPPDA had just devoted so much of its time to establish trust and credibility. Nevertheless, in his previous public addresses to these same groups, Hays had shown an almost cunning sensitivity to the star scandals by his indirectness and by his rather systematic avoidance of discussing the issue openly. It makes sense, of course, that Hays would concentrate most of his efforts on censoring film scripts since complaints about inappropriate film depictions were long-standing concerns with relatively wide public acceptance. Yet, his censorship priorities were also determined, no doubt, by the long-term investment that the studios had in their stars—by then the most bankable commodity the film industry had at its disposal—as compared to the relatively short-term investments they might have had in any particular story properties or film scripts. The regulation of film scripts immediately became and would remain the principle censorship task of the Hays office, with the MPPDA continually implementing new formulas, guidelines, and regulations for film scripts right up to and including the creation of the Production Code Administration in 1934. Surveillance of the private lives and affairs of film performers would only ever be a distraction from what Hays considered the real regulatory work of the MPPDA. Therefore, Hays's decision allowing Arbuckle's return to work, coming less than a week after the revelations of Wallace Reid's drug addiction, was, from this perspective, more of a calculated risk to measure the intensity of the response to this sort of action from those sectors of the public with a continuing interest in censoring previously popular and very valuable film celebrities such as Arbuckle. It is quite possible that the reinstatement of Arbuckle was done more with the future of Reid's career in mind than with Arbuckle's well-being. The timing of this action, coming as it did in the wake of yet another major celebrity scandal, was sure to draw more negative attention to the film industry, but the resulting headlines would at least be about the now familiar and seemingly intractable scandal of Arbuckle's fatal gin party in a San Francisco hotel suite and not about another Paramount star's current struggle with drug addiction in a Hollywood sanatorium. The Arbuckle scandal had proven itself as something with which the newspapers and their readers seemed endlessly fascinated, and the film industry may have sought to give the press and industry reformers something to preoccupy them at this most precarious moment in Reid's star career. It was, after all, important that the recovering actor receive peace and quiet, and publisher William Randolph Hearst reportedly printed special copies of his newspaper without coverage of Reid's addiction so that the actor might be spared the knowledge of his newfound notoriety. In any event, while Reid has quietly disappeared from popular memory, the media continues to speak about the Arbuckle scandal to the present day.[17]

What the Public Doesn't Know

It is important to note that during the period of the early scandals, regulating the identity of the film performer entailed much more than simply banning a notorious star's films from the nation's cinemas, though, as in the case of Arbuckle, that was sometimes considered a satisfactory if not an entirely efficient method of control. Hays explained his reinstatement of Arbuckle as the simple recognition of a troubled actor's right to earn a living just like anyone else, but the public sentiment that continued to keep Arbuckle off the screen was not primarily concerned with punishing the acquitted comedian further. What was objectionable about Arbuckle and his films were the kinds of inappropriate or delinquent audience receptions they were now imagined to support. When Senator Myer laid the blame for the "perniciousness" of motion pictures on the behavior of "those who pose for them," he may have been voicing nothing more than the belief that immoral people will "naturally" produce immoral entertainment or decadent works of art. However, within the historical context of film censorship, that belief itself implied that the character and personal habits of those who produced and appeared in motion pictures had a significant and measurable influence on the health and well-being of the nation's film audiences. In short, attempts to contain and control the identity of the film performer were also attempts to regulate film audiences, and that prospect, of course, was something of great interest to both the film industry and its many critics.

Sometimes the pernicious influence of motion pictures was described by reformers as a type of contagion whereby the very appearance of an immoral star on the screen tended to infect members of the audience who then spread the "disease" to the communities in which they lived. Senator Myer described Arbuckle as "odoriferous," and he compared Hollywood unfavorably to "a colony of lepers or an institution for the propagation of smallpox" when he argued against a fanciful reform plan to move the Hollywood community closer to the nation's capitol so that the federal government might keep a closer watch over it. While the model of infectious disease was somewhat silly and was often employed only facetiously, it did powerfully represent the scandalized star as a serious public-health menace, an idea that was gaining wider credence for reasons which will become clear shortly.

A far more typical understanding of this public threat was that films with scandalous stars would promote immorality and criminal behavior to the extent that the film medium necessarily glamorized the personalities of featured players, making them objects of public fascination, adulation, and envy. Many reformers and social critics were frightened by the idea that members of their own communities, citizens who on most other occasions would show proper judgment in condemning immorality in all of its guises, might be drawn to personalities who had publicly proven themselves to be either criminals or moral delinquents. The basis of this concern was the recognition that it was now virtually impossible to separate in one's mind any film appearance by a star who had been damagingly linked to a scandal through the publicized details of that scandal. Every film appearance of the immoral performer was an occasion for the imaginative return of some nefarious affair, the particulars of which, it was thought, might best be forgotten. Moreover, those events would be remembered in relation to a personality made attractive through cinematic presentation. Given the intertextuality on which the star system had developed, the validity of this reception theory was quite compelling. Those wishing to support Arbuckle found it necessary to claim that not only was it possible to consider the work of the star performer quite apart from the scandal that had attached itself to him, but that the scandal could only continue to be of interest for those whose concerns were already in some way morbid or perverse. Shortly after Arbuckle's acquittal, a New England woman writing in *The New York Times* argued that, in fairness, the comedian should be restored to the screen, and she attacked what she saw as the movie reformers' own unhealthy obsessions with the subject of vice: "In this instance fair play seems to mean to some superior (?) editors and Christian (?) clergymen filthy-mindedness. For my part, I fail to see anything clean-minded, great-souled, or praiseworthy in persistently harping on scandal for the sole purpose of persecuting victims."[18] The major difficulty with such a position (what we might think of as a "New Critical" approach to the work of the star performer) was that it went against ten years of industrial practice and film audience expectations. However, the very fact that alternative models for the popular consumption of film stars could be offered and debated in the nation's newspaper speaks to the ideological cracks in the star system's traditional mode of production which were opened up, at least in part, by the scandals of the early 1920s.

As deCordova's study of the emerging system has shown, the film star's identity was based on a previous elaboration of what he terms "the picture personality," an identity constructed principally out of the performer's repeated appearances in film. To know a picture personality was to be familiar with the multiple screen roles undertaken by a particular player. While stardom entailed an expanded discourse about the off-screen and private existence of film performers, the film star still needed to be a picture personality first and only later a star, to the extent that stardom ultimately rested on one's regular featured appearance in motion pictures, or at least this is how the system developed. Yet the traditional basis of film stardom, the picture personality, was called into question from outside the film industry by Clara Smith Hamon when she announced in March of 1921 that she planned to appear in motion pictures.[19]

Hamon had just been acquitted of murdering her employer, Jake L. Hamon, an Oklahoma oil and railroad magnate and member of the Republican National Committee that had helped place President Warren G. Harding in office. Clara Smith Hamon had been his stenographer and his mistress before shooting him in November of 1920; Hamon's arrest and trial for murder made national headlines continually throughout the first three months of 1921. During the trial it was revealed that Jake Hamon had arranged for Clara Smith to marry his nephew, Frank Hamon, so that the late millionaire and his secretary could have the same last name, making travel and hotel bookings easier under the pretense of being husband and wife. The defense successfully argued that Jake Hamon had entrapped Clara Smith in a sexually exploitive and physically abusive relationship and that she had shot her employer in self-defense during an exceptionally brutal episode in which Jake Hamon attacked her with a chair.[20] The newspaper reports of their relationship told a compelling story and created a large popular audience for the case. Immediately after her acquittal on the grounds that the shooting was a "justifiable homicide," it was reported that Clara Smith Hamon "[had] signed a two-year contract with the Oklahoma Moving Picture Company of Oklahoma City under the terms of which she [was to] receive $25,000 as an advance payment and fifty percent of the profits of the company."[21]

The first and probably only motion picture that Clara Smith Hamon made was *Fate* (W. E. Weathers, 1921), in which she played herself while John Ince took the part of Jake Hamon.[22] The film was in production at the Warner Bros. studio during the summer and was ready for release just prior to the arrest of Arbuckle on charges of rape and murder. Film historian Kevin Brownlow maintains that *Fate* may have met with much greater success and acceptance had it not been for the unfortunate timing of the film's release and the decision to open the film in San Francisco, since that city was "the wrong town in which to open. The Arbuckle case had aroused deep feeling against the entire motion picture profession."[23] Ultimately, however, it was not so much the Arbuckle scandal that impacted *Fate*'s reception and censorship; in fact, the production of *Fate* was potentially a far more disruptive event for the industry than the famous comedian's troubles. Instead of the Arbuckle scandal determining the reception of *Fate*, the film actually provided the grounding context for the many star scandals that immediately followed, and this is why the Hamon murder trial was an important event in the development of the star system. The Hamon case significantly exacerbated the damage to Arbuckle's career by dramatically posing the possibility that film celebrity could be based solely upon the notoriety of the featured performer and that audiences were primarily interested in scandalous stars not in spite of their transgressions, but precisely because of them.

Fate's fate had already been determined as early as March of 1921 when movie theater owners in California announced their opposition to any film appearance by Clara Smith Hamon and declared "that an exhibition of this sort would unduly and improperly put a premium on violence."[24] Exhibitor organizations in other states quickly followed suit, calling for self-imposed bans on any and all films in which Clara Smith Hamon might appear. The Motion Pictures Exhibitor's League of New York went on record as "emphatically opposed to the exploitation of criminal sensationalism as illustrated in a proposal to film Clara Smith Hamon." Exhibitors were not alone in their calls for voluntary censorship. Apparently, many film producers and distributors also supported a nationwide ban on any and all pictures featuring Hamon. William Brady, president of the National Association of the Motion Picture Industry (NAMPI), the principal regulatory agency in the film industry before the formation of the MPPDA, reported that members of his organization were "unilaterally opposed" to Hamon's appearance on the screen and that they were actively seeking means to stop the production and distribution of any such films.[25]

Even though Hamon had been a defendant in a highly publicized murder case and was known to have suffered sexual exploitation by her employer, why was there all this fuss about a small independent production company's plans to feature this young woman in films, even before the production of any such pictures had begun? While the industry's concerns were real and not so much public posturing,[26] these concerns are explained less by a commitment to social propriety and an adherence to professional standards of decency than by the sheer disruption that Hamon's film celebrity would have surely caused to the regular functioning of the Hollywood star system. Since the film industry had continually represented itself as the ultimate source of film stardom and the supplier of stars to the public, the popular appeal and success of a film performer such as Clara Smith Hamon would mean that Hollywood was no longer capable of authorizing film celebrities in the same way it had in the past. At stake was not just the idea that movie stars were stars because they had proven themselves through long apprenticeships as picture personalities in the industry, but also the increasingly real possibility that star identities could actually be defined and sustained by a public interest that had little or nothing to do with the ostensible products of the industry: motion picture stories. While it might be argued that the nation's newspapers were the real usurpers of Hollywood's prerogative to create compelling mass celebrities, the threat to the star system posed by Hamon, and then so dramatically enacted a few months later by Arbuckle, was more a result of the internal logic of the system itself.

By the late 1910s, as more and more information about the private lives and the personal experiences of Hollywood's most successful actors and actresses was revealed to the public, the star system functioned as a fairly coherent and codified system of knowledge. For film audiences, the screen appearances of the stars were not just pleasurable displays of the faces, the bodies, and the wardrobes of their favorite players, but a unique way of knowing each of them and the industry in which they worked. The American cinema was presenting itself to the public as a new and particularly powerful way of understanding personality, and there was absolutely no substitute for the knowledge to be gained by the appearance of a particular player in a featured role. As the private lives of the stars became more and more a part of the information that constituted the star's identity, the epistemological gap between a star's screen appearances and his or her private life became less and less; in other words, the star performer brought to the screen an elaborate biography that was available for further inspection by the film audience. Any information revealed about the stars in magazines or newspapers could quickly become an integral part of their identities on the screen.

Since the motion picture screen had become such an important instrument for producing knowledge about the stars, it was only a matter of time before the screen was proposed as a way of knowing other interesting individuals, ones who lived quite apart from the film industry but who shared with Hollywood stars a lifestyle that was in some way exceptional and indicative of the most current social trends. Clara Smith Hamon had proposed to perform in pictures immediately after her acquittal because she believed that a large portion of the American public had a particular interest in her life experiences and might welcome the opportunity to learn more about her at the cinema. Such an interest on the part of the public was, however, a rather radical appropriation of the star system, one that went far beyond the film industry's own deployment of personalities in order to build and sustain a mass market for its products. The film industry's initial responses to these developments were entirely defensive. Besides rather disingenuously claiming that Hamon and her associates were "attempting to commercialize [her] life history,"[27] industry leaders also felt it necessary to portray any audience interest in any such personalities as deviant. However, the activity of this pathological audience had to be carefully distinguished from the will to knowledge that characterized the Hollywood star system proper.

One way to make this distinction was to claim that the reception of scandalous celebrities was essentially static and defined only by a morbid fixation on a particular individual's transgressive behavior or immoral condition, whereas the reception of genuine Hollywood stars was a dynamic process that continually revealed new aspects of a performer's identity. In the latter case, fame was well deserved since the star was talented enough and, by implication, healthy enough to support an ever-changing popular interest in his or her identity. In contrast, audience fascination with notorious individuals was portrayed as perversely arrested by a single quality.

Consider the example of Fred Beauvais. Beauvais, a professional wilderness guide from Quebec, had been named as a co-respondent in the highly publicized Stillman divorce case, one of the major news stories of 1921. His name had featured quite prominently in the extensive coverage given to the legal proceedings by the nation's newspapers where he was often identified as a "half-breed Indian."[28] A prominent figure in financial circles, James Stillman was president of the National City Bank of New York when he filed for divorce from his wife, Anne Urquhart Stillman, by claiming that Fred Beauvais was the actual father of their youngest child, Guy. In her repeatedly appended answers to her husband's suit, Mrs. Stillman named a former showgirl of musical revues along with several other young women, all of whom had been allegedly "kept" by Mr. Stillman at one time or another during their marriage. The intense and protracted publicity given to this case forced Mr. Stillman to resign his post as bank president, and several love letters purportedly sent to Anne Stillman by Beauvais were published as part of the press coverage.[29] Subsequently, when Mrs. Stillman claimed that Florence Leeds, a former chorus girl, had been one of her husband's mistresses, *The New York Times* reported that the young woman possessed both "beauty and personality" and was contemplating taking a role in a motion picture about the Stillman affair. During the summer, rumors also began circulating that Mrs. Stillman herself was considering offers to appear in motion pictures.[30] Finally, when some exhibitors in New York State began advertising the appearance of Fred Beauvais in *The Lonely Trail* (Credit-Canada Productions, 1921) at the end of the year, NAMPI president, William Brady, once again spoke out strongly against the screen appearances of immoral individuals, and this time he attempted to define the type of audience reception that such appearances necessarily entailed.

> If Clara Hamon and Roscoe Arbuckle are barred by popular sentiment from appearing on the screen, the same holds good in the case of Fred Beauvais. *He is an attraction only because of his connection with a notorious divorce case*, the details of which might best be kept from the public in the papers, on the screen or in the courts. If one can become famous through murder, divorce or scandal, then encouragement only goes to spread the present wave of crime.[31]

Brady's condemnation of exhibitor sensationalism suggests that the only possible interest that anyone could still have in pictures featuring performers such as Arbuckle, Beauvais, or Hamon was a prurient fascination with their immorality or their crimes; in other words, there was nothing left to be gained or anything new to be learned by patronizing the motion pictures in which they appeared. Furthermore, by permitting movie audiences to publicly indulge a continued interest in such people by displaying their images and screening their films, exhibitors were inadvertently allowing a misguided sector of the public to make these individuals into celebrities to be envied and emulated, and that is why, Brady claimed, such films ultimately "encourage" crime.

What is interesting in Brady's account of the problem is how far his representation of the scandalous celebrity in motion pictures departs from the industry's previous discursive construction of film stardom. Unlike traditional film stars, the appearance of immoral or criminal individuals in motion pictures was considered nonproductive of any new or useful experience. More importantly, their very status as celebrities was represented as entirely derived from and supported by the public's interest in them; the industry no longer bore primary responsibility for authorizing the identity of the film performer in such cases. These individuals could only continue as prominent public figures in spite of the efforts of the majority of the film industry to ban their film appearances. Furthermore, the possibility that film audiences could have a more dynamic interest in the personalities of notorious individuals, a reception that sought to further understand the different situations and experiences of these people, was completely discounted in the industry's condemnation of showing the films of Arbuckle, Hamon, or Beauvais. Yet, since *Fate* was more or less a recounting of Clara Smith Hamon's exploitation at the hands of the Oklahoma oilman, and since Fred Beauvais played a character quite similar to himself in *The Lonesome Trail*, it is clear that there was a potential public interest in their individual stories. Though some film exhibitors denounced any attempt to tell the Hamon story at all, regardless of who performed it, the film industry as a whole was far less concerned with the suitability of the Hamon murder or the Stillman divorce for the motion picture screen than it was with controlling the screen appearances of the individuals involved in these public scandals. The industry's bottom line was that these individuals were undeserving of attention and did not properly belong in feature films.

As *Variety* stated, "there is a movement on the part of the industry to blacklist stars recruited through the medium of sensationalism and with no other known talents to recommend them than the notoriety accruing through court proceedings."[32] However, the industry's attempt to regulate the identity of the performer faced a major contradiction by the fact that Arbuckle, a major Hollywood star who had performed in hundreds of films before his arrest, was now included on a list with the likes of Hamon and Beauvais. This contradiction centered on how to adequately explain Arbuckle's troubles. If Hamon and Beauvais were not suited to motion pictures because they were immoral people, then Arbuckle proved that moral deviance was not simply a given identity that was innate and obvious. The film star who was revealed to be immoral or criminal had to be explained in terms that avoided the possibility that the film industry and its associated media had in some way been deceiving the public about the true identity of the performer. This meant that the star had to be represented as *having become*

FIGURE 1. While this cartoon that appeared in the *Rutland Herald*
(Vermont) February 20, 1922, sought to point out the hypocrisy of those
attacks on the film industry which were increasing in the wake of the
Taylor murder, it also inadvertently posed Hollywood—despite its
contrition—as a vortex for any number of publicized scandals and outrages
around the country, some of which are seen here personified and turning
their attentions toward the film colony.

perverse or criminal through a set of circumstances and that he or she was in no
way congenitally deviant.

This, in turn, meant that the scandalous star was, or at least could be, an important object of inquiry. However, the cinema screen could not be the place to
provide further information about the causes and development of a scandalous
star's condition, despite the central position that film appearances then held in

the production of popular knowledge about the stars. In 1921 and 1922, the film industry was battling for discursive control over the explanations for the existence of deviant celebrities. Within the historical context of film censorship and the industry's development of its star system, the Arbuckle scandal posed a seemingly insoluble dilemma: either the actor's excesses were indicative of the larger corrupting influences of the Hollywood environment as many reformers had claimed, or the industry had been negligent in its celebration and promotion of an individual who had been of unsavory character all along. If Hollywood was essentially all-of-one, at least for those who visibly occupied positions at the top levels of the film industry, how else does one explain Arbuckle? This is a false dilemma, of course, since it was possible and quite likely that film audiences sought to understand the scandalous star by recourse to ideas about education, moral development, and social justice then available elsewhere in American society. Audiences therefore might turn their attention to understanding a star's film appearances as moments in the social and psychological development of a particular personality. What the industry needed was to find a way to gain control over and to deploy those discourses about personal development then in vogue and circulating in the American culture at large.

THE MANUFACTURED PERSONALITY

After 1922, one can detect an important change in the industry's promotion of its stars. No longer was the star easily represented as a member of some extended corporate family. Instead, after the early scandals, more emphasis was likely to be placed on the contractual nature of the star's employment. Additionally, the post-scandal coverage of the stars' personal lives typically stressed their unique and idiosyncratic tastes and interests instead of their attainment of some definitive Hollywood lifestyle. Since studio contracts were an important part of earlier star publicity, especially when a particular studio wished to announce that they had signed a prominent and popular star for a set number of pictures, these changes in the star discourse of the period were more matters of degree than any radical transformation of the previous system. Even so, the differences between the pre-scandal representations of films stars and those of the post-scandal period are easily discernible and, more importantly, these changes significantly altered the terrain of star reception in America. What ultimately changed in the latter period is the representation of the institutional basis of stardom.

During 1923, public discussion about the excesses of stars' salaries began in earnest. This was also the year that Rudolph Valentino was absent from the screen because of contract disputes with his production and distribution company Famous Players-Lasky, an absence given enormous significance in the fan press and generally viewed as the catalyst for the industry's importation of several new stars to fill the void left by Valentino's departure. Ramon Novarro, one of the most important and successful of the Valentino replacements, was favorably compared to John D. Rockefeller by *Photoplay* because of the financial acumen he supposedly evidenced in his contract negotiations with Marcus Loew, president of Metro Pictures.[33] There was an industrial enthusiasm for the "new face" during this period which made the separation of the star from the film industry that much easier to accomplish.[34] Unlike the first generation of Hollywood stars who were rapidly subsiding from prominence by the end of the First World War, very few of the second and third generations, those who had achieved stardom in the early and mid-1920s, could claim to have grown up within the industry. These newer stars could not be equated with the industry as an historical institution, as had the film stars who were involved in the first wave of major scandals. These new personalities were more easily represented as being difficult, as having domestic problems, and as walking out on their contracts. The leaders of the industry could always question their Hollywood credentials in ways they could never question, say, Mary Pickford, Douglas Fairbanks, or Charlie Chaplin, renegade stars who broke from the ranks of the studios to found United Artists, an action that was actually represented in both the trade journals and the fan magazines as more of a development within industrial practice than as any radical break from it.

It is by now almost a cliché to mention the stardom of Theda Bara as an important turning point in the development of the star system. Her overnight success as the dangerous and exotic vamp in *A Fool There Was* (Fox, 1915) is generally viewed as a master stroke of publicity in which the studio more or less manufactured a fully formed star identity for Bara even before she had appeared in a single film. In many ways, she represents a trend that would come to dominate the manufacture of stars in the 1920s. While it might appear that a star like Bara would benefit (or suffer as the case may be) from an especially close association with the film industry since her stardom was fully a product of the studio system, in fact, just the opposite was true. Fox could justify the outrageousness and potential excesses of Bara's star identity by claiming that people had paid to see her and she was, thus, just what the public wanted. Her stardom was marked in numerous ways by a notion of supply and demand, and the vamp character, with whom she was most associated, lived by her seduction of those who were fool enough to fall under her spell. Bara's appeal was figured as a type of addiction to a thoroughly synthetic thrill. The need to justify in some way a star's decadent sex appeal would never arise for someone like Gloria Swanson, who had worked her way up to stardom at the Essanay studios and then at Triangle-Keystone. Moreover, Swanson had been made into a star by Cecil B. DeMille, an unquestionably authentic Hollywood type and not some ambitious exhibitor such as William Fox who had entered film production through backward integration, but who was still catering to the indiscriminate desires of the masses. The trend that began with making the public largely responsible for Bara's celebrity came to fruition in the 1920s when Will Hays said he was going "to clean house." After that, film stardom would never be the same, and immoral performers would only have themselves or their audiences to blame for their misfortunes.

The star scandals of the early 1920s had disciplinary effects on film performers, film audiences, and the relationship between movie stars and the public. Not simply useful diversions for maintaining corporate autonomy or public relations crises requiring quick rectification, the early star scandals extended and elaborated knowledge about modern personality and how personality relates to and is determined by the conditions of mass industrial society. The star scandals changed the way film stardom was represented and how the individual film star was understood. As the rest of the book will show, the modern scientific discourses of criminology, psychology, sociology, and ethnography often provided different ways in which to represent and understand the film star's transgressions, and star biography quickly became a new aspect of the case study. No longer a foundational identity partially hidden from public view, now the film star's personality was continually under transformation, conditioned by the social environments in which it would develop or deteriorate. To know a star, at least certain prominent stars, was more than just knowing the facts of a career; it was to understand those facts as evidence of a particular type of personality and the conditions under which that personality came into being. In this way, the scandals were events that positioned film audiences to understand themselves in particular ways and to take both themselves and the stars they watched as objects of an ongoing investigation.

UNDERSTANDING WALLACE REID AND HIS PUBLIC

Despite the difficulties that the circumstances of Reid's death posed for an industry already attempting to circumvent growing demands for outside censorship, Reid's use of narcotics was made consistent with his earlier star image through a set of industry-directed discourses that purportedly sought to extend the public's knowledge about the social basis of drug addiction. In newspapers, trade journals, and fan magazines, the coverage of the scandal drew upon specific psychological and sociological images of drug addiction and drug trafficking in order to represent Reid as a tragic but heroic figure who sacrificed his life to an adoring public. By examining some of the specific strategies of this coverage and its stages of development both during and in the aftermath of the scandal, we can draw some conclusions about the ways his contemporary film audiences were encouraged to understand Reid's stardom and their own relation to his death.

The major interpreter of Reid's identity, once his addiction became widely known, was his wife of nine years, actress Dorothy Davenport Reid. Putting an end to over two years of rumors, she went public about her husband's addiction on December 17, 1922, shortly after committing him to a Los Angeles sanitarium for treatment, and approximately one month prior to his death. Davenport Reid was, at this time, almost always referred to in the press as "Mrs. Wallace Reid." Whether pressured by the film industry or seeking on her own to put an end to mounting press speculations about her husband's condition, Mrs. Reid gave an extensive interview to the Hearst newspapers, detailing her husband's life in order to explain just how he had become addicted to drugs.

A primary aim of the interview was clearly to counter the damaging image of Hollywood as a "den of iniquity," an image that had been so recently promulgated by the tabloids and by many of the would-be reformers of the industry. Mrs. Reid explained her motives:

> I am being criticized severely by some of our acquaintances for having talked so much, but I feel that if the public knows the truth it will not condemn Wally any more than I have condemned him. His is not an individual case [but?] symptomatic of a community. The battle Wally is making is the battle that thousands—I might say a million—of men and women are making. . . . If then through telling the truth I can do my part to arouse public sentiment against this nefarious traffic I am willing to suffer criticism.[35]

The idea that an open discussion of Reid's addiction would serve the public good by fostering a greater public familiarity with an important social problem allowed the industry to use the scandal to its own advantage. A commitment to honest disclosure and frankness in the service of social hygiene was a self-congratulating component of the media coverage of Reid's stardom that would continue in the fan magazines throughout the 1920s, long after his death.

To sever further any connections between her husband's drug use and Hollywood, Mrs. Reid reiterated several times that she was absolutely certain that Reid's drug addiction had begun in New York when he traveled there in the summer of 1921 to work on the film *Forever*, a lavish adaptation of the novel *Peter Ibbetson*. Reid fell ill and began to worry that his "illness was delaying production and adding to the expense." He asked a local physician for morphine in order to "nerve him for his daily and arduous task."[36] Nevertheless, the place, date, and nature of the commencement of the addiction were continually disputed, and later disclosures and explanations attributed to Mrs. Reid often contradicted one another wildly, sometimes even within the same interview or article.

While making New York the site of Reid's affliction, Mrs. Reid also felt it necessary to mention several accidents earlier suffered by her husband while performing motion picture work. She also indicated that her husband had had enormous demands placed upon him by an intense production schedule. The incident most remarked on later and mentioned by Mrs. Reid in her first interview occurred early in 1919 when the actor was involved in a train accident while making *The Valley of the Giants,* an adventure picture about lumbering in northern California. Various accounts of this particular incident exist, but what is certain is that several members of the film's crew sustained injuries when a caboose carrying them jumped from the tracks and tumbled off an embankment or from a small bridge. Reid mentioned this train wreck in a newspaper interview in July 1919 on the occasion of his signing a new five-year contract with Famous Players-Lasky, a most unusual length of service obligation. Calling *Valley of the Giants* "a tough picture to make," Reid remembered how "in one scene, we were all 'messed up' in a train wreck, and then we had to travel seventy-five miles away from the hotel during the photographing of certain scenes."[37] At the time of the accident, Reid was apparently given morphine to ease the pain he experienced from a head injury; according to later statements by Mrs. Reid, the treatment did not lead to an addiction and Reid continued to work after the train accident despite suffering lingering pain.

This incident is extremely important because it quickly became the single biographical moment that was most often mentioned in explanations of Reid's death and, even today, it is often cited as the event most likely to have been responsible for his morphine addiction.[38] Whether it actually was so or not is beside the point. The incident accomplished several things that made it a compelling explanation of Reid's fate, both in terms of his established star persona and in terms of popular sociological ideas about drug risks. On the one hand, this story somewhat de-pathologized Reid by characterizing his addiction as the result of a beneficent medical treatment, thereby making it recognizable as an older and more genteel form of morphine dependency. On the other hand, the staging of Reid's first exposure to morphine at the scene of a train accident pushes his addiction closer to an emerging set of representations that linked drug addiction to industrial waste, such as the etymology of the word *junkie.*

The idea that Reid would be susceptible to morphine addiction because of physical exhaustion and injury brought about by arduous working conditions would have been problematic for the film industry since it suggests that the studio contributed significantly to Reid's illness and impending death. Indeed, only two weeks after her first interviews, we find Mrs. Reid writing a new account of the illness in the *San Francisco Examiner.* Here, she begins by emphatically stating that her husband's misfortune was a "personal tragedy" and an "isolated case," and that it had nothing whatsoever to do with motion pictures or with Hollywood. Nevertheless, she retells the story of the 1919 train wreck; however, now the accident no longer takes place during the filming of a scene, but occurs as the film's personnel travel to a chosen outdoor location. Reid is also given a more heroic role in this new version of the event as he selflessly attends to the other passengers, neglecting his own injuries for several hours. In addition to changing these important details, Mrs. Reid attributes a somewhat nebulous significance to the injuries suffered by her husband in the train wreck: "Against the advice of physicians he went to work [the] next day and the picture was made on schedule. But from that hour Wallace Reid was never the same. I do not know why; it is an intangible thing. I will try to explain as we go along."[39] Together with the very nature of these revisions, the fact that Mrs. Reid was allegedly even writing so many different narratives of her husband's addiction, presumably during a time of great personal stress for her, suggests that she was working at the behest of the industry. Since Reid's illness and impending death constituted a major Hollywood scandal, it is more than probable that both Famous Players-Lasky, the studio to whom Reid was still under contract, and the MPPDA had a hand in determining the changes of the particulars and in controlling the overall direction of Mrs. Reid's accounts. As media scholar Danae Clark has demonstrated with respect to the industry's regulation of film labor in the 1930s, the MPPDA often sought to control public representations of the labor of motion picture actors as well as the representations of the conditions of that labor. At times, this function would even take priority over the organization's need to protect actors from harmful publicity.[40] The news coverage of Reid's morphine addiction indicates that the MPPDA had made the concealment of film labor a priority from the very beginning of its existence.

Within two weeks, the "explanation" of Reid's addiction had shifted from being about an injury sustained at work, to being vaguely related to an accident that occurred *on the way to work*. Whereas in Mrs. Reid's first accounts the film star felt compelled to work while experiencing intense physical pain because of the possibility of costly delays in production, he now returns to work "against the advice of physicians." The picture of Wallace Reid the actor, presumably drawn by the person who knew him best, had quickly changed from one of a worker who was also the victim of an industrial accident, to one of a hard-working but ultimately self-destructive individual who often placed himself at risk in his desire to serve others.[41] In other words, through these stories Reid had become an addictive personality; he was being posed in the media as a compelling individual to whom the public was addicted and as an identity whose compulsions were available for multiple interpretations and diagnoses. This attention to Reid's personality was an important intermediate stage in refiguring the scene of his addiction. The question remains, however, as to why the image of the train wreck continued to play such a central role in Mrs. Reid's and others' accounts if the aim of many of these explanations was to dissociate Reid's illness from the industrial conditions under which he labored.

Several possibilities for the recurrence of the train wreck suggest themselves. First, there is evidence that the story of this injury was already in circulation as a part of the rumors surrounding the star, and it was important to incorporate as much of what people already knew or believed about Reid into the news stories about him. Second, it is quite possible that even while choosing to protect what she believed were the interests of the industry and of the community to which she belonged, Mrs. Reid understood her husband's addiction to have resulted from the exploitive film work that he was required to perform, and thus felt obliged to telegraph to the public the demanding nature of her and her husband's occupation. Third, once Mrs. Reid had incorporated the train wreck into her account, any dramatic shift in the scene of addiction would have called attention to the very constructedness of her disclosures. Finally, as film scholar Lynne Kirby has so amply demonstrated in her article "Male Hysteria and Early Cinema," the fantasy of the train wreck was an important way of organizing the experiences of the perceptual dislocations that were entailed by modernity, in general, and by the cinema, in particular.[42] Mrs. Reid's apparent compulsion to repeat the story of the train wreck thus suggested to the public that the nexus of trauma described by Kirby was an appropriate context for understanding the film star's addiction to drugs. In 1922, such a reception would have still been available to the public and recognized as related to a previous historical mode of film spectatorship. In this way, the scene of the accident and the resulting trauma provided a model for dealing with the disruptions caused by news of the addiction, and the train wreck helped link Reid's present condition to the pre-classical era of cinema in which he began his film career.

While it is probably the case that all these considerations played some part in the sustained attention given to the injury in the press coverage of the scandal, the train wreck was also highly compatible with Reid's star identity. Reid's insatiable love of automobile racing had become one of the most often remarked-on interests of the star after he began performing in a popular series of car racing pictures for Famous Players-Lasky in 1919, films that included *The Roaring Road* (1919), *Double Speed* (1920), *Excuse My Dust* (1920), *Too Much Speed* (1921), and *Across the Continent* (1922). Aimed at young male audiences and usually based on the racing stories of popular fiction author Byron Morgan, these films had heroes with names such as "Speed Carr" (*Double Speed*), "Jimmy Dent" (*Across the Continent*), and "Dusty Rhoades" (*Too Much Speed*). In many ways, of all the films that Reid made during his eleven-year career, the racing pictures were represented as the most autobiographical. Reid was himself an adept auto mechanic, and he had acquired an amateur racing license. Reportedly, he even had aspirations to compete in the annual race at the Indianapolis Motor Speedway.[43] The type of character played by Reid in these films was usually possessed by a compulsion to compete, either as a successful racer or as an automobile designer with a seemingly in-satiable desire to set speed and time records with his inventions. While never entirely reckless, his great love of auto racing often gets him into trouble and he is sometimes placed in great physical danger by an unscrupulous competi-tor or by other, less competent drivers. Yet, in the end, it is this same love of the sport together with a consummate mastery over the machines that pull him through.

During the same period that Reid was making these pictures, he also com-pleted at least twenty-three other feature films before collapsing on the set of *Thirty Days* in late September or early October 1922.[44] Reid suffered a temporary loss of vision at that time and was reported to be suffering from a severe case of "Klieg eyes," a not-uncommon industrial hazard for film performers. Named after the powerful arc lamps that had become standard studio equipment in the mid-1910s, Klieg eyes resulted from prolonged exposure to the ultraviolet radia-tion of the lamps, which produced corneal lesions on the eyes. *Thirty Days* had to be completed with an assistant on hand to provide Reid with a constant verbal description of the film's sets so that the actor could convincingly portray a fully-sighted person.[45] At the very height of his stardom, Reid was appearing in twice as many pictures as other stars of his caliber and he was performing in practi-cally every variety of the studio's product, from cheap action and adventure pic-tures, to romantic social comedies, to specials and prestige costume dramas.

In *The Love Special*, a railroad romance made in 1921, the themes of strenuous labor and physical exhaustion are central to defining Reid's character, Jim Glover. Glover is a construction engineer who designs large architectural structures for Great Western, a powerful railroad firm. The film begins with Glover not behind a drafting table, but at a flood site where a rising river threatens to destroy the total expanse of an important bridge. We learn that he has been awake for over ninety-six hours, stubbornly refusing to rest as he directs rotating crews of workers in a valiant attempt to divert the rising waters away from the bridge. Of course, all his suffering and sacrifice is eventually rewarded when the bridge is saved from ruin. When word of Glover's accomplishments reaches the nearby company offices, Morris Blood (Clarence Burton), a division superintendent, joy-ously exclaims how invaluable Glover is as an employee and asks, "Who wouldn't give his right hand saving a man like that?" The question refers to Blood's right hand, which appears to be a black rubber prosthesis, though the loss of the origi-nal is never fully explained or pursued. While there is no immediate narrative motivation for this particular disability, the missing hand does function as an index of the danger involved in railroad work, though it is somewhat odd that a regional manager should have to suffer such an injury. Blood is preparing for a visit to the flood site by Great Western's owner and president, Rufus Gage (Theo-dore Roberts), and, in an effort to make a good impression on the boss, he asks the now exhausted Glover to be the chief executive's guide. Gage admires Glover for his heroic efforts and sheer physical stamina, but equally taken with the young man's abilities is Gage's daughter Laura (Agnes Ayers) who is accompanying her father on the tour. When Laura learns of Glover's remarkable feats, she quickly decides to pursue a romance with the dashing young engineer. The missing hand does, then, work at a symbolic level to signify the rail company's need for the aptly named Glover, a sort of "right hand man" to whom president Gage must eventually forfeit the oedipal battle. In the end, it is Glover who wins Laura's hand from the rail magnate by bravely commandeering a locomotive and driving it full-steam through a dangerous mountain pass during a snowstorm, arriving just in time to save Gage from a devastating betrayal by an unscrupulous business partner.

When Mrs. Reid first revealed her husband's addiction, the nation's news-papers sought to represent his illness as a heroic life-and-death struggle by a "strenuous actor" against "the drug menace" and as "a human interest story as gripping as many depicted on the motion picture screen."[46] Both in fan magazines and in his film roles, Reid had demonstrated an adventurous enthusiasm for the speed of automobiles and trains, and, at least in his film roles, he often placed his life under the threat of mechanical disaster. So despite the fact that the story of his part in the 1919 train wreck ran the risk of making the industry responsible for his drug use, it did stage an important moment in Reid's life in a melodramatic way that was consistent with his star image. After all, Reid was still alive when these accounts were first given to the newspapers, and it was important that his illness be integrated into a coherent popular identity which could continue to be profitably exploited.

The relation of Reid's addiction to the excesses of modern industry also had to be negotiated in terms of class identity. When not using generic terms such as "dope" or "narcotics," Mrs. Reid and the nation's newspapers almost always discussed Reid's addiction in terms of morphine. Yet two years earlier, when *Variety* reported that a "dope-peddler" who claimed to be delivering heroin to a well-known star had been arrested on a studio lot, many people in the industry were certain that the star in question was Wallace Reid. In fact, it is likely that Reid was a user of heroin at the time of his breakdown and throughout much of his addiction.[47] Heroin, a semi-synthetic derivative of morphine and generally considered more pharmacologically potent and more addictive, had appeared in the 1890s as a treatment for certain respiratory conditions. Unlike morphine, heroin had a much shorter therapeutic history and was medically prescribed for a fairly limited range of illnesses. Addiction to heroin, therefore, was not as easily associated with legitimate medical treatment as was morphine. From the mid-1910s on, heroin usage was popularly identified with crime and with the so-called criminal classes, those unemployed and unskilled laborers who lived in America's largest cities and who spent much of their time on the streets as members of informal gangs.[48] This transformation of the social identity of the drug addict was also shaping the medical understanding of drug addiction as well and, from available information and statistical data, it does appear that the urban poor were disproportionately affected by heroin addiction in the 1910s and 1920s.[49] While it was important for the film industry to present Reid's drug addiction as determined, in part, by the arduous conditions and demands of modern life, it was also important to thoroughly disassociate his plight from the experiences of an urban working class. This was not simply a strategy to make Reid's illness appear more respectable. The insistence that Reid suffered from morphine (as opposed to heroin) addiction helped to cover over important relations between economic class and narcotic addiction, thereby making Reid's illness compatible with contemporary liberal reform discourses that sought to represent drug addiction as an affliction that could "happen to anyone."[50]

What occurred after Reid's death was more or less a continuation of the changes that were already well under way in the representation of his drug use. Because modern medical discourses and public health practices were addressing drug addiction as an environmentally determined condition, it remained important for the media to establish a social milieu for Reid's addiction. However, in subsequent accounts given by Mrs. Reid and by others, the industrial world of film production as the scene of Reid's drug use was rapidly being replaced by the private world of domestic consumption. Not only did Reid's posthumous publicity quickly turn to images of a family bereft of a husband, a son, and a father, but the preferred explanation of his addiction now became Reid's private encounters with the "wrong element" during his leisure hours away from the studio and at his home during parties. Drawing on popular fears and fantasies about wild Hollywood parties, the newspapers now told of how Reid's indiscriminate hospitality and the fabulous amenities of his luxurious Beverly Hills home "had drawn to him a mob of hand-shakers which he could not be persuaded were not his real friends."[51] Furthermore, Reid's addiction had become public knowledge in the midst of a moral panic about illicit drug use in the United States, a panic that was in no small way aided by the sensational stories then appearing in the Hearst newspapers about criminal "dope rings" and fraudulent clinics purporting to cure wealthy addicts by providing them with illegal narcotics.[52] This propaganda campaign ultimately sought to strengthen the powers of the police, to create public support for new federal anti-narcotic legislation increasing the penalties for those convicted of trafficking, and to establish international agreements halting the production of stimulants and narcotics overseas. While Reid was only sometimes portrayed as an habitué of wild Hollywood parties, he was increasingly represented as the innocent prey of a criminal traffic in narcotics. Both the Hearst newspapers and the film industry quickly latched on to this image of the dead star and used the publicity generated by Reid's death in their efforts to militarize drug addiction as a public health issue and to win the "war on dope."

Nowhere is this transformation in the understanding of Reid's addiction more evident than in the film *Human Wreckage* (1923), a Thomas Ince production about drug addiction, directed by John Griffith Wray and made with the support of Mrs. Reid and with the cooperation of various public health officials and law-enforcement agencies, including the Los Angeles Anti-Narcotic League and the Los Angeles Police Force.[53] Released nationally only six months after Reid's death, *Human Wreckage* tells the story of Ethel MacFarland (Mrs. Reid) and her slow and devastating realization that her husband, Alan (James Kirkwood), is a drug addict. Alan MacFarland is a prominent lawyer who spends many of his evenings at home working on pressing legal cases. In order to help sustain the attorney's flagging attention to an important murder defense in which an innocent man may be sentenced to die, an incautious physician gives Alan an injection of morphine. This physician is later revealed to be a "dope doctor" connected with the illegal trade in narcotics. As Alan's work continues to place demands on his strength, he comes to rely more and more on the drug, and he is eventually blackmailed by a drug syndicate for whom he must perform legal services in order to procure more narcotics for himself. Even when Alan seeks a cure by going into the seclusion of a countryside cottage with Ethel, a drug dealer is sent to follow Alan and to keep him addicted. Sick and demoralized, Alan fails in his every attempt to break with the drug habit until Ethel pretends that she, too, has become addicted to morphine. Alan, in moral revulsion at what he believes he has done to his wife, finally finds the willpower to conquer his addiction.

The main story of *Human Wreckage* is told against a pair of subplots about two young working-class youths who are not as lucky as Alan MacFarland: both are social welfare cases of Ethel MacFarland, both come from homes without fathers, and both end up dying because of the illegal traffic in narcotics. One of these youths, Mary Finnegan (Bessie Love), is a single mother who has become addicted while mourning the loss of her late husband. When Ethel discovers that Mary has been giving morphine to her infant, she takes the child from Mary and places Mary in a clinic for treatment. Unfortunately, the young mother is too frail for complete withdrawal, and Mary dies "a broken flower" in her own mother's arms, an event the continuity script suggests be treated as "a fairy-book scene."[54] Mary's death prompts the intertitle, "THE BEAST is driven back." The other working-class youth is Jimmy Brown (George Hackatorne), a young man arrested for theft while under the influence of drugs and sent away for a cure. Unlike Mary, Jimmy is hardy enough to withstand the cure, and he returns home to his mother, finding employment as a taxi driver. Unfortunately, because the city's drug dealers know he is an addict and continually tempt him with narcotics, Jimmy eventually suffers a relapse. Deciding that he cannot face the tortures of another withdrawal, he suddenly determines to kill himself and his current fare at that moment, Steve Stone (Harry Northrup), a notorious drug dealer who has been blackmailing MacFarland. Jimmy accomplishes this spectacular murder-suicide by driving his taxi full-speed into a stationary street car. The continuity script describes the taxi in the aftermath of the collision as "practically in splinters," and indicates that, "lying in the wreckage, and partially covered by it are Jimmy and Stone; they are both dead and the scene should be so shot that there is no doubt of this." Here, the train wreck is no longer the privileged scene of drug addiction or relevant to its explanation. Instead, *Human Wreckage* has made the mechanical disaster a part of the cure.

Human Wreckage worked to unify the differing and potentially disruptive discursive positions of social worker, actress, and widow that Dorothy Davenport Reid occupied and from which she spoke. The film was promoted and popularly received as based on the particulars of Wallace Reid's drug addiction, though not only because Mrs. Reid plays the wife of a drug addict. She also appears at the beginning and at the end of the film as herself, Mrs. Wallace Reid. In a direct address to the camera and with her two children at her side, Mrs. Reid explains: "The picture I have made deals with this great danger and every incident depicted has its parallel in fact." While the script for *Human Wreckage* was officially credited to C. Gardner Sullivan, the film was widely represented as authored by Mrs. Reid, such as when *Photoplay* published a photograph of Mrs. Reid pensively writing at her desk in mourning attire. The accompanying caption identified her as "at work on her propaganda film to fight the narcotic evil."[55] Preparations for a novelization of the film, entitled *Powdered Death,* credited Mrs. Reid, first, and Sullivan, second, as the book's co-authors.[56] When the picture was released in June, Mrs. Reid's name appeared above the film's title on both cinema marquees and in newspaper advertisements.[57] She also made several public appearances with the film, lecturing on drug addiction as a medical disease and calling for an end to the unsympathetic representations of drug addicts as moral degenerates and criminals. Asking her audiences to dispense with the common term *dope fiend,* she stressed the need for greater drug education and for the establishment of clinics devoted to the care of those suffering from narcotic addiction. Yet even as Mrs. Reid publicly supported the greater medicalization of the addict, others were using her and her husband's death to criminalize drug addiction further. U.S. District Attorney John T. Williams, for instance, blamed Reid's death on "a growing disregard of the law within our own country."[58] The contradictions between law enforcement and the clinical treatment of narcotic addiction had been greatly exacerbated in 1919 when the U.S. Supreme Court interpreted the Harrison Act of 1914 as proscribing all medical treatment of narcotic addiction through drug maintenance. Because of this decision, scores of treatment centers across the country were forced to close their doors out of fear of prosecution.[59] Ironically, even *Human Wreckage*, a motion picture promoted as Mrs. Reid's effort to create greater public sympathy for the drug addict, actually supported the further criminalization of narcotic addiction by emphasizing the criminal gang in the addiction process and by portraying maintenance-free withdrawal as the sole possibility for effective treatment, a therapy that was, undoubtedly, the single most significant contributor to Reid's death given his state of physical exhaustion at the end of 1922. That Mrs. Reid could be presented as the author of *Human Wreckage*, a film that in many ways ran counter to and eventually undermined her own efforts to obtain better and more humane medical treatment for drug addicts, demonstrates both her importance as a national spokesperson on the issue of narcotic addiction and the power of the industry to determine what she was capable of saying about addiction.[60] Her own reasons for participating in such a project are unclear, although she, like many others, likely believed that the discourse on the criminal traffic in drugs was ultimately compatible with the re-medicalization of the addict.[61]

What is certain is that *Human Wreckage* was an important final step in containing the scandal that Reid's addiction posed for the film industry, despite claims that the film required a "special dispensation" from Will Hays in order to be made and released.[62] With Mrs. Reid's guarantee that everything in the film "has its parallel in fact," *Human Wreckage* helped to refigure her husband's drug addiction as the unfortunate result of his personal ambition and his desire to serve the public and to please his friends. Through the story of the MacFarlands, *Human Wreckage* neatly combined both the demands of modern work and the influence of the criminal gang as contributing to narcotic addiction, but it firmly privileged personal contacts with other addicts and with dope peddlers as the most typical, determining, and dangerous cause of habitual narcotic use. Drug addiction spread in the society only by an alien and contagious criminal element. The film urges sympathy for the drug addict since addiction is shown to cut across class lines, but gone is any sense that addiction is a disease tied to the excesses of mass industrial society. The only remnant of such an idea in the film would appear to be its title, *Human Wreckage*, a title that effectively telescoped the scene of the industrial disaster onto the individual, much in the same way that the word *junkie*—a term that once so forcefully called upon an active understanding of modern urban life—soon gave way to the absolute identity of the narcotic addict as the American public knows this figure today. As the philosopher Theodor Adorno observed in his dedication of *Minima Moralia: Reflections from Damaged Life*, "in an individualistic society, the general not only realizes itself through the interplay of particulars, but society is essentially the substance of the individual."[63] If, however, a substance cannot be controlled, then its meanings can. The scandal of Reid's addiction had the real potential of affirming for a

Mrs. Wallace Reid

in

"Human Wreckage"

The Picture that is staggering the entire nation

SUPPORTED BY

JAMES KIRKWOOD

BESSIE LOVE, ROBERT McKIM, GEORGE HACKATHORNE
CLAIRE McDOWELL and ALL STAR CAST

STORY BY
C. GARDNER SULLIVAN

DIRECTED BY
JOHN GRIFFITH WRAY

© 1923 BY R.C. PICTURES
DISTRIBUTED BY
F.B.O.

mass audience something about the deformation of life under the conditions of twentieth-century capitalism. Clearly, there were many who had not previously concerned themselves with Wallace Reid or his films, but who had turned their attention to his life and to the terms of his illness in order to learn something.[64] What that something was could not, of course, be abstracted from the very apparatus that made Reid a compelling figure in the first place: the star system. Reid's death helped to pose the star system as a unique source of knowledge not only about the star himself, but about cinema as a social institution. Would the star system be used to think about the totality of social relations under monopoly capitalism? The "proper" use of the star system was the ultimate stake which the film industry had in controlling the discourses about Reid's use of narcotics.

Reid's narcotic addiction aided a reception of his identity as susceptible to a set of conditions entailed by the nature of mass communications, by the supply of and demand for media personalities. Just how those conditions of supply and demand were finally represented and understood through the repeated biographical inscriptions of Reid's life and death points to the importance of film stars in constructing, addressing, and maintaining a mass audience. Reid's personal desire to please others, whether his friends or his vast public, was a pivot on which the institutional representation of Reid's drug use turned. Though images of wreckage, waste, and ruined efficiency continued to dominate the media's coverage of Reid's addiction, these negative qualities of his stardom were effectively detached from the demands of industrial film production and transferred to the excesses of private life and consumption. While it is usually assumed that rumors of wild Hollywood parties were essentially harmful to the interests of the film industry, *Human Wreckage* demonstrated how the image of the lavish dope party could be used to portray narcotic addiction as an expression of excessive domestic consumption. Increasingly, the larger institutional context of Reid's addiction became the box office through which the public expressed its adoration for him.

The posthumous coverage of Reid in fan publications usually took the form of either short elegiac pieces written by friends or, more commonly, published letters from loyal fans remembering the great film star. Much of this material emphasized Reid's courage and determination in his fight against addiction and represented his death as a victory against a major social evil and, therefore, a great contribution to the world. One letter from "a lady" living in New York City claimed that, even in death, Reid was still hard at work: "And I have a conviction unshaken, that his spirit will be at work, MORE EFFECTIVELY for what has happened than it could had he been left here. He is on LOCATION working on a much bigger picture."[65]

FIGURE 2. Advertising for *Human Wreckage* repeatedly portrayed Mrs. Wallace Reid as the author of the film, as in this 3-sheet poster issued by Film Box Office.

In 1924 his friend Buddy Post explained Reid's addiction to *Motion Picture Magazine* this way: "I shall not attempt to tell when and why Wally started on that fatal journey. A number of circumstances brought about this trouble. To sum up in a philosophical way I might say that Wally did not kill others with kindness but killed himself with kindness to others."[66] Reid's very selflessness and his popularity were now seen as major contributing factors in the etiology of his disease. And if the studio had been initially portrayed as exploiting Reid's popularity with grueling work schedules, his death was now represented as a consequence of an excessive demand placed upon the star by a desiring public for whom Reid sacrificed himself and the happiness of his family. The desire of millions replaced the demands of the studio as the source of the damage to which Reid was so susceptible. In 1929, movie-magazine columnist Gladys Hall wrote of the difficulty Dorothy Davenport Reid faced in explaining to her son, Billy Reid, who his father really was: "Difficult to give the boy his father as a human being broken on the wheel of his most endearing qualities. Difficult to explain that dreams are not always best, that the love of millions can break a man as well as make him, that idealism and flattery can lead to degradation, that prowess of body is not always pride of spirit."[67] Yet the public's adoration of and addiction to Wallace Reid was by no means faulted or condemned in such representations. Instead, Reid's death functioned in the posthumous publicity as an uncritical demonstration of the simultaneous emotional proximity of the motion picture star to his public, and the alienated nature of mass communication. The adoring public was very much welcomed by the media as a part of his addiction.

In 1927, a young college student named Ray Harris organized an international effort to erect a large bay to the memory of Wallace Reid in the Cathedral of St. John the Divine in New York City. Harris had no difficulty convincing several prominent personalities to endorse publicly the construction of the bay and to serve on the executive committee for the memorial project. Members of this committee included film stars Richard Barthelmess, Richard Dix, Douglas Fairbanks, Wanda Hawley, Conrad Nagel, and Mary Pickford; film executives Cecil B. DeMille, Thomas Edison, and Carl Laemmle, as well as Reid's old production supervisor, Jesse L. Lasky; and politicians James Rolph, Jr., the mayor of San Francisco, and John W. Smith, the mayor of Detroit. Many of these individuals were quoted in the publicity materials for the fund drive, and several of them testified to the "cleanliness" of Reid's character. Still others employed a language of transcendence to suggest that Reid had been purified in death and that he was exalted in his family's loving remembrance. DeMille told potential fund subscribers how the late star's "mind and soul and spirit was [*sic*] untouched and always clean, clear and fine," and the national president of the Daughters of the American Revolution, Mrs. Alfred Brosseau, gave her personal endorsement to the memorial campaign by stating how she was "in sympathy with the aims of the wife and mother of

Wallace Reid."[68] Fundraising was complicated by advertising restrictions that the Episcopal Diocese of New York placed on Harris's organization and later by the onset of the Depression in the early 1930s. After ten years in existence, the Wallace Reid Memorial Association was only able to raise $792.79, less than one percent of the money required to build the cathedral bay.[69] With the exception of Thomas Edison, who contributed twenty dollars, no major studio executive pledged any money to the fund.

ACCOUNTING FOR THE LOSS

The social historian Frederick Lewis Allen saw the celebrity scandals of the early 1920s as a kind of misdirection, a distraction for the masses that necessarily kept them from pursuing their real political interests. Discussing the rise in circulation of the tabloids in the period, Allen maintained that it was not simply a "coincidence . . . that as they rose, radicalism fell." Allen portrayed the scandals of the early 1920s as devoid of any real relevance for the lives of working people, and he assumed that the only mode of reception possible for these media events was an uncritical prurience: "Workmen [sic] forgot to be class conscious as they gloated over pictures of Miss Scranton on the Boardwalk and followed the Stillman case and the Arbuckle case and studied the racing dope about Morvich."[70] However, it is clear that the scandals spoke to the public's real needs and experiences in some way and that they were not simply the mindless diversions that Allen and, not incidentally, the tabloids, news media, and the film industry would have us believe. Lecturing to the students of the Harvard Graduate School of Business Administration in 1927, the popular film actor Milton Sills explained the importance of maintaining the illusion of the film star as a harmless diversion for the masses who, he admitted, must work at "routine jobs [that] represent so much inevitable drudgery, and for the most part in the drabbest surroundings." Citing this situation as the reason for "the menace of revolt against our economic system," Sills stressed how the film star "performs an important public service, ameliorating the dreary lives of countless millions, bringing them charm, romance, laughter, grace, and high adventure."[71]

As we have seen, the film industry had to struggle with the media representations of Reid's drug habit in order to make the star's addiction practically incoherent within the terms of industrial production and labor. Instead, the damaged life was finally made into the life that had to be lived and lost at home, where only the grief of a friend, a fan, or a family remained to explain how it all had come about. With the privatization of his addiction complete, newspaper and tabloid attention to Reid actually ceased after his death, leaving his posthumous celebrity to the fan magazines. In fact, less than one week after Reid's funeral, an editorial in the obituary section of *Variety* angrily noted Reid's disappearance from the nation's headlines. Attacking two groups perceived to be serious threats to the industry during this period, the anonymous writer of this editorial blamed tabloid journalists for exploiting the scandal only to deliver women readers over to the department stores who advertise in their papers, and the writer similarly blamed social reformers for discussing drugs and drug trafficking only in order to "attract morbid crowds of attentive listeners." The really important lesson to be learned from Reid's death is given in the editorial's very first sentence: "Wallace Reid died in a fight against the drug habit at 31, more than thirty years before his time and his potential earning capacity of half a million dollars a year."[72] With an astonishing lack of irony, even for a trade journal, the tragedy of Reid's death is here accounted for as loss of an already calculated future income. The appeal is for readers to understand and to remember Reid's death as a lesson about the threat that drugs and drug use pose to the efficiency of rational planning and the realization of future revenue. Throughout the 1920s, the major newspapers did remember Reid in the manner advocated here. During this period his name usually only came up in the recurrent news stories about the enormous salaries paid to film stars. His final salary of $2,500 a week was often used as a sort of benchmark against which to measure other star earnings.[73] The callous honesty with which the *Variety* writer could invoke Reid only a week after his death had already been made entirely unremarkable by the previous manner in which the publicity around the star had succeeded in evacuating the site of production as a meaningful place from which to understand Reid's addiction. Furthermore, it is Reid's very death, the dead certainty that he will work no more, that allowed the anonymous *Variety* writer to remember Reid as already forgotten, as someone about whom the newspapers would have nothing left to say.

2
_____

Psychoanalysis and Fandom
in the Leopold and Loeb Trial

I'm a bit interested every time some witness testifies we said something
which we never did say; in this way I learn many things about myself I
never knew before.

—NATHAN LEOPOLD[1]

The newspapers could not stop writing about Nathan Leopold and Richard Loeb during the summer of 1924. From the time the two young men were arrested for the abduction and murder of fourteen-year-old Bobby Franks in late May until they were each sentenced to life plus ninety-nine years in early September, Leopold and Loeb made banner headlines in the nation's newspapers almost daily. The case has become a cultural and legal landmark, in part because defense attorney Clarence Darrow successfully avoided the death penalty for his clients by presenting psychiatric evidence of the young men's developmental abnormality so as to explain their criminal actions. Darrow did not seek to prove that Leopold and Loeb were insane; instead, he avoided a jury trial by having his clients plead guilty to the charges so that he might present to the court the details of these two young men's unusual life stories as mitigating evidence to be considered by the judge in sentencing. It was the first time such extensive psychiatric evidence was presented as mitigation in a criminal case, and Darrow's successful avoidance of the death penalty for the two defendants continues to be viewed as marking a significant transition in legal considerations of criminal responsibility. What Darrow was able to demonstrate that summer was that the kidnapping and murder had been, at least in part, the result of that most modern of all forces: chance, or the sum total of environmental influences that come together in a particular fashion to produce a deviant personality. American historian Paula Fass has argued that the case and its public dissemination through the national press "offered Americans the new terms *normality* and *abnormality* to understand transgressive behavior."[2] Nevertheless, the sustained media coverage of the courtroom

49

testimony given about the emotional lives of the defendants presented those lives as compelling developmental histories available to modes of public investigation already established. Like the coverage of Wallace Reid's narcotic addiction the previous year, the press provided readers with the means to understand the abnormal personality and their own relationship to that personality as members of an interested public. The Hollywood star system provided the grounding context for the public's interest in the intimate details of these two young killers cum media celebrities.

In order to attend to the historical mass-media context of the trial in 1924, it is first necessary to acknowledge a continuing fascination with the Leopold and Loeb case that has produced various retellings of the case, many of which, I would argue, seek to contain or distort its implications for mass culture. The trial is not only a celebrated legal case of the early twentieth century, but a story that has, at different moments, been a compelling narrative for the cinema of North America, as is evident in the films *Rope* (Universal, 1948), *Compulsion* (Twentieth Century-Fox, 1959), and, more recently, Tom Kalin's independent production *Swoon* (1992), all of which draw heavily from the particulars of the case. The sheer heterogeneity of these film texts makes it clear that the filmic reappearance of this story is not a simple repetition, but one that serves different purposes at different historical junctures. What gets repeated in these films is not so much a monumental crime and legal trial but the origins of a "modern" understanding of human behavior; what gets repeated is the purported introduction of the concept of the unconscious into mass culture. There is often an insistence on the traumatic nature of the public trial, as if its revelations were widely met with horror and astonishment, Leopold and Loeb becoming, thereby, emblematic of a violent loss of innocence in the midst of Jazz Age exuberance. The repeated cinematic recalling of this case allows it to be both reinvented as a decisive development in modern criminal law and reinvested as a popular memory that can articulate and contain present anxieties about human sexuality.[3] For instance, *Rope*, while making no explicit reference to the Leopold and Loeb case, nonetheless makes that case readily available to an audience twenty-four years later by conforming its story to many of the well-known and notorious details of the Franks murder. By making Leopold and Loeb elements of its textual system, the film brings into play a reading strategy that places the spectator in a position of historical, psychiatric, and criminological knowledge. Film and literary scholar D. A. Miller has analyzed the representational strategies of *Rope* and discussed the way a subsequent critical technicist history of its production that is obsessively concerned with the unusual editing ensures a continuous homophobic reading of the film. Though he does not historicize his analysis, Miller reads *Rope* as a specific deployment of homosexuality that constructs sexual difference between men while, at the same time, furnishes a deniability that homosexuality is a major factor in the film's disjunctive scopic regime: "No less busily than *Rope* excites a desire to see, it [gay male sex] inspires a fear of seeing; the object of voyeuristic desire is precisely what must not catch the eye."[4] Yet, if gay male sex is the repressed of the film, the spectator is already assured that it is what *cannot* be seen, since the unconscious can be known only through its traces; the more it remains hidden, the more it exists as an object of knowledge for the psychoanalytically informed spectator. The repressed of *Rope*, then, can only be knowable because it is repressed.

One can begin to historicize the "panic" of *Rope* by noting that it was released in 1948, the year the Kinsey report on male sexuality initiated a renewed public debate about what constituted normal nonprocreative sexual behavior. More importantly, though, *Rope* sets out specific relations between criminality and homosexuality that would be in need of further analysis. Social historian Estelle Freedman has discussed how the historical construction of the sexual psychopath gave way in the post-World War II period to the coupling of homosexuality with violent and aggressive behavior, masculine characteristics that were more valued during the war years:

> The psychopath literature did reinforce the fear of male homosexuality. At times it appeared that the major motive of psychopath laws was to prevent the contagion of homosexuality from spreading from adults to youth. Such contagion might affect the entire community and might ultimately result in violent death. For example, a 1948 article in the *American Journal of Psychiatry* argued that when adults indulged in homosexual acts with minors, "The minors in turn corrupted other minors until the whole community was involved." As evidence the authors cited "the recent killing of a 7-year-old boy by a 13-year-old because he [the younger child] would not perform the act of fellatio."[5]

Freedman points out that this increased concern about the criminal effects of homosexuality came at a time when some gay and lesbian communities were making gains in social visibility and political cohesiveness. Miller's argument about *Rope*'s simultaneous surveillance and disavowal of "the" homosexual act and the film's construction of sexual difference on and between male bodies becomes even more convincing when placed within this context of a growing anxiety about homosexual recruitment and a felt need to define "normal" male sexuality on its own terms.[6] But what Miller's reading does not account for are the specific linkages of homosexuality and criminality that the film undertakes and how *they* might function as a homophobic discourse (or, possibly, even a queer-loving discourse). Throughout his article, Miller reads the criminal identities and behavior presented in *Rope* as a rather transparent, if ultimately deniable, index of homosexuality "where the conventional assumption of the classical detective story that *anyone might have committed the murder* at once conveys and culpabilizies a universal potential for homosexuality in men."[7] If the connotative system operates in *Rope* as Miller says it does, the question still remains as to whether that system recruits all signifiers in the same way or whether certain signifiers function to specify "the homosexual," even within the ubiquity of connotation.

This question cannot, perhaps, be answered through a textual reading of the film and its criticism alone. I raise it only to return to the fact that *Rope* is a film that makes a certain refusal to represent homosexuality and that that refusal is maintained through a continued and systematic representation of criminality. This is not simply to say that the homosexual stands behind the criminal here; rather, it points to a mythic operation that both constructs a specific homosexual subject who supports the criminal through his desire for him, and connects the film to other epistemologies and discourses about celebrity identity and mass audiences. An important vector in this genealogy of *Rope* is the Leopold and Loeb case itself. However, a return to the case itself is made difficult, beyond any of the usual problems with any such return, by the manner in which subsequent retellings have positioned themselves as far more sophisticated and knowing than the public representations and popular discourses of the day allowed. Indeed, Fass maintains that the novel *Compulsion*, Meyer Levin's 1955 fictional account of the crime and trial upon which the subsequent motion picture was based, was far more direct in its depictions of the psycho-sexual motives that led to the crime than was possible "in the atmosphere of the twenties [where] the public discussions were choked off."[8] I would argue, conversely, that the so-called frankness of later accounts results from a far more rigid application of seemingly settled categories of pathology and identity formation that make it fairly difficult for us to appreciate the way popular appreciations of deviance in the 1920s sought to understand it as tied more broadly to the conditions of modern life and as available for at least partial identifications. In other words, one could still be moved by the deviance of others, contemplate one's relation to the deviant, and thereby see deviance as a condition greater than the individual.[9] *Compulsion*, in both its literary and cinematic manifestations, is far more paranoid in its mobilization of psychological discourse and its insistence on naming deviance (so as to deliver the deviant to the hands of beneficent justice) than the open, unsettled, and, at times, incoherent newspaper coverage of the Leopold and Loeb trial where vitriolic condemnation, claims to scientific expertise, and fan appreciations coexisted on the pages of the dailies for an ever fascinated public. It is this distant and difficult media situation wherein the public was seeking to use the publicity around the trial to make their own investigations that I pursue in this chapter.

The popular reception of the Leopold and Loeb trial reactivated many of the expressed concerns about the pathological audience that had defined the film industry's discourse (particularly the discourse of film exhibitors) on the nonproductive, meaningless, and morbid interest in disgraced stars during the scandal period. Also, by successfully consigning the accumulation of information about particular personalities—whether garnered from news accounts or publicity—to either an imaginative flight from reality (the scrapbook designed for the daydreams of the fan) or the instrumentality of official institutional actions (the marketing of an entertainment film by studio), these same concerns would eventually be important in changing the way fandom was understood and the ways in which it might be lived out. Take the example of playwright John Logan, whose stage drama, *Never the Sinner*, retells the Leopold and Loeb story. Writing in 1998, Logan recounts his inspiration for the play and the preparations he made prior to writing. Logan narrates a significant change of life occurring after gaining access to documents held by Leopold's former parole attorney.

> I buried myself in Leopold and Loeb. I read an endless stream of intimate letters between Leopold and Loeb and Darrow. I read one of two existing copies of the full trial transcript. I read dozens of encyclopedic psychiatric reports made at the time of the trial. I held the actual ransom note in my hands. I devoured newspapers from the day, from stories on the case to the comics to the wedding announcements. I hunted down every legal cite and contemporary reference. I scoured the *Chicago Tribune* morgue and the Chicago Historical Society for photos. I haunted the areas of Chicago where the events occurred. I watched hours of newsreels, I listened to music from the period. I read only books Leopold and Loeb read. My apartment was a chaos of period street maps and phrenology charts and time lines and Nietzsche quotes and ornithology texts and police reports and the whole swirling world of 1924 Chicago.
>
> My friends, quite sensibly, thought I had gone mad.
>
> I was not mad. I was seduced. I was completely captivated by Leopold and Loeb. Their flash and panache and smug brilliance had taken hold. To my mind, they were two of the most magical human beings who had ever lived.
>
> All that ended on the single most important day in the writing of this play. I was flipping through a very dusty file (from a source who must still remain confidential) when a photo caught my eye. And then another. And another. I was holding the autopsy photographs of Bobby Franks.
>
> Then I wrote the play.[10]

Logan accurately describes the activities of a fan that are, not coincidentally, remarkably similar to the activities of a sociological or historical researcher. He refers to the passion that overtakes him as a type of seduction, a wanting to be close to the subjects of his fascination, finding in the preserved record of their lives a possibility of thinking and experiencing the world differently. What Logan experienced was something approximate to a portion of the public's involvement in the news media's attention to these two troubled young men in 1924.

Significantly, this captivated involvement with media personalities by a mass audience was a part of the coverage itself. Logan, however, must disown his affective attachment to his objects of study in order to claim the authority to speak or write about them. His previous interest is figured as an error in judgment despite the knowledge gained, a sort of fanciful flight from reality with sobering ethical consequences. Citing the forensic evidence of a child's dead body as the reality principle that returned him to a socially responsible outlook on the case, Logan recasts his earlier relation to Leopold and Loeb as having been without social purpose, a useless inquiry and one without a future. Logan here recapitulates the process by which early Hollywood fandom was made incoherent by the discourse on morbid reception in which the social context for any popular interest in deviant stars was reduced to a question of individual pathology. Still, the question of the audience was not completely settled in 1924.

The 1920s was a period when significant changes in the popular understanding of male homosexuality were underway. This was an era when homosexuality, previously viewed as a category of vice or moral perversion, was beginning to be represented in both sexological discourse and clinical practice as an organic or developmental abnormality. This shift, in part, seems to depend on the linkage of homosexuality with criminal behaviors. Criminology itself had only recently begun to dispense with models of heredity and anatomical types to consider environmental and psychological factors as important determinants of criminal behavior.[11] While it is impossible to locate any single event or moment that could explain the arrival of a "modern" popular view of homosexuality, the Leopold and Loeb case can be used to demonstrate how this new understanding depended on the work of diverse institutional practices and various discourses that ran through and across these institutions, including the new mass media and the Hollywood star system. I focus principally on psychoanalysis in my discussions of the trial since psychoanalysis as a method of diagnosis was crucial to the publicity of the case—at least one contemporary observer claimed that the trial was really "a contest in psychology,"[12] with psychoanalysis often identified as the most modern and sophisticated school contender—and because psychoanalysis more completely furnished the necessary concepts for constructing this new relationship between the homosexual and the criminal. However, one needs to understand that psychoanalysis is always articulated at this historical moment through and alongside other discourses, and any understanding of its social effects must acknowledge its interaction with these other forms of knowledge.

It is difficult to make complete sense out of the respective diagnoses of the psychiatrists for the prosecution or those alienists who testified for the defense by reading through their testimony or consulting their summary reports. The problem is in part due to the heterogeneity of psychiatric theory and practice in the United States at the time, and in part because the diagnoses are themselves inherently contradictory and sometimes incoherent. They become especially difficult to untangle where competing and commingled discourses of biology, psychoanalysis, constitutional theory, phrenology, endocrinology, vice reform, and determinism are debated within and outside of the courtroom. One can somewhat reductively say that the prosecution simply dismissed evidence about Leopold's and Loeb's fantasies and childhood experiences since everybody fantasizes about something. It was just that Nathan Leopold and Richard Loeb chose criminal (and homosexual) fantasies whereas most boys choose to fantasize about being a doctor or a fireman. Thus, the state's experts viewed their criminal and homosexual identities as types of vocations and their childhoods were seen as years of apprenticeship.[13] The defense alienists, on the other hand, argued that the fantasies and behaviors of the two young men signaled abnormalities of psychological development that were traceable to events in their early histories. Leopold was diagnosed as a paranoiac, a diagnosis based, it seems, on his withdrawal of affective response to social life, his immense amount of psychical energy, and his fantasies of megalomania and persecution. Loeb was diagnosed as a split personality because of his supposed confusion of fantasy with reality and the eruption of those fantasies into his everyday life. Again, these diagnoses are not reducible to a purely psychoanalytic theory of human behavior but owe as much to the same social process theories of imitation that the prosecution used. For instance, in discussing the contributing factors to Loeb's personality disintegration, the defense psychiatrists repeatedly pointed to his life-long interest in detective fiction and true crime stories which constituted the bulk of his reading and which, according to the alienists, provided significant material for his fantasies. The salient difference, though, between the two groups of alienists was the defense's insistence that Leopold and Loeb were mentally abnormal because of psychic conflicts that resulted from their early familial relations and their experiences with those popular staples of psychoanalytic case studies, controlling governesses.[14]

THEIR PICTURES IN THE PAPER

Since both groups of psychiatric experts in the trial gave inconsistent opinions and often shared the same paradigms of delinquency, it is impossible to pose an opposition of schools of thought at the trial or to determine how one particular view became hegemonic. What is important about this testimony are the kinds of conditions that allowed such a debate to take place and to have the kind of social effects that this case supposedly did. The raising of Leopold and Loeb to a type of celebrity status in the press allowed this debate to enter into a field of public fear and fascination where the public was given a lesson in ostensibly the most thorough methods of understanding the causes of crime.

The major U.S. newspapers provided front-page coverage of the trial throughout the summer of 1924. The initial press coverage of the case, after the confessions were given to the state's attorney, centered both on the details of how Leopold and Loeb carried out the kidnapping and murder and on their respective histories and personalities. This information was taken from their released confessions, preliminary examinations by the state's alienists, press and police interviews with relatives and friends of the accused, and continual press interviews with Leopold and Loeb themselves. While the press often suggested that the importance of this case for the public rested on larger issues of criminal justice and modern concepts of morality, it became clear immediately that the case was interesting to the public precisely because of the economic exclusivity of the defendants' social class, their extraordinary intelligence, and their "peculiar" relationship. The case was interesting because of its uniqueness, and any light the crime might shed would not come from a purely empirical analysis of specific criminal practices or individual motivations; this crime would, through some sort of emblematic signification, tell us something about the state of the nation's soul. Yet it was the singularity of the crime and the defendants' personalities with which the press justified its exhaustive reportage. On May 31st, the day of the confessions, the *Chicago Tribune* explained its view of the case:

> In view of the fact that the solving of the Franks kidnapping and death brings to notice a crime that is unique in Chicago's annals, and perhaps unprecedented in American criminal history, the *Tribune* this morning gives to the report of the case many columns of space for news, comment, and pictures.
> The diabolical spirit evinced in the planned kidnapping and murder; the wealth and prominence of the families whose sons are involved; the high mental attainments of the youths, the suggestion of perversion; the strange quirks indicated in the confession . . . combined to set this case in a class by itself.[15]

The tension expressed here between the social relevance of this case and its "being in a class by itself" is a tension that played itself out over and over again throughout the trial. It is ultimately a tension that expressed an anxiety about the nature of the public's interest in the two defendants and the possible effects that sustained media attention might have on the mental health of susceptible readers.

The newspapers were already in the awkward position of fulfilling Loeb's fantasies of sensational crime, fantasies that were said to have been formed through and fed by his unchecked consumption of both fictional and journalistic accounts of famous criminals. It was further revealed during the trial that Loeb had reconciled himself to a life in prison as long as he could have a complete collection of news clippings documenting the crime and trial.[16] The newspapers balanced "the public's need to know" with the possibility of more prurient interests by continually reporting on Leopold's and Loeb's own narcissistic desire for publicity. On the day they pleaded guilty to the kidnapping and murder of Bobby Franks, the *New York Times* noted their eagerness to talk to members of the press and said that "they were curious about the ticking telegraph instruments in the court. They wanted to know how big a crowd waited outside and whether the headlines that told of them would be as big as the ones that announced the World War armistice."[17] Such stories attempted to displace the possibility of an unhealthy interest in the case by locating such an interest in Leopold and Loeb themselves, thereby making the newspapers and their readers observers of a process of morbid influence to which they were somehow immune. At the same time, these stories also tended to collapse the differences between the audience and the defendants, since Leopold and Loeb were shown to be a part of that same audience. By reading the same newspapers and listening to the same reports, they bore witness, along with the rest of America, to one of the greatest crime trials of the century.

The professed concern about publicity, however, was that some youngsters might be induced to emulate Leopold and Loeb, and reports began to circulate that some young criminals had begun to justify their crimes by reference to these most famous of criminals.[18] But it is not simply a fear of copycat crimes that explains the ambivalence in the newspapers' coverage of the two killers; instead, the coverage demonstrates a more abstract worry about creating sympathy and sentiment for these boys who, by several accounts, were quite charming. By reporting on the minutiae of Leopold and Loeb's daily life—their demeanor inside and outside the courtroom, their dress, their countenances, the letters that they wrote home, the gifts they received—the press, in its desire to appear as objective as possible, placed Leopold and Loeb in the specularized and fetishized position of cinematic stars. The ambivalence expressed in the press about the uniqueness of the case and its social relevance was a quality of the publicity that also attached itself to the coverage of the defendants who were at once exceptional (young, intelligent, rich) and quite ordinary (members of caring families, college boys, bridge players). This paradoxical construction of Leopold and Loeb as both exceptional and ordinary allowed their images and personalities to function as stars within the media apparatus, and the fact that they were criminals only reinforced their star status by calling to mind the Hollywood scandals of the preceding years in which the press played such an important role.[19] The larger problem that the press publicity initiated was, then, a problem about fandom, and the previous creation of criminal stars played a central role in the creation of star criminals. It was psychoanalysis that made this transition possible.

FREUD GOES TO HOLLYWOOD

So he asked me if I really never wanted to do a thing that I did not do. For instance did I ever want to do a thing that was really vialent, for instance, did I ever want to shoot someone for instance. So then I said I had, but the bullet only went in Mr. Jennings lung and came right out again. So then Dr. Froyd looked at me and looked at me and he said that he did not really think it was possible.

... So then his assistant looked at me and looked at me and it really seems as if I was quite a famous case.

—LORELEI, IN *GENTLEMAN PREFER BLONDES*[20]

In 1925 Sam Goldwyn told *Moving Picture Classic* that he was going to Europe to attempt to secure a contract with Sigmund Freud who, the producer felt, would "inject into the pictures truth and reality, where now we have only tinsel and shadows."[21] Goldwyn's claim, whether true or simply studio promotion, was consistent with Hollywood's growing preoccupation with Freud and his theories of human behavior. Not only were writers and directors claiming to consult psychoanalysis in order to create moving picture stories, but audiences were being instructed in how to understand these new narratives in terms of a modern theory of personality. A year and a half before Goldwyn made his announcement to *Moving Picture Classic*, that magazine had run an article explaining how Charlie Chaplin was using Freudian concepts in his latest film to "stress the really important thing, the mental processes that brought about the action." This piece, entitled "Absolutely Mr. Chaplin! Positively Mr. Freud! Psycho-analysis Comes to the Movies," begins with a title illustration of Chaplin's tramp introducing an equally tramp-like Freud, whose body is bent forward in salutation, to his newfound companion and collaborator. The article that follows, an apparently fabricated interview with Chaplin who was working after hours on his film, *Public Opinion* (released as *A Woman of Paris* in 1923), informs the moviegoer about the new method of understanding character and motivation. The basic idea behind this method turns out to be that every opinion, affect, or desire will always be represented by its opposite. Chaplin is described as feeling confident about the audience's ability to laugh at the tragic moments of the story and to cry at the seemingly lighthearted: "And there's a man that all the characters in the story hate and the audience will love him. All because the story is treated subjectively. D'ye see?"[22] These ideas appeared in *Motion Picture Classic* the year before Freud wrote his important essay on negation.[23] Chaplin goes on to discuss how the audience will be in complete sympathy with the heroine, in spite of the fact that she has caused the death of two characters and the derangement of a third. He explains that "there are no heroes or villains in life *per se*, but only ephemeral things called people: twisted and bent into myriad absurd patterns by infinite, indifferent life."[24]

Similar ideas were expressed throughout the Leopold and Loeb trial; Clarence Darrow said in his closing statements: "I know that every influence, conscious or unconscious, acts and reacts on every living organism, and that no one can fix the blame."[25] Such ideas were not so new to an American movie audience that had been become accustomed to viewing movies and to understanding personalities as if there were an unconscious, as in those complicated narratives of Wallace Reid's narcotic addition which depicted his deviance as stemming from some obscure trauma. In this way, the popular interest in this trial and the meaning that it had for the public were, in part, sustained by this prior articulation of psychoanalytic understanding within the entertainment industry.

At the same moment that psychoanalysis was becoming a factor in the cinema, Hollywood was experiencing a new wave of pressure from reformers and social hygiene groups to submit to outside censorship. As explained in Chapter 1, these concerns were, in large part, initiated by several scandals in which well-known movie personalities were implicated in murders and other criminal acts. While earlier censorship efforts had focused on the lurid conditions of the theaters and the perceived moral value of motion picture stories, the new reformers became increasingly concerned about the influence that individual performers might have on their audience, and they began to take an interest, just as the fans did, in the on- and off-screen lives of screen stars. Knowledge about the star and his or her private life was already an important part of attending the movies. As Richard deCordova has shown, the early star system was already functioning through a model of surface and depth, where, behind the more glamorous and excessive aspects of the star's screen image a conventional and domestic lifestyle guaranteed the moral wholesomeness of the star's identity. The coverage of the star's personal life by fan magazines became an important part of the film-viewing experience, since it established an intertextual system of meaning in which it was important to know something about a star's private life in order to fully appreciate that star in a particular film. Within this process, the films themselves continually promised to reveal more information about the star's identity with each new enactment of that personality in a film appearance.

DeCordova points out that the star scandals of the early 1920s were more or less an extension of this surface and depth model that was already in place. Another possible layer could now be added to the model, where behind the apparent health and conventionality of the star's personality lurked an immoral or criminal identity. Since film audiences generally understood there to be a signifying connection between what was known about a particular star and any screen appearance she or he might make, reformers felt justified in calling for the removal from the screen of any product that made use of an immoral star's image. Thus, the star scandals of the 1920s opened up popular debates about the moral status of particular stars and, more significantly, made the relationship between the star and fan a site for intervention. The banning of certain stars from the screen was not necessarily a punitive action taken against the performer, but an action that insured that audiences would be protected from the corruptive influences of these identities.

Early in 1923, after the MPDDA had lifted its national ban on new Arbuckle products, the warden of Sing Sing prison, following the example of film exhibitors and mayors across the country, continued to prohibit the screening of Arbuckle's films in the prison since "they might be considered a bad influence."[26] Unless one wanted to object to the frequent appearances of Arbuckle in drag, there was not anything really objectionable in his films, yet the actor continued to be the target of reform groups and censors who felt that any public use of the comedian's image was a danger to the morals of the community. These bans were usually rationalized, often with the apparent support of the film industry, by the need to protect children and youth who were highly impressionable and who usually tended to idealize screen personalities. But sometimes the expressed concern was that everyone was at risk and that these films might influence all the members of a particular community through a type of contagion. As an editorial writer in the *New York Times* put it in his commendation of the original ban, "Fortunately . . . fellows of a baser sort will not have the opportunity to disease themselves and the rest of us by applauding the man the jury pronounced 'not guilty.' "[27] Such comments demonstrate that what was troubling about Arbuckle was not anything he had done, but the kinds of desires his appearance might indulge or awaken in members of the audience. What was objectionable was the kind of affection that his films might allow, a type of love that would be typical of "fellows of a baser sort." The bans, then, were not only an effort to remove Arbuckle's image from the screen, but also an attempt to control the desires of an audience. Arbuckle's films, by the reformer's logic, could only be appreciated by an immoral or degenerate population whose displays of affection would have harmful effects on the entire community.

But why would someone be attracted to a personality as notorious and immoral as Arbuckle? Even though he had been acquitted, "an odor [clung] to him," as the *New York Times* put it.[28] Concerns about children and other impressionable types notwithstanding, the possibility of "normal" members of the community being corrupted by a picture personality was made cogent by a new understanding of the relationship between the audience and the film. The kind of audience response that was being privileged in fan magazine articles, like the one on Chaplin and Freud in *Motion Picture Classic*, stressed the easy reversibility of normal affects and the way films were capable of promoting sympathy for the most despicable of characters. If Erich von Stroheim could be billed as "the man you love to hate," audience members would be attracted to Arbuckle, not in spite of his association with criminal conduct, but because of it. Psychoanalysis had become a significant term of mass culture by this point. As the historical research of Nathan Hale Jr. has confirmed, "Publicity fed an apparently insatiable hunger for more news about the new psychology, psychiatry, and 'mental hygiene.' 'The demand for information is so great that we are simply swamped with inquiries and appeals,' Frankwood Williams, a psychiatric and medical director of the National Committee for Mental Hygiene observed in 1924."[29]

While the traditional reform movements operated under models of morality that had nothing to do with a psychoanalytic understanding of human behavior, their surveillance of picture personalities tended to be informed by and to support a system of film reception that made use of psychoanalysis and, at least implicitly, figured fandom as a troublesome type of object choice. If this importation of psychoanalysis into the film industry tended to give rise to homophobic fears about the nature of star worship, then the star system itself has to be viewed as an important contributor to an emerging understanding of homosexuality. The larger issue raised here is the need to determine to what extent the critique of the entertainment industry in the 1920s was informed by a homophobic discourse and to what extent this same discourse was fundamental to the industry's continued development.

THE STARS COME OUT IN CHICAGO

Dr. Kirby said that the fact that the youths had been reading the literature of abnormality did not mean that their minds had been affected by such reading.

—*NEW YORK TIMES* (JUNE 2, 1924)

If there was a star witness at the Leopold and Loeb trial it certainly would have been Dr. William Alanson White, superintendent of St. Elizabeth's Hospital. In the novel *Compulsion* (1956), Meyer Levin's fictionalized account of the crime and trial, the author describes Dr. White's literary stand-in: "He had been many times to Europe, he had studied Charcot's work at the Salpêtrière in Paris, he had been to Nancy, he had known Jung in Switzerland and Bleuler in Vienna and lastly, the great Freud himself."[30] White's relation to Freud here, along a metonymic chain of psychoanalytic stars, not only signifies the rising stature of the "new psychology," but makes that stature dependent upon Freud himself.[31] It has often been noted that Freud was asked to come to Chicago in the summer of 1924 to comment on the personalities of the defendants. It was not Clarence Darrow who made this request but William Randolph Hearst. Hearst offered Freud passage on a private luxury liner and an unnamed amount of money to come to North America and give exclusive commentary to the Hearst newspapers. Freud turned down this and a similar offer of $25,000 by the *Chicago Tribune* saying, "I cannot be supposed to provide an expert opinion about persons and a deed when I have only newspaper accounts to go on and have no opportunity to make a personal examination."[32] Here, Freud sought to protect psychoanalysis as a science and clinical practice from the distortions and abuses to which it was seemingly being subjected in the mass media by de-authorizing the newspaper audience as having adequate information with which to understand the personalities involved. The psychology of everyday life was in danger of becoming everyday psychology, as the newspapers daily reported the detailed testimony of the alienist psychologists.

Dr. White's testimony at the trial centered on the interplay of the two young murderers' personalities as a type of alter-ego relation. This interplay hinged on the interweaving of their respective fantasies. Loeb was characterized as having delusional fantasies about being a famous criminal who enjoyed the adulation of other lesser criminals and the sympathy of young girls. Leopold's predominant fantasy revolved around certain master-slave narratives in which he was either an especially valued slave who was completely devoted to his master or a king who maintained a close and beneficent attachment to a chosen servant. In the defense psychiatrists' joint summary, Loeb's position within Leopold's fantasies was made explicit by claiming that Leopold's "ready acceptance of Loeb's suggestions with respect to their joint criminal activity fitted precisely with [his] phantasying for years himself in the role of a slave, . . . transferring his allegiance to his idealized king-like companion."[33] Stressing the interdependence of the personalities further, White claimed at the trial that "Dickie [Loeb] needed an audience. In his fantasies the criminalistic gang was his audience. In reality, Babe [Leopold] was his audience."[34]

It is important to understand that, given the publicity surrounding the trial, White's formulation of Leopold and Loeb's relationship as one of audience to star threatened to place the entire public in a position akin to Leopold's fascination with his companion. This threat was kept in check by continual reassurances from various quarters about the moral quality of the coverage, and anxieties about recruitment were relieved by the guarantee of "no filth." The *Chicago Tribune* had campaigned for radio coverage of the trial on its station WGN with promises that "the censor will be as discriminating with his button as the copy editors are with their pencils. The *Tribune* can appear at the breakfast table of any family in the country."[35] The implied audience in need of protection here were women and children, and the susceptibility of this group was underwritten by the repetitive coverage of "real fans" at the trial, young girls who crowded the courtroom to pledge their unflagging devotion to the boys.[36] As was the case with the film industry's response to social reform arguments, there was a felt need on the part of the press both to repeat the concerns about the effects of indiscriminate coverage of criminals and perverts and to portray itself as entirely responsible to public standards of morality.[37]

Yet both the press and the defense were able effectively to communicate the "unspeakable" to a public that had become accustomed to interpreting personalities and motivations in the absence of visible evidence. When Dr. Bernard Glueck, head alienist at Sing Sing prison, testified for the defense, he described Leopold's egomaniacal personality by noting, "When I asked him whether he would object to having me detail some of the intimate things with respect to his instinctual life in a court room he said he would rather hang than have me do so."[38] Statements such as this, both in the courtroom and in the press, were constantly calling attention to Leopold's hidden sexuality, making this secret the most important element of his personality precisely because it was so secret.[39] Thus a closet was constructed for Leopold because it allowed the defense a way to demonstrate that his "instinctual life" was a determining cause in this relationship, and any judgment about this crime would have to take into account the role of Leopold's unconscious.

THE MATERNAL CAST

Before conception his mother was not healthy, and during his childhood he was not healthy.

—HULBERT AND BOWMAN JOINT MEDICAL REPORT[40]

I want to return to the legitimate yet absent star of the Leopold and Loeb trial, Sigmund Freud. Fourteen years earlier, Freud had theorized a type of love relation that approximates the relationship of fan to star. In "A Special Type of Object Choice Made by Men," he sets out to explain a particular type of erotic love by outlining the conditions that this love places on its object. Freud divides these conditions into four separate categories: (1) that the love object belong to another or in some way be unavailable; (2) that the object possess a bad reputation, generally taking the form of sexual infidelity; (3) that there is a compulsive overvaluation of the love object; and (4) that there exists a felt need to rescue the object from its fate or defend the love object's social standing. All these conditions were present, to a greater or lesser extent, in the defense alienist's description of Leopold's attachment to Loeb. Loeb's sociability and numerous romantic relationships compelled Leopold to negotiate for his attention. Loeb's self-identification with criminals and other transgressive types was conducive to Leopold's own fantasies of inferiority and superiority. Leopold idealized Loeb's accomplishments and believed him to be the "ideal man." And Leopold often saw himself as rescuing Loeb, both in his master-slave fantasies and in the practice of their criminal activities. White testified at the trial, "In several joint experiences, whenever Dickie fell down in the role of leader, Babe stepped in to fill the breach and picked up the situation."[41]

Freud relates these various conditions placed on the love object by this type of patient to a fixation of infantile feeling for the mother. His tracing of these different conditions to a group of feelings for the mother is not as important as the manner in which the love object functions as a mother-surrogate. Freud describes this fixation by recalling an obstetrical metaphor:

> In our type, on the contrary, the libido has dwelt so long in its attachment to the mother, even after puberty, that the maternal characteristics remain stamped on the love-objects chosen later—so long that they all become easily recognizable mother-surrogates. The comparison with the way in which the skull of a new-born child is shaped comes irresistibly to mind; after a protracted labour it always bears the form of a cast of the maternal pelvis.[42]

The "irresistibility" of this comparison is curious if not outright confusing. If Freud is theorizing a type of object choice that has not given up a fixation on the mother, how is it that the skull of the child, and not the object of the child's love, bears her mark? The child here seems to be both "stuck on" the mother and "stuck in" the mother at once. But Freud is not talking about the patient's subjective alignment and identification with the mother as an object of desire for the father, so whose head is Freud talking about here? Whose mother? This comparison becomes particularly ironic considered in the context of the Leopold and Loeb case, where phrenological readings of the defendant's heads were offered to the readers of the *Tribune*.

Freud is presumably discussing a type of heterosexual love relation in "A Special Type of Object Choice Made by Men." Yet his use of the "maternal cast" suggests that a type of identification with the mother is at work here in some way, an identification that elsewhere in Freud's work defines male homosexuality in terms of a narcissistic object choice.[43] Since, for Freud, the type of object choice under analysis in this essay is merely an extension, intensification, and delay of the "normal" successful negotiation of the Oedipus complex, homosexuality, in its "retiring in favor of the father,"[44] must be kept separate from this most passionate form of heterosexual love. And yet it "comes irresistibly to mind."

Homosexuality, if mostly hidden, was also the irresistible in the Leopold and Loeb trial. While the defense alienists gave testimony about the details of Leopold and Loeb's sexual relationship "in camera"—at the Judge's bench, out of the hearing of the press, and off the public court record—the pair's "perverse" relationship was a continuing subtext of the press coverage and the trial itself. The defense ostensibly wanted to employ sexual perversion as an index of the defendants' developmental abnormality, while avoiding any explicit link between homosexuality and the Franks murder itself. The prosecution, conversely, wanted to link the two together directly in order to provide a further motivation for the killing and to encourage a public understanding of the crime as a sexual assault perpetrated by a pair of perverts. In other words, the defense tried to mobilize an understanding of homosexuality as indicative of a type of abnormal personality that entailed certain types of antisocial behavior and that, though not criminal in itself, could combine with and encourage criminal behaviors and preoccupations in others. This is precisely the effect that the defense wanted to say Leopold had on Loeb. It is Leopold's homosexual love for Loeb that is the determining cause of the crime;[45] according to the logic of the defense alienists, this was not a homosexual relationship, only a relationship with a homosexual. Such a conclusion was also a view that could be arrived at by a more traditional ideology of inherited degeneracy. As Harry Olson, chief justice of the Municipal Court of Chicago, stated in a legal symposium on the case, "I believe, from this report that the Leopold and Loeb case is not an environmental calamity, but a hereditary catastrophe! . . . This case is not so unique from a psychological standpoint that it will not frequently repeat itself. On the contrary, it is very common in criminology where one of the parties is homosexual."[46]

The importance of Leopold's mother, who died in 1922, is given special stress in the defense psychiatrists' summary that makes no direct reference to inversion or homosexuality. The summary emphasized Leopold's extreme idealization of his mother *and* his identification with her:

> As a young child he placed his mother and a favorite aunt on the same level with the Madonna, about whom he came to know through having a Catholic nurse at four years of age, as being the most wonderful person of whom he had any conception. And later in life, as he looked down with contempt on women on account of their intellectual inferiority to him, he steadily maintained the above exceptions. He thus transferred his own abnormal egotistical standpoint to his own immediate family life and what is more significant psychologically, to his own origin.[47]

By citing the model of the virgin birth as a determining factor in Leopold's developmental history, the defense was able to articulate his devotion to his mother and his identification with her as simultaneous factors in his psychic life. Thus, to the extent that his worship of Loeb approximated Freud's conception of the mother-fixated object choice made by men, it also figures that choice as an inverted one, returning the repressed of Freud's essay (identification with the mother) to the foreground. What this suggests is that the separation of certain psychical processes that psychoanalysis originally attempted to maintain—here, the conceptual separation of maternal fixation and maternal identification for the male child—became more difficult and eventually collapsed as psychoanalysis was enacted within various institutions and articulated within other discourses of knowledge production in North American society.

In 1920 Freud again discusses this special type of object choice, and this time he formulates it explicitly as a type of star worship. He also discusses its role in a case of homosexuality, albeit a lesbian one. In "The Psychogenesis of a Case of Homosexuality in a Woman," Freud reiterates throughout the analysis both the patient's masculine subject position and the fact that she has chosen a feminine love object. Detailing her overvaluation of the love object, Freud notes that "all these little traits in her resembled the first adoration of a youth for a celebrated actress whom he regards as far above him, to whom he scarcely dares to lift his bashful eyes." He goes on to mention other conditions characteristic of this type of object choice, most importantly, the unavailability and questionable reputation of the loved one: "But already her first passion had been for women who were not celebrated for especially strict propriety. The first protest her father made against her love-choice had been evoked by the pertinacity with which she sought the company of a cinematographic actress at a summer resort."[48] Freud conceives star worship here as a specifically masculine trait that must seek a feminine object. This formulation is the exact opposite of the way that star discourse typically depicted the phenomenon of star worship in North America during the period of the Leopold and Loeb trial, an understanding of the devoted and adoring fan that still has particular valence today. Newspaper coverage of the trial usually mentioned only young women who swooned or showed other signs of intense devotion to the young defendants. Likewise, as discussed in the next chapter, many accounts of Valentino's funeral in 1926 commented on women who appeared to be overcome by mourning and grief while existing photographs and film footage of the crowds outside of Campbell's Funeral Church show that a majority of the spectators were men.[49] The *Chicago Herald and Examiner* even went so far as to provide a front-page column for Lenore Ovitt, "a lately graduated school girl," to convey her "impressions of the [Leopold and Loeb] proceedings." When offered this opportunity, Ovitt maintained that while she had had a "choice of a matinee at 'Topsy and Eva' or a ring side seat at the trial," she "chose the latter because I thought the Loeb-Leopold Company would put on a better show." Ovitt, who must pinch herself to make sure she is not dreaming, continues her description of the trial as show businesses. "The curtain rises upon the stage. 'Master Mind' and 'Baby Face' make their grand entrance. They are dressed immaculately—the 'glass of fashion' and the 'mold of form.' Dickie saunters along with all the grace and bearing of Valentino promenading on the screen. Nathan Jr. smiles more condescendingly and hurries to his seat." Ovitt also reported on the activity of the courtroom audience who "do not look like morbid curiosity seekers—rather do they seem like sixty (or perhaps less) authors in search of a plot." And, as was becoming standard practice in the press, Ovitt also remarked on how Leopold and Loeb were part of this same fascinated public. "Leopold and Loeb sit together reading the same newspaper. They laugh at the headlines that shriek forth the facts of the 'direst, most cruel murder in the history of American jurisprudence.'"[50]

This need to represent the devoted if somewhat disaffected fan as a young woman results, in part, from a nascent psychoanalytic understanding of sexual-

FIGURE 3. Former girlfriends of Richard Loeb who testified at the trial were also featured in the newspapers as devoted fans. Lorraine Iris Nathan and her sister Rosalind Nathan at the Leopold and Loeb murder trial. Chicago Historical Society.

ity in North America. As was the case in the Leopold and Loeb trial, this modern view of personality tended to interpret certain obsessional characteristics and behaviors in males as both indicative of homosexuality and conspiring with criminality: the homosexual and the criminal—two identities presumably unthinkable for women and children, but from which they also needed protection. When the former girlfriends and dancing partners of Loeb testified about his character at the trial, newspapers prominently featured photographs of them in fashionable attire, while sob sisters reported on the young women's continuing devotion to the "college-bred murderer." Betty Walker reported in *The Chicago Herald and Examiner*, for instance, that the case had brought Lorraine Nathan and Germaine "Patches" Reinhard, former rivals for Loeb's affection, together as friends in their mutual support for the troubled young man. Walker reported that when Nathan returned from the witness stand, she reassured Reinhard about testifying. " 'There's not a thing to be nervous about,' the quivering little co-ed volunteered excitedly. 'And you'll see Dickie.' "[51]

At the end of "A Case of Homosexuality in a Woman," Freud reiterates the need to separate object choice from mental sexual characteristics, especially in understanding homosexuality, but he still does not acknowledge how this "special type of object choice," which plays such an important role in star worship, could ever take a masculine object. Unable to take his own advice, he ties this type of object choice so closely with a masculine need to search for mother surrogates that its presence in a woman is what ultimately defines this case, for Freud, as a case of *homosexuality in a woman.*[52] Again, North American conceptions about star worship's compatibility with homosexuality reversed this formulation to stress the subjective inversion of the male fan regardless of the gender characteristics of his chosen object. Any intense devotion to popular stars exhibited by males tended to be viewed as effeminate and perverse, the stereotype of the "stage-door Johnny" notwithstanding. The compulsive nature of star worship was thought to be more suited to women and children whose affections were seen as less sexual and therefore more innocent than the desires of adult males.[53] This situation is in part explained by the recurring concerns about the attractiveness of criminals in the 1920s and 1930s. The effects that famous criminals were thought to have on young boys, and the fact that these criminals existed in a system of media publicity, forced reformers and sociologists to construct the criminal-audience relationship as a dangerous and mutually sustaining one.

The anxieties about the representation of criminals in the cinema produced a mass of research and studies on different audiences' responses to these representations, thus expanding the already well-organized surveillance and bureaucratic control of the movies and their audiences. As mentioned earlier, the relationship between movies and crime was an important component of the Payne Fund studies that were conducted in this period to measure the effects of motion pictures on children. While these studies adopted the appearance of using the most rigorous sociological approaches for the study of social behaviors, with little room for a concept like the unconscious, they also tacitly registered the previous effects that psychoanalysis had had on star-fan relations. Many of these research projects made the mutuality of the criminal-audience relation an assumption of their methodology. In one of the studies, different groups of grade school children were asked to examine a list of men and to determine which of them were "bad" and which of them were "good."[54] The fact that Al Capone and Lon Chaney could coexist on this list suggests that the researchers understood the categories of "badness" and "goodness" as media effects which were determined by the kinds of object choices a particular audience might make; in other words, for some audiences bad was going to be good. The more radical implications of this assumption were quickly covered over when the study groups were then asked to indicate which persons on the list they would like to be, with the girl respondents being told to "indicate [instead] which you would like to have as a friend." This was an attempt to maintain heteronormativity through the partitioning of identification and desire, with questionnaires continually assuming that girls would want to have (as a friend) what boys would want to be. Such partitioning recurs constantly in the Payne studies, especially those that attempt to measure audience attitudes toward criminals.

Another of these studies concluded that children who frequented movies were more likely to "believe that the love of a woman is more apt to reform [a criminal] than fear of the police." The study found that, if given a scenario about the sudden reform of a criminal, "movie children" were more likely to choose the answer that "He fell in love with a girl who insisted that he go straight" as a way of explaining such a transformation.[55] This response confirmed the assumption that movie audiences tended to understand identity in terms of desire. What was not foregrounded by the researchers in this study was that the believed change effected in the moral status of the criminal through heterosexual love implied that his previous identity would have been understood by the audience to have depended on some *other kind of desire*. The criminal was glamorous to the extent that he was represented by a publicity industry, a necessary condition to be sure, but his glamour also assumed a dependence on the adoration of others. The star criminal, who had little time for children and little respect for women, needed a male audience in order to remain a star and, sometimes, even to remain a criminal.

3
_____

Queer Valentino

Almost every biography of Rudolph Valentino begins with a dramatic description of the popular film star's death in August of 1926 and with the notorious riot that erupted on the first day of his lying in state at Campbell's Funeral Church in New York City.[1] Tens of thousands of his fans—as well as admirers, well-wishers, and the morbidly curious—stood in line all morning just to get a glimpse of Valentino's corpse. They stood there until after two o'clock in the afternoon, when at last the doors to Campbell's were opened and the riot began. The screenwriter and Valentino biographer Irving Shulman describes the crowd this way: "Psychologically blind, emotionally drunk, intoxicated by steamy human contact, increasingly defiant of the impotent police force—the mob, transformed into a human juggernaut, stormed the doors. It shouted and screamed and cried out in a masochistic ecstasy that transmuted pain into joy."[2] Such scenes repeatedly portray Valentino's public as a ritualistic cult whose transgressions of the law were accomplished by crossing the sacred with the profane and by alternating beatific reverence with destructive ecstasy. In privileging this particular representation of Valentino's public, these biographies suggest that the cult of Valentino was constituted and sustained by exotic rituals and collective behaviors suitable for ethnographic investigation. However, the sheer repetition of the funeral riot as the central trope of Valentino's life actually works against any such analysis since it represents his public as a "primitive" cult whose spectacular appearance in the modern city is as fascinatingly remarkable as it is inscrutable.

To begin a biography of Valentino with the spectacle of his funerary rites poses the film star as a sort of false idol for an adoring but misguided and sometimes manipulated audience whose intensity of devotion (filtered, as it was, through the manufactured publicity about the star) helped create the myth of the star's charisma. The Valentino biographer can thus acknowledge the prominence and importance of the star-audience relation for Valentino's popular identity, only to dismiss that relation as a source of any valuable or reliable information about Valentino himself. The biographical work of the author can then be limited to an empirical project of getting at the truth of the individual *behind* the myth. Of course, this is a rhetorical gesture common to most exposés of celebrities, but, in the case of Valentino, the continual repetition of the scene of a violent and re-gressed audience is also important for containing potentially disruptive sexual and racial meanings which circulated around and were facilitated by Valentino's stardom. As much feminist scholarship on the star over the last two decades has shown, part of the historical significance of Valentino is the way in which his stardom complicated static notions of masculine identity and, just as im-portantly, produced more dynamic possibilities for audience receptions and self-definitions.[3]

More than just an index of the great star's popularity, the chaotic public vio-lence that followed Valentino's death represents his mass appeal as powerful and potentially destructive, though ultimately irrational and impossible to analyze. Ironically, to begin the story of Valentino's life with the mass spectacle of his death means to turn away from mass-cultural reception as a site appropriate for understanding that life; the star's public must be explained (away) by an investi-gation into the individual man, since the public can never be relied on to produce acceptable knowledge. In this view of the situation, a mass audience is only ever able to passively guarantee the talent or appeal that a star is already presumed to possesses, but it cannot, in any significant way, qualitatively determine the iden-tity of a star or contribute to his or her life experiences. Interestingly, this notion of the star audience is precisely opposite of the increasingly more prevalent man-ner in which film stardom was being represented during the early and mid-1920s. As discussed in Chapter 1, film audiences of the period were not only being cred-ited with the power of shaping the content of Hollywood films, but also of influ-encing the respective fates of their favorite stars.

The riot at Valentino's funeral has proven so successful a moment for initiat-ing and legitimating the project of empirical biography that it has even been used to begin the life story of someone other than Valentino. In his monograph on Natacha Rambova, who was Valentino's second wife, biographer Michael Morris ostensibly wants to demonstrate the unique and various contributions Rambova made to twentieth-century culture as a dancer, a costume designer, and an Egyp-tologist. Yet *Madam Valentino*, too, begins with the now well-known but still intriguing scenes of the riot outside of Campbell's Funeral Church in 1926. By beginning his book with the cliché of Valentino's dead body, as well as entitling his biography *Madam Valentino*, Morris inadvertently suggests that perhaps

FIGURE 4. James Abbe's double portrait of Rambova and Valentino on the cover of Michael Morris's book poses the question of gender transience to construct Morris's authority as an historian. It also sells books.

Rambova was not entirely "someone other than" Valentino himself.[4] Additionally, the use of James Abbe's photograph of the famous couple in visually rhyming and overlapping profiles on the book's dust jacket implicitly poses the question: which one of these two is the real "Madam Valentino?" It is Morris's job to straighten these two personalities out, and while such ambiguities cannot be said to call into question the very possibility of an objective biography, they do suggest that an intractable instability of identity is crucially important to Valentino's cultural legacy, and was, as well, a factor in his ascendancy to stardom in the early 1920s.

Like previous treatments of Valentino, Morris's biography of Rambova-Valentino trades on the mysterious and disruptive erotics of their personae in order to validate the author's task of describing the actual lives of Rambova and Valentino that are to be found behind all the publicity, rumor, and historical re-appropriations of their identities. The ambiguities of gender and sexual identity that the book's dust jacket sets forth function only as a lure whose more sugges-tive and queerer meanings are then denied by the "real" work of the social histo-rian and biographer. In many ways, *Madam Valentino* illustrates the immense difficulty of thinking about the past reception of film stars with any sustained or sophisticated attention to the ways that those receptions were informed by his-torically and socially divergent notions of sexuality and gender identity.

The very idea that Valentino could have glamorized a version of male queer-ness within the star system of the 1920s seems worth pursuing to Morris only if Valentino can somehow be proven to have been actually queer himself. For example, Morris is compelled, with an urgency bordering on panic, to put a stop to all the "controversy and innuendo" concerning Valentino's homosexuality, a lamentable state of affairs that has lately come about, according to Morris, almost solely because of an arrogant post-Stonewall gay sensibility and because of Ken-neth Anger's treatment of Valentino in his "gossip-filled" book on star scandals, *Hollywood Babylon*. Emily Leider makes a similar maneuver in her 2003 biogra-phy of Valentino, *Dark Lover*, when she quotes Valentino's close friend, the cine-matographer Paul Ivano, as having vexedly dispelled more recent gossip about the silent star's deviant sexuality by pronouncing Valentino "a nice, normal human being."[5] Most recently, film scholar Amy Lawrence has described the way Valentino's film roles often queered his identity and relations to others, only to circumscribe these deviant erotica within the sphere of a personal and inscruta-ble reception.[6] However, the necessity to once and for all clear up any misunder-standings about Valentino's sexual identity is most forcefully broached by Morris in a section of his book cordoned off from the rest of the biography by being placed *after* the epilogue. Apparently, Morris must quarantine his discussion of Valentino's sexuality from the rest of the text since even the insinuation of Valen-tino's and Rambova's homosexuality threatens to devour all the details of their lives.

Despite Morris's claims, Anger had not, in fact, maintained that Valentino was homosexual, only that Valentino's masculinity was often questioned in the 1920s and that the star was "blamed for the mannerisms of a bunch of Clark Street faggots," who were presumed to have taken their cues from the matinée idol in matters of dress and public comportment. Nevertheless, Morris attempts to res-cue Valentino's reputation. Morris narrates his own diligent and thorough search for an "autographed art deco-style dildo fashioned of black lead," a purported present from Valentino to Ramon Novarro which Anger claimed was found rammed down Novarro's throat after he was murdered by two young hustlers he had picked up in 1968.[7] Morris tells the reader how he had "felt it necessary to check the veracity of Anger's story." By marshaling the testimony of family, church, and state, Morris presents his refutation:

> The coroner's report filed for Novarro revealed no evidence of any object thrust down his throat. Mr. C. Robert Dambacher, the coroner's investigator assigned to the case, has written that no "Art Deco Dildo" was found at the scene of the crime. An interview with the Reverend Edward Samaniego, a Jesuit priest and nephew of the slain actor, revealed that nothing of the sort was ever inventoried in his uncle's estate, and, according to Novarro's relatives, the actor was never on friendly terms with Rudolph Valentino, since they were in competition for the same roles. Finally, United States District Judge James M. Ideman, who was at the time the deputy district attorney responsible for prosecuting the killers of Ramon Novarro, answered my inquiry on this matter: "With reference to the claim that Mr. Novarro was choked to death by means of an 'Art Deco dildo,' I can tell you that that did not happen. . . . I certainly never made any statement to the effect that such an instrument was used. I did not even know of its existence."[8]

Finding no trace of this "Art Deco dildo" anywhere, Morris concludes: "if this murder weapon is fictitious, then so is the insinuation that Valentino and Novarro were connected to it in 'friendship.' Likewise, the convenient and related allegation that Natacha Rambova was a lesbian collapses when one scrutinizes the facts."

Aside from the fallacious logic of these conclusions and the ludicrous image of the historian scouring the archives in search of a tell-tale dildo, Morris's inability to read Anger's work as anything other than "straight" history is telling in its refusal to countenance queer reception as culturally significant or as having a historical lineage that precedes the late 1960s. From a historiographical point of view, his resistance betrays, more generally, the empiricist historian's reduction of sexual identity to the "truth of the individual," a reduction that always assumes, not incidentally, that an individual is heterosexual until proven otherwise. Furthermore, the demand for empirical evidence to support claims about the significance of sexual meanings and identifications involved in specific audience receptions continually seeks to assign those meanings and identifications to isolatable and verifiable subjectivities. In other words, the reasoning goes, if there are, say, lesbian meanings or identifications detectable for a specific historical event, or generated through a particular confluence of cultural texts, then there must be lesbians somewhere in the vicinity; the historian's task, then, is to seek them out and document them. Not only is such a demand politically problematic and ethically suspect, but it also obscures the historical force and complexity of sexuality as a popular way of knowing and living in the Western world during the nineteenth and twentieth centuries. By acknowledging these problems with the ideological work of star biographies, I am not suggesting that all historical work on cinema and sexuality that aims at or incorporates the biographical is necessarily retrograde or flawed. By way of a counterexample, Judith Mayne, while ambivalent about her "discovery" of the surviving correspondence between film director Dorothy Arzner and Arzner's life-long companion Marion Morgan, comments on the letters' political importance: "For too long clichés of spinsterhood, of asexuality, of careers managed at the price of any personal satisfactions, have not only rendered lesbianism invisible, but insignificant and meaningless as well. There, written in her own hand, was a declaration of her relationship with Morgan."[9] Even here, the demand for proof is still functioning on its own paranoid terms of skeptical (but fascinated) disbelief, and the visibility of lesbianism is achieved only by satisfying hegemonic empirical criteria about what can be reasonably claimed concerning the existence and relevance of non-normative sexualities in the past.

Compounding this problem of sufficient historical evidence is the way deviant sexualities and subjectivities have been defined and theorized within queer theory in terms of their very "spectrality," "insubstantiality," and "deniability."[10] Queerness is often seen as a type of haunting of historically normative modes of thought or being, and queerness, while facilitating the very intelligibility of the normative, is also its perpetual blind spot. There would seem to be little place for such deconstructive notions about sexuality and identity within the parameters of current film scholarship on historical reception where methods of audience demographics, audience sampling, and analyses of specific institutional receptions predominate.[11] However, one of the areas where queer theoretical work has been more fully integrated with film studies is in scholarship on film stars and star culture.[12] This is partially explained by the way that the star system functions in tandem with the sexual as sources of knowledge. As Richard deCordova has explained, "The dynamic of secrecy and confession, concealment and revelation that supports discourse on sexuality supports discourse on stars as well."[13] Again, a return to deCordova's work is instructive. According to deCordova, the public's consumption of film stars takes the form of an investigation and, because this investigation is structured around binaries such as presence/absence and public/private, film stars not only recapitulate sexual knowledge, they constitute, in the very terms in which they appear and disappear, acts of sexual knowing and learning and, thus, they constitute important instances of historical receptions, ones that can tell us a great deal about the interests and expectations of historical cinema audiences.

In this chapter and the next, I argue that Valentino constitutes a particularly complex example of a celebrity whose stardom enacted deviance and the epistemological conditions under which that deviance could be understood. In this way Valentino functioned as a type of meta-sign for the possibilities of understanding the social relations that subtended personality, sexuality, gender, and race for U.S. audiences in the 1920s. Valentino's stardom is examined in this chapter through its relation to popular and scientific ideas about gender, sexuality, and vision. In Chapter 4, I consider the ways that Valentino, through rather intricate scenarios of presence and absence, enacted a particular version of modernity in which racial hierarchies underwrote the experiences of industrial production and mass consumption.

Like Kenneth Anger and many other biographers of Valentino, Morris chooses to discuss those attacks on Valentino's masculinity that appeared with some regularity in the nation's newspapers and, less often, in the fan magazines. The public questioning of Valentino's gender identity has come to be seen by Valentino biographers as a significant part of the star's career and, as we shall see, possibly the most important contributing factor in his early death. Also, like some contemporary commentators and most present-day historians, Morris reads Valentino's gender deviance, a deviance that manifested itself in the star's obvious investments in beauty culture, as primarily the projection of a conservative, white masculinity that was insecure and jealous of the glamorous Italian's success and popularity. It was Valentino's professional association with powerful women and the sex appeal he presumably held for women audiences that Morris and others see as the catalysts for these public attacks.

> Valentino's olive skin, oiled hair, and Italian grace projected a feline yet virile exoticism that made women swoon. His limpid, heavy-lidded eyes suddenly bulging with sexual passion became his much caricatured trademark. His posturing, decorative image was focused to seduce women in the audience, and this made their husbands and boyfriends uncomfortable and envious. The Latin-Lover's self confidence in his own attractiveness was eyed suspiciously by those who had been conditioned to believe that beauty had but one gender, and that was feminine. Valentino was a women's sex object, he was a woman's actor, and women were his most loyal fans.[14]

Morris here, as in his discussion of Valentino's sexual orientation, seeks to explain Valentino's gender deviance as the conditioned response of an audience he defines as conflicted and unreliable since they were seeking to maintain their own narrow views of proper masculinity. Morris does concede, however, that Valentino's effeminacy was an issue during the period of his celebrity career and was not simply an invention of more recent times.

In this respect, Morris's work concurs with the views of other cultural critics such as Gaylyn Studlar and Marjorie Garber, both of whom see Valentino's departure from traditional masculinity as having challenged essentialist notions about gender identity and a dominant cultural order that still depends on such notions to sustain itself.[15] Studlar has discussed Valentino as resembling the Progressive-era model of "the woman-made man," a creature who was viewed as symptomatic of the feminizing influences of the modern city, consumerism, and the disappearance of strenuous physical activity in the lives of white, middle-class men. Valentino was woman-made in several respects: his star potential was reported to have been discovered by a woman, June Mathis, the famous script writer; he was accepted into a circle of well-known lesbian artists that was headed by theater and film actress Alla Nazimova; and he was often represented as dominated by his more sophisticated and pretentious wife, Rambova, whose slave bracelet he wore at all times. Perhaps more at issue in the charge of woman-made man was the idea that Valentino's celebrity was sustained and held in place by an exclusively female audience who were manipulated and seduced by the star. For Studlar, those attacks on Valentino that characterized him as some sort of lounge lizard, or as a "tango pirate" who made his living off the misplaced affections of women are evidence of attempts by socially conservative forces of the era to reaffirm the ideals of masculine health, virility, and citizenship that had been in ascendancy since the Roosevelt era.

Garber offers Valentino as an example of what she terms "unremarked transvestitism." In unremarked transvestism, performers do not necessarily don the clothes of another gender, and yet "the way they are received and discussed in the media, and, increasingly, the way they emphasize their own trademark idiosyncrasies of dress in response to audience interest all suggest that the question of cross-dressing, whether overt or latent, is central to their success, and even to the very question of stardom."[16] Garber gives three examples of this type of transvestism: Liberace, Valentino, and Elvis Presley. All males, these three performers, while almost never indulging in the literal practice of cross-dressing, signaled their transvestism through the very excesses of their haberdashery and through a noticeable and stylized use of cosmetics. By referencing those psychoanalytic theories of "masquerade" which have traditionally approached femininity as a social mask or as a theatrical ruse used to assuage male anxieties, Garber maintains the these three male celebrities, each with his respective relation to sartorial spectacle and physical display, drew upon prevalent cultural definitions of the feminine as artifice. In other words, because these performers were emphatically marked as in some way fake or artificial, the star identities they performed, whether highly masculine or otherwise, were structured and popularly received as feminine in their very lack of authenticity and naturalness.[17] For Valentino's glamorous beauty and his menacing sexuality were often received as a type of drag performance. Of course, Garber notes, as have many others, that the ability of men to employ strategies of masquerade demonstrates that masculinity, too, is nothing but the performance of a social mask.[18]

Since Valentino's somewhat humble background as a struggling Italian immigrant was generally well known, his overstylized acting, his association with the theatricality of costume spectacles, and his apparent admiration for aristocratic manners and other forms of cultural refinement all helped to portray the star as a sort of grand poseur. Valentino's falseness of character was further enhanced by the historical moment of his film stardom.[19] As discussed in Chapter 1, the very terms of Hollywood stardom were rapidly changing in the immediate postwar period, due in large part to the disruptions caused by the public scandals of the early 1920s and by the attendant contradictions that developed in the industrial regulation of star personalities. As in the case of Wallace Reid, the Hollywood film industry successfully shifted the basis of film stardom away from an emphasis on the star as a public representative of corporate quality and integrity, and instead emphasized the film-going public's role in the production of stars, a role that had to be rather quickly contained and pacified so that it would amount to little more than a passive expression of a star's popularity at the box office. This alienation of the film star from any close and easy association with the emerging Hollywood studio system meant that the star's status as a *manufactured* product, subject to ever changing market demands and conditions, was made more apparent in both the lives of stars and in the discourses that spoke about those lives. No male star of the period reflected this change in the star system more than Rudolph Valentino. The oft-noted indeterminacy of Valentino's gender and ethnic identity needs to be situated both in relation to this change in the star system and in relation to the repeated inscription of Valentino as a manufactured celebrity.

Despite having worked as an actor for several years before achieving international stardom in 1921, Valentino was touted as a new kind of male star, an overnight sensation who was anything but genuine. He was a beautiful false idol whose appearance and affectations were calculated to secure and flatter a fascinated female audience. Valentino was regarded by some commentators as the male version of the vamp character,[20] another gender deviant who was most closely associated with the career of Theda Bara. Interestingly, Bara was a film actress whose star identity was, perhaps, the very first to have been considered a pure fabrication of studio publicity.[21] By marking and marketing such deviant stars as the fictive creations of the movie marketplace, studios neatly avoided the possibility of a negative backlash should that deviance deeply offend those who would hold the studios accountable for the moral quality and emotional health of the persons they employed as well as the types of personalities they promoted in their products. Since the star persona could be shown to have little or no basis in the real life of the performer, the very appearance of the deviant star could be attributed to a public demand for such personalities, and not to any moral laxity on the part of the studio.

In September 1922, Valentino decided to walk out on his contract with Famous Players-Lasky for a number of reasons, which included disputes over his salary and the studio's refusal to allow Valentino a role in choosing the films in which he was to appear. He claimed that the studio had taken away his previously granted right to pre-approve film projects and to suggest film stories. While Valentino charged the studio with breach of contract, Famous Players-Lasky won a permanent injunction against the actor preventing him from appearing in any motion pictures or from taking on any theatrical work for a period of two years, the length of time remaining on his studio contract.[22] While a compromise between the star and the studio was finally reached in the summer of 1923, Valentino ended up being absent from the nation's movie screens for almost an entire year at the very height of his stardom. The fan magazines, which typically gave only scant coverage to industrial antagonisms and labor conflicts in Hollywood (and always downplayed or completely ignored the major Hollywood scandals), made Valentino's contractual battles with Famous Players-Lasky into a major story. *Photoplay* even decided that the occasion of Valentino's absence from the screen merited the serialization of his life story, "written by himself—not by his press agent, for he hasn't any."[23] Such coverage foregrounded the arbitrariness of the film star's relationship to the studio and even to Hollywood itself, and it suggested that since Valentino was no longer employed by a film studio, the "truth" of the man behind the mask of publicity could finally be revealed. While it might be thought that the film industry stood to suffer from all the media attention given to Valentino's complaints about the abuses of the studio system, the fact is that, at that moment of star scandals, the industry had a much larger investment in emphasizing the legal and moral autonomy of movie stars. Ironically, this autonomy could be best represented through the stars' complaints about their contractual obligations to the studios.

Both Valentino and Rambova attacked the studio system in the fan magazines. They justified their decision not to give in to studio demands by claiming that they were more interested in protecting and promoting the artistic integrity of the screen—a pursuit that was, they felt, greatly compromised by the sheer greed of the producers. In an interview printed in the December 1922 issue of *Photoplay*, Rambova described the studios' methods of star exploitation:

> Some producers find an unusual personality. They use up thousands of dollars to exploit it. They put the personality into a picture and the picture goes over and makes millions. Then, instead of letting the actor who does fine work go on doing it, they give him cheap material, cheap sets, cheap casts, cheap everything. The idea then is to make as much money from that personality with the least outlay.[24]

While such statements ran the risk of portraying studio work as deadening and highly degraded, as had the initial newspaper coverage of Wallace Reid's drug addiction, the emphasis here was almost always on the integrity of the artwork and how the American public was being cheated out of the finest that Hollywood had to offer. In the same interview Rambova predicted that film audiences would soon "refuse to take second-rate products even when a big personality is exploited." This lament about the loss of artistic integrity under the profit-driven aegis of the Hollywood producer system did little to establish any sense of authenticity for Valentino; in fact, this discourse had the effect of further counterfeiting Valentino's star identity to the extent that it necessarily dwelt on the reification of that identity as it had been exploited in cheap film productions. Proof of the relationship between studio exploitation and the liquidation of Valentino's unique individuality can be found in the advertising materials for *The Young Rajah* (1922), the last film the young film star made before his tempestuous break with Famous Players-Lasky. The press kit for *The Young Rajah* recommends that exhibitors of the film "play up the fact that the public has seen Mr. Valentino as a picturesque gaucho of the South American plains—as a soldier of France—as a popular society idol—as a barbaric Sheik—as the virile American youth and sailor—as a courageous torero—and now they will see him as an East Indian prince."[25] Rather than emphasizing Valentino's acting virtuosity, studio publicity tended to promote Valentino as a highly adaptable and easily consumable fantasy figure, and this was precisely the type of routinized manufacture of personality to which Rambova and Valentino so strongly objected.

The couple's appeals to the sanctity of art were, however, often represented as elitist, pretentious, and entirely out of touch with the majority of the film-going public. Morris includes in his biography of Rambova a cartoon that appeared around this time in *Photoplay* showing a large, tightly packed cinema audience excitedly gathered to watch the films of Ramon Novarro and Antonio Moreno while Valentino and Rambova stand off to the side, pontificating from a soapbox about the importance of art to the only person who will listen: a fellow member of the idle class, a lone hobo. Valentino's continuing unemployment also ran the risk of confirming his status as a "woman-made man" since it would make him financially dependent on Rambova, a danger she tried to somewhat anticipate when she disclosed how "Rudy gets horribly excited when I say this, but I do declare that if they keep him from working for two more years then I will work and support us both."[26]

Both Rambova and Valentino also spoke about the radical disjunction between Valentino's star image and his real-life personality. While other film historians have pointed out that the star discourse in this period generally tended to draw attention to itself by giving examples of how the real identity of the star was quite distinct and different from the star's public image,[27] Valentino's star identity constituted a rather extreme case of this tendency. "Rudy's personality on the screen is entirely different from the Rudy I know," Rambova told readers of *Pho-*

FIGURE 5. Valentino's identity as a defender of high art, though widely known, was seldom convincing. *Photoplay*'s cartoon hints that such posturing actually connected Rambova and Valentino to the lowest elements of American society.

toplay;[28] discussing his own stardom a month later, Valentino explained to these same readers how he felt "quite unreal." Valentino attempted to garner public sympathy for his dispute with Famous Players-Lasky by declaring that his stardom belonged to "the fans, who made me." By making his public entirely responsible for his star identity and his success, Valentino was inadvertently aiding the film industry in relieving itself of its own responsibility for complications in the public images of its stars as well as its responsibility for the very real problems many stars faced in their immediate work-a-day lives. Valentino forfeited a lot of ideological leverage in his struggle for a better contract by representing the creation of his stardom as a public ritual imbued with a tragic fate: "Idols were made to be shattered. My pedestal is at present a little too high to be entirely comfortable. I feel too humble for such an altitude. In the very nature of things I know that I cannot occupy such a position very long."[29] It was through such utterances that the cult of Valentino was born.

Because this representation of Valentino as an idol of a mass cult worked to publicly figure his star image as a sort of ritualistic mask, his gender transience has to be finally understood as more than just the effect of particular details of dress, physique, manner, or biography. In other words, what we might call, following

Garber, Valentino's "masquerade," or what I would term his "counterfeit masculinity," cannot be fully explained by any set of character traits that marked the star as in some way feminine, but was, instead, determined by specific developments in the star system that were also significant moments in the institutional history of the American cinema. One of the implications of this is that Valentino's queerness, which was only in part based on the particular way he performed masculinity, was a structural component of American mass culture in the 1920s, one which helped to determine the subsequent development of star culture and fandom. The work of Alexander Doty and others have confirmed that mass cultural texts, as well as mass cultural production and reception practices, very often destabilize rigid gender categories to offer queer pleasures and meanings to a public capable of recognizing the queer possibilities and positions historically present or available within it.[30] As Doty formulates it,

> Queer positions, queer readings, and queer pleasures are part of a reception space that stands simultaneously beside and within that created by heterosexual and straight positions. These positions, readings, and pleasures also suggest that what happens in cultural reception goes beyond the traditional opposition of hetero and homo, as queer reception is often placed beyond the audience's conscious "real-life" definition of their sexual identities and cultural positions—often, but not always, beyond such sexual identities and identity politics. . . . I don't want to suggest that there is some queer utopia that unproblematically and unpolitically unites straights and queers (or even all queers) in some mass culture reception area in the sky. Queer reception doesn't stand outside personal and cultural histories; it is part of the articulation of those histories.[31]

What Doty's insight means for my consideration of Valentino's stardom is that the star's involvement in the production of queer meaning does not entail that there must be an assignment of a recognizable queer identity to any particular person, including Valentino himself, though this might and undoubtedly did happen quite often. What queer mass cultural reception does entail is the confirmation, production, and dissemination of knowledge about queer identities and queer sexuality generally, within the limits of the discourses about sexuality then available at that historical moment and in relation to people's lived and shared experiences. But which discourses about sexuality were available to film audiences in the 1920s? What were the lived and shared experiences of sexuality and sexual identity in America at that time? Before attempting to answer these questions, it is first necessary to examine the mass media's own representation of Valentino's audience.

Because Valentino was portrayed as a film star who was almost entirely dependent on his public for his identity, he is particularly useful for investigating the mass reception of film stars during the period. In many ways, Valentino was held up as the embodiment of a grand collective wish, an obvious consequence of his function as a cult figure. Who Valentino was and what he stood for supposedly had its source in the desires of a public who admired and adored him. When, in 1923, *Motion Picture Magazine* published an analysis of Valentino's popularity that was supposedly written by "one of America's most eminent psychologists," the fan magazine was doing nothing more than participating in the already well established practice of using film stars for the purpose of performing social and cultural criticism. Stars had become interesting during the previous few years precisely because of what they might tell audiences about themselves and the society in which they lived. The anonymous psychologist of the *Motion Picture Magazine* article reminded her or his readers that, as with any social fad, all extreme expressions "of popular enthusiasm have their source in some deep psychological need. Psycho-analysts call these needs repressions, and tell us that when a repression grows strong enough there is always a psychic reaction. No great public demonstration, no burst of popular passion just happens."[32] Portraying Valentino as a symptom of psychological repression was not in any way unusual or remarkable during this period, but the more interesting possibilities of just whose deep-seated needs might be met by such a public fantasy figure were almost always circumscribed by an appeal to a rather predictable set of ahistorical and universal archetypes representing normative heterosexual desire and gender relations. Valentino had become the symbol of the eternal lover, readers were told, "because he embodies those qualities and characteristics which, from the dawn of history, have fascinated the impressionable feminine heart." The historical circumstances for the expression of this eternal need occurred, so readers were told, because "the business men of this country have not made good with their women."[33]

As discussed in Chapter 2, unlike most European theatrical traditions where young men often held lasting crushes on popular actresses, the ardent fan of any movie star in the United States—whether the star was male or female—was almost always assumed to be female, in part because of the gender deviance that resulted from any male's display of an obsessive attachment to another person. Such emotional dependency was invariably understood as a feminine quality. Interestingly, Valentino's passionate portrayals of life-or-death romantic attachments in his films were used to help explain his attractiveness to women since he obviously "spoke their language of love." Yet it is questionable just how sincere and how successful were the attempts to characterize the cult of Valentino as a thoroughly feminine expression of heterosexual romance. One could well wonder, for example, what was actually meant by characterizations that described the matinée idol as "the masculine counterpart of Sappho."[34] Therefore, since Valentino was often positioned as having an uncannily close familiarity with feminine psychology and female desires, the very possibility of a male fandom for Valentino would have been doubly suspect as a manifestation of gender deviance and sexual abnormality. No, as the newspapers and the fan magazines of the period would have it, all women adored Valentino and all men hated him.

Undoubtedly, the cult of Valentino represented the existence of a unique female public sphere where some women, however tentatively, found a space of leisure and sociality outside of entrenched patriarchal forms of organization.[35] Yet these very women and their concerns were represented in the media, both positively and negatively, as a rather homogeneous bunch, and female fans of the star were encouraged to imagine themselves from a white, middle-class perspective. No one has done more to provide an account of this historical and cultural context for the reception of Valentino than Gaylyn Studlar, whose writings on female audiences and Valentino illustrate the extent to which the discursive construction of the cult was dominated by white, middle-class concerns. By showing how the public discussion of Valentino was tied to and fairly consistent with social concerns about the "New Woman"—her abandonment of traditional domesticity and her experimentation with new forms of leisure that was made possible by her financial independence—Studlar demonstrates that Valentino was represented as a threat to traditional middle-class values. Those purported to be at risk from the seductive charms of Valentino were women of some affluence and with disposable incomes upon whom the wily tango pirate was thought to have set his sights. Whether titillating or terrifying, the scandal of being a kept man could only have this sort of meaning and valency from a middle-class point of view. Who was to "blame" for this scandalous state of affairs? As the anonymous psychologist of *Photoplay* had testified, it was "the business men of this country [who] have not made good with their women," and the warning to these men was to learn to participate with their wives in the new pleasures and "freedoms" now offered by an ever-expanding consumer culture.

The thoroughness of Studlar's historical recovery of a dominant white, middle-class reception context for Valentino can be seen in her analysis of the textual pleasures offered by Valentino's screen performances and the mode of their spectatorial address. Take, for instance, her reading of the famous tango scene at the beginning of *The Four Horsemen of the Apocalypse* (Metro, 1921) where Valentino plays a brash young gaucho who uses his whip to select a suitable dance partner from one of the many lower-class women and female prostitutes populating the mise-en-scène of the rough but lively Buenos Aries saloon. Studlar writes:

> [T]he female spectator of *Four Horsemen* did not necessarily participate in a simple masochistic fantasy reproducing the dance partner's submission to a dark, mysterious, brutal, man. She may savor the tango as a "safe display" of dangerously eroticized heterosexual relations because she can rely on the conventionalized patriarchal dynamics of dance to displace responsibility for her own arousal onto the powerful male dancer. The actualities of casting and presentation offer the specta-

tor the imaginative space to enjoy being superior—in class, ethnicity, and/or physical beauty—to the woman in Valentino's arms.[36]

Studlar had previously outlined how exotic dance can function as a "'safe display' of dangerously eroticized heterosexual relations" in her discussion of the American success of Diaghilev and the Ballets Russes, and the promotion of ethnic dancing by high cultural institutions such as the Kosloff School of Dance.[37] The possibility of dance offering an escape from the responsibility of sexual feeling for the many working-class women who frequented and worked at the numerous small dance halls of the period seems rather remote, however. I will discuss Valentino in relation to working-class dance culture in the next chapter. At this point, suffice it to say that those freedoms that may have been won by the women's movement or that patriarchy may have been willing to grant to women's erotic imaginations were, in this particular instance, freedoms only to be enjoyed by women of an established, genteel middle class. Furthermore, the "actualities of casting" in the initial tango sequence of *Four Horsemen* could only have afforded a sense of superiority to those who had already consented to a particular justification of race and class privilege. This specific invitation to a dance may well have been an attempt to place the female spectator in step with white middle-class standards of taste and beauty, as Studlar's reading implies, but whether or not the great majority of the film's contemporary viewers accepted this invitation is another question entirely and an historically important one.

While many middle-class men genuinely believed that Valentino posed a threat to white, middle-class womanhood, and while probably just as many white, middle-class women genuinely indulged in what they took to be a transgressive worship of the film star, this was not the only, or even the most important challenge that Valentino's stardom posed to bourgeois ideology. The real scandal of Valentino's stardom was, in fact, its utter *indifference* to American middle-class culture. The radical indeterminacy of Valentino's star image had opened the possibility for diverse mobilizations and appropriations of his identity, many of which would conceivably have little or nothing to do with the dominant cultural order. This indifference helps to explain the repeated insistence in the press and in the fan magazines that Valentino's popularity was a provocation *for* the middle-class, not *against* the middle class. While historians and theorists of the mass media have noted the devastation of traditional rural, local, and immigrant cultures caused by mass culture's rationalization of everyday life,[38] it is also true that, at times, a fully democratic and participatory society could be glimpsed in the universalization of access that mass production promised. It is important to remember that mass culture was, and still is, a site of social struggle and political resistance despite the fact that a particular group is able to invisibly impose itself in seemingly every instance of culture and, more importantly, control almost every public remembrance of the historical past. Representing Valentino's stardom as a challenge to traditional middle-class Anglo propriety was (and continues to be) an attempt to shape mass culture according to middle-class values and to curtail the participatory nature of the star system.[39]

In *Babel and Babylon,* author Miriam Hansen has made a similar point about how culturally privileged discourses on Valentino's audience has had exclusionary effects.

> It would be a mistake to overrate the masculinist attacks on Valentino or to take them at face value. To a certain extent they were part of the ritual. If not exactly self-ironic, the paragons of American virility were aware of performing a rhetorical role, playing straight man as it were to women's follies. . . . We should not forget that this rhetoric only presumed to speak for all men. It thus obscured Valentino's popularity with a large number of men, gay and straight—a dimension that Kenneth Anger, among others, has tried to restore to the history of Valentino's reception.[40]

Hansen points toward the real diversity of receptions that must have taken place but has been obscured by the entrenched mythologies of Valentino's cultural importance in defining a new romantic hero for American audiences. I would, however, suggest that the problem of historically submerged receptions of the star might best be pursued along the axis of class and not that of gender since social class, as we have just seen, was the primary category through which issues of gender, sexuality, and ethnicity were finally articulated to construct what came to be known as the cult of Valentino.

One of the great difficulties of investigating alternative and nonhegemonic receptions of mass culture is the problem of locating records or artifacts that would disclose and document such receptions. While scrapbooks, fan letters, and oral histories have been used extensively in many fields to construct revisionist social histories from alternative points-of-view, such materials have yet to be highly valued by film archives, and they are generally unavailable to film historians.[41] Far more time and effort has gone into preserving and making available the papers of prominent individuals in the film industry.[42] However, the ultimate goal of any inquiry into the historical participation of subaltern groups in both the production and reception of mass culture should never be to recover some lost, authentic voice of an oppressed or marginalized group who is assumed to have some pure existence outside of its relationship to the dominant group. The very fragmentation, dispersal, and unavailability of evidence for these alternative receptions are part of the material histories of these different groups who have, thus far, been unable to gain control of the means of representation or to finally influence the terms of what might count as an important historical legacy. One can, however, begin to think about how the unique material conditions, social institutions, and cultural practices of historically nondominant groups would have supported interpretations, evaluations, and engagements with mass culture at odds with those whose memories of the past have been officially enshrined.

One thing we know about both the popular representation of sexuality and sexual identity in the United States is that our current confidence in object-choice as the primary basis for understanding sexual identity was not by any means universally conceded during the first half of the twentieth century. As was made evident in the trial of Leopold and Loeb, where several competing and contradictory definitions of male sexual deviance combined to make male sexuality one of the central problems of the case, there simply was no single, stable homosexual identity with which medical, legal, or journalistic discourses were comfortable. Hormonal theories were proffered alongside of psychoanalytic explanations that were then, surprisingly, combined with phrenological descriptions of the defendants' heads. How individuals might have related all of these various ideas about deviant sexuality to their own lived experience is anybody's guess, but the sheer polyphony of expert opinion on the matter shows how unsettled and conflicted was the question, at least at an institutional level, of what we would now call "homosexual identity." In the most general terms, what many of these theories held in common was a fairly widespread understanding that male sexual deviance typically took the form of gender inversion and that the personality of the male invert was not, in the first instance, determined by an erotic attraction he held for other men. Instead, inverts were considered men with feminine characters or sometimes men with feminine physiologies, who constituted for some, such as the influential British sexologist Havelock Ellis, a unique "third or intermediate sex." Gay men in the early part of the century who "lived and loved as women" preserved or recapitulated heterosexual object-choice since they quite "naturally" (so the logic of attraction went) chose masculine men as their sexual and romantic partners. The same or quite similar assumptions about gender inversion were at work in the well-known figure of the "mannish lesbian" who populated both sexological studies and the popular literature of the period.

Even though gender continues to play an important role in the way sexuality and sexual identity is understood and represented in contemporary America, it is now less an individual's subjective alignment with a particular gender position which finally determines sexual identity than it is the relationship between the presumed anatomical sex of a person and that of her or his preferred partner(s). Indeed, outside of a finite set of rather stereotypical representations of effeminate gay men and masculine lesbians, it is now difficult for many of us to think about how markers of gender alone could have so easily signified familiar queer sexual identities to a relatively large number of people. This very difficulty manifests itself in the work of cultural historians and critics such as Morris, Studlar, and Garber who can discuss, sometimes in great depth, Valentino's fairly radical departure from traditional white masculinity, as well as his close association with feminine tastes and desires, without then being able to even suggest that male homosexuality was an important factor in Valentino's historical reception. In addition to this problem of the alterity of sexuality a mere eighty-five years ago, there is also the unstated assumption on the part of these writers that gender identity is much more fluid, because it is more socially constructed and therefore more easily transgressed, than sexual identity which is thought to be more stable and only knowable by the evidence of certain declarations or certain types of genital acts with other people.[43] Of course, there have been, and there still are, other ways of knowing sexuality and experiencing sexual identity.

In his history of gay male social life in New York City during the first half of the twentieth century, George Chauncey recounts the 1922 arrest of two young working-class Italian men in Prospect Park. These two friends, one eighteen and the other seventeen, were picked up by a police detective who pronounced them "fairies" upon discovering their plucked and shaped eyebrows which they had kept hidden beneath their caps. Chauncey cites this incident as evidence of how the stylized details of masculine grooming were often used by young men to signal their deviant gender status to other men whom they sought for sexual and romantic encounters. Chauncey quotes one of the young men arrested as explaining how "men with full faces, long delicate fingers, tweezed eyebrows and well-shaped lips were [known as] inverts" in his Italian Harlem neighborhood.[44] Chauncey takes great care to point out that the meaningful contexts for the various stylistic signifiers of male sexual deviance were often specific to particular ethnic communities, outside of which such styles of dress and personal appearance were either unremarkable or just unusual. He does, however, demonstrate that the use of facial cosmetics (penciled eyebrows, rouged lips, powdered faces) was a relatively well-known and common way for many men to signify their status as fairies. While the wide variety of dress styles that could be associated with male sexual deviance in the 1920s was as much a reflection of the real diversity of gay life as it was lived in relation to locality, class, and ethnicity, the visible center of gay life for the wider public was the figure of the effeminate fairy who, in Chauncy's study of New York, populated several of the clubs along the Bowery and who participated in many of the highly publicized and well-attended drag balls that were held in the city throughout the decade, often in major venues such as Madison Square Garden and the Astor Hotel. Although there were large numbers of gay men in the 1920s who thought of themselves as "queers" but did not identify with the flamboyant styles and feminized identities of the fairies, drag balls were an important part of a broad gay culture at that time, and they were common occurrences and popular events for both gay and straight audiences in other major U.S. cities.[45]

Chauncey's previous work on the lives of gay men in Newport, Rhode Island, during the late 1910s and early 1920s demonstrated that many people there, both straight and queer, felt quite confident in their ability to correctly identify inverts on the street and in social clubs solely on the basis of effeminate appearance or behavior. It was only when pressed by official authorities to explain precisely how a person could know that someone else was a fairy that the confidence of a previous identification was shaken by a general lack of agreement on precisely what constituted the signs of the male "sex pervert."[46] While clearly there was no single set of codes for reading male sexual deviance at that (or any other) historical moment, many people believed that there were a set of stable indicators, and they acted accordingly. Undoubtedly, Valentino's highly visible use of and association with beauty products—both in his films and in his product endorsements—suggested his sexual abnormality to some members of the motion picture audience and to readers of the fan magazines. Chaw Mank, another biographer of the star, reports that Valentino's close friend, the film actress Nita Naldi, remembered that Valentino began receiving "a lot of crank mail accusing him of being a queer and a pansy" on the release of *Monsieur Beaucarie* (Famous Players-Lasky, 1924), a film in which Valentino appeared in the sprightly attire of the late eighteenth-century French aristocracy, which included various wigs, face powder, silk garments, and fancy lace.[47] Moreover, the somewhat effusive and ethereal off-screen pronouncements he made about the timelessness of art and beauty, rather than providing an alibi for the sartorial extravagances of his film appearances, would have likely confirmed the suspicions of those who believed Valentino was more than just a little eccentric. Chauncey writes: "Observers often considered the unusual—even fairylike—dress of entertainers, artists, and other professionally colorful personalities to be just another sign of their special status rather than a sign of their sexual deviance. As a result, however, describing someone as 'artistic' could be a coded way of calling him a homosexual, and observers often played on the ambiguity of their criticisms of artists."[48]

Of course, the codes that were used on the street and in the tabloids by any given social group or community were not necessarily always translatable to their experience with the cinema or to their reception of star discourses. Nevertheless, the details of Valentino's stardom provide a rather startling number of points of similarity with the visible aspects of a contemporaneous gay male culture in America's largest cities. The important point is not that Valentino was thought to be a sexual deviant by some, though there were those who obviously thought he was. Of larger social and historical significance is the very mode of Valentino's star presentation and his appearances within a mass cultural context, the kinds of expectations his various performances encouraged for investigating the relations between sexuality and gender. In short, Valentino's star personality helped establish a queer space for the reception of mass culture.

Two other aspects of male sexual identity in the 1920s are important for the queer reception of Valentino and for a fuller understanding of the various attacks on his character and masculinity. First, though men from many different social positions participated in fairy culture, that culture was developed and thrived in working-class neighborhoods. It is no accident that many of the most important saloons and clubs catering to or controlled by fairies were located in the Bowery in New York City. Chauncey notes that the practice of "slumming" by the genteel middle- and upper-classes during the early part of the century quite often included a visit to the resorts of "male degenerates" on the Lower East Side.[49] The location of such establishments in the Bowery was, in part, due to the fact that the area was the city's center for prostitution and other forms of commercialized vice, but these haunts also sprang up and flourished there because of the relative tolerance afforded fairies and queers by working-class society. Though never entirely out of danger from the bigoted violence of both moralistic and physical attacks, fairies were an unexceptional sight on the Lower East Side and a familiar part the vibrant working-class culture of the Bowery and its dynamic mix of immigrant populations.[50]

A second feature of male sexual identity important for understanding the public attacks on Valentino is the relative lack of stigma that was attached to "masculine" men who had sex with fairies or accompanied them on dates. A straight man, who was at that time likely to be referred to as "a normal," might choose to engage in sexual relations with fairies without any questioning of his own sexual identity provided that he maintained an active masculine position and attitude in every aspect of such encounters, and provided that such encounters did not develop into prolonged and protracted relationships. While today such men might be more easily identified as homosexual, the prevalent notion that gender identity was the basis on which to determine male sexual normalcy and deviance allowed many men who considered themselves physically and psychologically masculine to engage in sexual relations with inverts while maintaining their status as healthy, normal men.[51] Chauncey's historical work on this issue is extremely enlightening since it demonstrates a rather radical divergence between prevalent popular understandings of male sexual deviance before and after World War II. Chauncey concludes that, in twentieth-century America, male sexual definition exhibited the uneven development characteristic of class segregation, with the historically older and popular figure of the gender invert defining the most typical and recognizable form of male sexual deviance for the urban working class. For at least three full decades after the middle classes had presumably acceded to the fully modern understanding of the male homosexual, which Michel Foucault describes as being consolidated at the end of the nineteenth century when "homosexuality began to speak in its own behalf," inversion remained the predominant way for an urban proletariat to understand male sexual deviance.[52] Foucault does point out, however, that "the working classes managed for a long time to escape the deployment of sexuality."[53]

Chauncey's historical research helps to clarify the scandal of Valentino by providing a more nuanced social context for understanding how Valentino's stardom responded to the disparities within male sexual definition that resulted from class differences and class antagonisms. Again, while the popular attacks on Valentino have been previously discussed and explained by others in relation to issues of gender and ethnicity, relatively little attention has been paid to the importance of social class in the star's reception. Beyond the acknowledgment of the contradiction between his being an Italian immigrant who worked his way to success in America and his identity as a "lazy gigolo" who became wealthy by manipulating the affections of lonely women, Valentino's importance for a class struggle over mass culture has been virtually ignored.

If the riot at Valentino's lying-in-state is the single most repeated and privileged event of his biography, then a likely candidate for the second most remarked upon incident would have to be the editorial about Valentino which appeared in the July 18, 1926, edition of the *Chicago Sunday Tribune*. The anonymous writer of this editorial blamed Valentino for thoroughly corrupting the values of traditional masculinity. By popularizing masculine cosmetics through his celebrity, Valentino was, the writer maintained, responsible for the increasing effeminacy of a whole generation of young men who favored the film star by following his example. Subsequently known as the "pink powder puff" affair, this questioning of Valentino's masculinity in such a prominent newspaper so enraged the star that he publicly challenged the anonymous editorial writer to reveal himself and to settle his differences with the film star in the boxing ring. When the writer remained silent in the face of this challenge, Valentino, in order to publicly prove his manhood, boxed an exhibition match on the roof of the Ambassador Hotel with Frank O'Neil, the sportswriter and boxing expert from the *New York Evening Journal*. After impressively holding his own against O'Neil in the ring, Valentino then went on an extended spree of semi-public appearances in restaurants and nightclubs at which he demonstrated his stamina for strong drink and late hours until, after a couple of exhausting weeks, he finally collapsed with severe gastric ulcers. Complications of this condition led to the peritonitis and endocarditis from which he finally died on August 26, 1926, a week after his hospitalization.[54]

This anonymous public attack on the film star is a tragic story that is most often understood by historians and cultural critics as exemplary of an ultra-conservative and masculinist reception of Valentino, whose hypersensitivity to such attacks was finally his undoing. According to this point of view, Valentino was killed by bigoted prejudice and his own stubborn naiveté. Because he had just applied for his American citizenship, Valentino has been viewed by some biographers as the victim of a masculinist attack which was, in reality, only a "journalistic subterfuge that masked the fact that the thief of hearts in America was a foreign-born Italian."[55] The editorial, entitled "Pink Powder Puffs," has been quoted extensively in biographies of the star and is sometimes reprinted in full; yet the motives of its author(s), the nature of Valentino's response to the appearance of the editorial, and the meanings the editorial had for a public are all treated by biographers and critics as relatively transparent. Studlar, Garber, Morris, and others cite the *Chicago Tribune* editorial as a rather unproblematic example of—to use Garber's words—"a xenophobic attack from middle America."[56] Here is the full text of "Pink Powder Puffs."

> A new public ballroom was opened on the north side a few days ago, a truly handsome place and apparently well run. The pleasant impression lasts until one steps into the men's washroom and finds there on the wall a contraption of glass tubes and levers and a slot for the insertion of a coin. The glass tubes contain a pink fluffy solid, and beneath them one reads the amazing legend which runs something like this: "Insert coin. Hold personal puff beneath the tube. Then pull the lever."
>
> A powder vending machine! In a men's washroom! Homo Americanus! Why didn't someone quietly drown Rudolph Guglielmo, alias Valentino years ago?
>
> And was the pink powder machine pulled from the wall or ignored? It was not. It was used. We personally saw two "men"—as young lady contributors to the Voice of the People are wont to describe the breed—step up, insert coin, hold handkerchief beneath the spout, pull lever, then take the pretty pink stuff and pat it on their cheeks in front of the mirror.
>
> Another member of this department, one of the most benevolent men on earth, burst raging into the office the other day because he had seen a young "man" combing his pomaded hair in the elevator. But we claim our pink powder story beats his all hollow.
>
> It is time for a matriarchy if the male of the species allows such things to persist. Better a rule by masculine women that by effeminate men. Man began to slip, we are beginning to believe, when he discarded the straight razor for the safety pattern. We shall not be surprised when we hear that the safety razor has given way to depilatory.
>
> Who or what is to blame is what puzzles us. Is this degeneration into effeminacy a cognate reaction with pacifism to the virilities and realities of the war? Are pink powder puffs and parlor pinks in any way related? How does one reconcile masculine cosmetics, sheiks, floppy pants, and slave bracelets with a disregard for the law and an aptitude for crime more in keeping with the frontier of half a century ago than a twentieth century metropolis?
>
> Do women like the type of "man" who pats pink powder on his face in a public washroom and arranges his coiffure in a public elevator? Do women at heart be-

long to the Wilsonian era of "I Didn't Raise My Boy to be a Soldier"? What has become of the old "caveman" line?

It is a strange social phenomenon and one that is running its course, not only here in America but in Europe as well. Chicago may have its powder puffs; London has its dancing men and Paris its gigolos. Down with Decatur; up with Elinor Glyn. Hollywood is the national school of masculinity. Rudy, the beautiful gardener's boy, is the prototype of the American male.

Hell's bells. Oh, sugar.[57]

While this editorial certainly does employ the sexist, racist, and homophobic discourses indicative of much of the conservative and paranoid anti-immigration politics of the era, the editorial's voice does not appear to be exactly identical to or coextensive with these discourses. Furthermore, the editorial also seems to rely on complicated notions of social class in order to produce its representation of deviant masculinity. By considering the authorial voice of this editorial and contextualizing its representation of male effeminacy within a class-based understanding of the history of male sexual definition, the obviousness of the writer's motives and the homogeneity of the editorial's reception become open to question. Indeed, it is the very uncertainty of what is being said about Valentino, the uncertainty of how and by whom the star is being addressed, that makes this attack into a scandal that urgently required an immediate act of declaring its utterances to be both obvious and familiar.

The powder puff editorial has been traditionally understood as an insult so scathing and as an accusation so demeaning that the mean-spirited author of the attack had to remain hidden out of necessity. By issuing a public challenge to the cowardly writer to reveal himself, Valentino (along with his business manager, George Ullman) appears to have preferred the public to understand the nature of the editorial in precisely this manner. But how serious was this attack on Valentino which closed with the insouciant and somewhat fey laments: "Hell's bells" and "Oh, sugar"? If such parting phrases were the sole evidence for a less malevolent intention on the part of the author(s) of the editorial, then these final words could only be read as mockery. However, the entire piece is so shot through with a grand self-consciousness about its own overstatements that it is actually quite easy to enjoy the editorial as a theatrical rave, a "bitchy" performance of those voices that often spoke about "male degeneracy" the loudest. Yet this editorial's playful sarcasm and fractiousness go far beyond the levity and humor that many of the other attacks on Valentino attempted.[58] Making light of Valentino's success and poking fun at "sheiks" who wore slave bracelets had allowed many conservative critics of the star to express their hatred of him while refusing to grant the Valentino phenomenon any social significance. The jocular tone of many of these attacks also gave critics the alibi of merely kidding about someone who was, in fact, only a celluloid hero.

Nevertheless, whatever the intentions of its author, the powder puff editorial is hysterical, both in the clinical sense of evidencing an intensity of reaction out of proportion to its purported concerns and in the vernacular sense of being convulsively funny. Part of the incoherence and frenzy of the piece comes from its rapid change of perspective in posing the question of male deviance. The editorial begins with effeminacy as a subcultural phenomenon observable in specific social spaces ("a men's restroom" and, a little later on, "an elevator"); moves quickly on to what Foucault might call the "speciation of homosexuality" ("Homo Americanus"); eugenics (Why didn't someone quietly drown Rudolph Guglielmo . . . years ago?"); behaviorism, environmentalism, and a masculinist critique of consumerism ("Man began to slip . . . when he discarded the straight razor for the safety pattern"); psychiatry ("a cognate reaction to the virilities and realities of war?"); mental hygiene and a conservative complaint that liberal mothers were ruining American men ("Do women at heart belong to the Wilsonian era of 'I Didn't Raise My Son to Be a Soldier' "?); and, finally, the educational effects of the mass media ("Hollywood is the national school of masculinity"). This is not to suggest that these positions or observations were necessarily read as incoherent or contradictory, for they were often found combined into the scientific and moral eclecticism that defined much of the rhetoric of conservative social reform of the period.[59] What makes the editorial so humorous and so hysterical is the sheer insincerity of its various positions, none of which are developed or sustained, and the manner in which they are quoted as so many familiar burning questions about how far modern society has sunk into moral degeneracy.

Nowhere is the insincerity of the piece more obvious than in its description of a colleague's outrage upon witnessing "a young 'man' combing his pomaded hair in the elevator." Demonstrating one's moral revulsion at a particular event by claiming that the event in question was even more shocking than a young man combing his hair in an elevator—a mundane and fairly unremarkable occurrence—is one of the surest was to parody and deflate the discourse of moral panic. Is Valentino really the object of scorn here, or is it, rather, those who were threatened by the actor's deviant masculinity? Is it possible that the powder puff editorial was what we, today, would term a public "outing" of Valentino by and for those who identified themselves as queers, or by and for those who participated in and were supportive of gay culture generally? Could the multiple moral and social discourses on male deviance in this editorial have been performed by those who were the objects of those same discourses, much in the way that the young gang members in *West Side Story* (United Artists, 1961) explain themselves to Officer Krupke by slyly mimicking the psychiatric, sociological, juridical, and social reform discourses that positioned and identified them as juvenile delinquents? More importantly, did some people read this editorial as satirizing the very ideologies and opinions that the writer of the editorial is usually thought to have unproblematically shared and supported?

Chauncey based some of his history of gay life in New York on articles that had appeared in *Broadway Brevities*, a monthly newspaper published in Manhattan from the mid-1920s through the early 1930s. This tabloid devoted extensive, accurate, and detailed coverage to gay life and cultural institutions, and, as early as 1924, the paper's writers were doing so by using the sensationalistic rhetoric of exposé and moral outrage. Headlines in the early 1930s included "Third Sex Plague Spreads Anew," "Fag Balls Exposed," and "Death Knell of Degeneracy," yet all these articles were written by authors with sexually suggestive and campy noms de plume, such as "John Swallow Martin," "Stephen O'Toole," "Connie Lingle," and "Buddy Browning." Chauncey cautions that it is virtually impossible to accurately reconstruct the reception context for this publication, nor is it possible to fully grasp the paper's political perspective on gay life. Nevertheless, concludes Chauncey, "while it overtly construed its writers and readers as straight, the paper was almost certainly read and written, in part, by gay people." Though perhaps more daring and explicit than other publications, *Brevities* was just one of several New York papers to cover places and events of gay cultural importance during this period. These papers, like *Brevities*, also typically reported on the flourishing of fairies and queers within the city as a more or less scandalous state of affairs.[60] What we can know from these news stories is that particular gay male identities had an astonishingly high degree of public visibility and recognition during the period, even though such recognition was usually condemnatory in tone. Despite the pretense to aversion, the accuracy of many of these reports and the amount of details they contained point to their function as sources of useful information about gay personalities and social life for anyone who might have been interested.

Given the historically established practice of using the rhetoric of public scandal to indirectly speak from, for, about, and to positions of male sexual and gender deviance, it seems more than likely that many who read the powder puff editorial, as well as those who soon learned about this scandal from the events that transpired after its publication, understood that Valentino was being acknowledged by the editorial's author(s) as an important mass cultural figure for fairies and other queers. For those who were practiced in queer exegesis, the scandal of the editorial would not only have been about some libelous affront to Valentino's character and reputation; instead, the scandal *as scandal* was the very means by which Valentino's sexual deviance was communicated and, just as importantly, through which an appreciative audience for that deviance was publicly acknowledged and addressed. The editorial writer's (or writers') sustained anonymity would have supported the surmise that the piece was queerly authored just as much, if not more, than it would have indicated that the writer was a cowardly and sheltered bigot, especially since nativism and sexism certainly had plenty of popular supporters at the time, even within the editorial offices of the *Chicago Tribune*. It seems rather silly to have to argue this point, but, as others have pointed out, the historical erasure of the active participation of lesbians and gay men in public culture has been so thorough as to make even the humblest claim about their significance prior to the Second World War susceptible to aggressive skepticism and the demand for irrefutable evidence. The ultimate purpose of such skepticism is often to maintain the historical erasure of lesbians and gays by protecting a definition of proper historical method and inquiry that denigrates the "truth" status of innuendo, rumor, and scandal. In his biography of Natacha Rambova, Morris is, as we have seen, one of the most tenacious defenders of a truthful and rumor-free historical past with respect to Valentino. Moreover, no film historian or Valentino biographer has ever suggested that the infamous powder puff editorial could have been anything other than the callous venting of sexism and homophobic hate. The biographical repetitions of Valentino's susceptibility to this particular attack and his subsequent self-destructive struggle to prove himself a "real man" continually construct the editorial as a violent manifestation of pure masculinist hatred which ultimately proved fatal to the great star. Unfortunately, such well-meaning condemnation and dismissal has the same result as paranoid empiricism: a diminution of the importance of queer identities and queer meanings in the development of mass cultural institutions such as the star system.

Significantly, socioeconomic class and sexual identity come together precisely within this historiographical and ethical problematic. Eve Sedgwick has succinctly pointed out how the knowledge systems of marginalized groups have often taken into account the real diversity of people in society and how they thus pose alternative ways of organizing experience and understanding identity:

> It is probably people with the experience of oppression or subordination who have the most *need* to know [that people are different from one another]; and I take the precious arts of gossip, immemorially associated with servants, with effeminate and gay men, with all women, to have to do not so much with the transmission of necessary news as with the refinement of necessary skills for making, testing, and using unrationalized and provisional hypotheses about what *kinds of people* there are to be found in one's world.[61]

Sedgwick emphasizes that it is neither scandalous topics nor secret knowledge that defines the social character and political effectivity of gossip. Instead, it is the very activity of questioning official appearances and received categories that lends gossip its productive role in identity (trans)formation. The threat posed by gossip, innuendo, and rumor—in short, all those unaccountable utterances which can, and so often do subtend public scandals, at least in their early stages has more to do with exposing the contradictions and limitations of dominate representations and classification systems than it does with embarrassing well-known or notorious individuals.

Gossip is thus often an act of resistance, the creation of an alternative space from which to pose questions about identity, questions that sometimes challenge both social propriety and scientific rigor as they are defined by the hegemonic order. With their concern for the systemization of psychological, social, and sexual identities, the human sciences that emerged to prominence at the end of the nineteenth century were often harnessed to social institutions for the management and control of both individuals and populations; those same sciences were also translated into the mass media, which had, not coincidentally, come into being at about the same time. These emergent mass cultural institutions soon took up the question of identity, and they had the potential of placing the means and the power to define and express identity into the hands of a vast and diverse public who might very well have actively called into question the accuracy and the rigidity of scientific methods through their own investigations, findings, and expertise. Such was the hope of cultural critics such as Walter Benjamin who embraced the new mass media (the metropolitan newspaper, the motion picture, radio broadcasting) as possessing a radical democratizing character and as expressing a revolutionary potential. While not entirely ill-founded, such enthusiasm was short-lived. In America during the 1920s, progressive critics like Walter Lippman were already claiming that the amount of information available in the mass media was more confusing than liberating to the average person, and that what was required for the proper functioning of democracy was, therefore, a professional class of semi-autonomous intellectuals and interpreters whose rational expertise could inform the masses about the relevant facts so they might live and act with correct opinions about their world.[62] In other words, unfounded opinions and fanciful rumors were to be avoided at all costs. The masses needed to be told about modernity; they were not to create it.

Public scandals within the developing mass culture were often shaped by class differences and registered specific class antagonisms. The disclosure of Wallace Reid's drug addiction, its subsequent reinterpretation through the discourses of disease and criminality, and its relocation within the sphere of private consumption worked to contain a more radical and critical understanding of the star's early death. Mass society often blurred the traditional spatial and cultural demarcations between social classes while heightening and highlighting their different and often competing interests. Because of its technical arrangements and its economic organization, a mass cultural institution such as the cinema could provide members from diverse communities, regions, and nations with the same points of reference for representing and understanding the world. Yet the cinema also, and especially in large metropolitan centers, provided new spaces for mass consumption, such as large public theaters, where different social and cultural groups could come together as a mass audience and contest the meanings and relevance of those same points of reference. Chapter 4 investigates how a sociological conception of the disorganized social world of public amusement and leisure was an important component of Valentino's popular reception, particularly for the ways in which his stardom related to culturally prevalent ideas about miscegenation and racial hybridity. However, at present, I want to briefly return to the powder puff editorial and inquire how aspects of class and class division were intertwined with its representation of Valentino's gender deviance. Should we, for instance, take quite seriously its question, "Are pink powder puffs and parlor pinks in any way related?"[63]

Whatever the ultimate intentions of the *Tribune*'s editorialist(s), the crisis of masculinity entailed by Valentino's stardom, both within the editorial and as a factor in his reception more generally, is only fully comprehensible as a crisis of middle-class cultural hegemony. As Chauncey has shown, the public culture of fairies in New York City drew upon an array of participants from diverse backgrounds and social positions; nevertheless, the sites of their participation were almost always confined to working-class venues or to the more bohemian haunts and establishments of Greenwich Village and Harlem. Even when the more elaborate drag balls went uptown to the finer hotels, fairies appeared there only as imported entertainment. Fairies as guests might well have been on display at the Astor Hotel, but they certainly did not control the space of its largest ballrooms. Because the historical development of fairy culture in the United States was largely the prerogative of the urban working class, the *Tribune*'s "complaint" about the presence of a pink powder vending machine in a men's washroom was launched through the incongruity and surprise of discovering such a device in such a place, that it was located within a "truly handsome" and "apparently well run" public ballroom on the affluent north side of Chicago. A sense of a surreptitious invasion of this men's room by some foreign element is established at the very beginning of the editorial, and even though this intrusion is partially about the questionable gender identity of any "men" who would use such facial cosmetics—jokes abounded then, as they still do, about which bathroom effeminate men should use—another real concern and worry tacitly expressed here is that the presence of fairies implied the presence of a larger, more vulgar, and possibly more dangerous element: those who were known to have little or no qualms about sharing their space or their time with fairies and other queers, as well as those men who, during their time away from home and work, sought out the company of fairies. In other words, the possible presence of straight-identified working-class men of the more rough-and-rugged variety was also part of "the problem." Whose bathroom was this anyway? Whose ballroom?

The working-class character of male gender deviance and the type of society it was believed to attract is a concern that is tacitly expressed throughout the powder puff editorial. If the "young 'man' combing his pomaded hair in an elevator" was supposed to have been taken by the reader as the stereotypical image of the narcissistic and effeminate male homosexual, then it was not so much his visibility in a public space alone that constituted a provocation. Instead, by grooming himself in a public elevator, the young man's breach of etiquette indicated a remarkable level of confidence, ignorance, or indifference to the manners practiced by those of the social level to which he pretended to belong. Such behavior could be seen as a more or less pretentious affront to members of the genteel middle class. Even more than their feminine affectations, the fairies' transvestism of social class could sometimes be represented as the most threatening aspect of their identities. At the very least, male gender deviance and working-class coarseness often functioned as indexes of each other, for both working-class and middle-class urbanites. Of course, letting one's working-class slip show, as it were, was all part of the fun. Those "failed" attempts by drag queens and fairies to achieve the glamour of the movie and theatrical stars upon whom they so often based their identities contributed much to the campiness of their appeal. What was often seen as a travesty of gender order could also be taken as a travesty of the order of social class.

The *Tribune*'s powder puff editorial represented Valentino's stardom as a sort of national catastrophe. We find, again, that Valentino's stardom was represented as the inexplicable return of a more "primitive past," a return which gives way to morally transgressive and uncivil behavior in the modern world. The author(s) explicitly posed the erosion of traditional bourgeois masculinity as a political conflict between social classes in which Valentino's popular success signaled a victory for the forces of social and historical disintegration: "How does one reconcile masculine cosmetics, sheiks, floppy pants, and slave bracelets with a disregard for the law and an aptitude for crime more in keeping with the frontier of half a century ago than a twentieth century metropolis?" The implied answer to this rhetorical question was that they are reconcilable by the fact that the elegant finery of the sheik is simply a ruse, a disguise behind which lurks the vicious street criminal. Valentino's previously noted "counterfeit masculinity," as well as his pretentious pronouncements about art and beauty, made the film star particularly well-suited as an example of the lower orders' undisciplined and unjustified rise into positions of public prominence and cultural importance.

Yet there is another possible answer to the problem of how to reconcile cosmetics with crime. The question poses a paradox about modern society where gender difference is, almost incomprehensibly, recapitulated within the male homosocial world of beautiful sheiks and rugged frontiersmen, a fantasy world to be sure, but one made readily available by a mass media catering to and easily appropriated by the meaner elements of American society. As was the case in the trial of Leopold and Loeb, a further possible solution to this gender paradox was to see the effeminate homosexual and the violent male delinquent as "partners in crime." While Leopold and Loeb belonged to wealthy and prominent families of Chicago, their identities and their relationship were represented in the courtroom and in the press as symptoms of a more general assault on traditional American institutions by young people who were made cynical and disaffected by the unprecedented slaughter of the First World War, and by the effects of an unregulated mass culture which, when not viewed as simply desultory, was often condemned for valorizing crime, sexual promiscuity, and viciousness on the nation's motion picture screens and in cheap novels and magazines. The media's apparent celebration of ruthless criminals and gangsters certainly produced widely voiced concerns about impressionable young readers and viewers who might be led into lives of crime through imitating star criminals. However, as with the publicity surrounding the Leopold and Loeb trial, a much more vexing possibility was that boys who obviously enjoyed reading about and seeing on screen the exploits of dangerous and violent criminals *might fail* to identify in important ways with these notorious men's more laudable masculine traits: courage, loyalty, strength, and a menacing threat of violence, however misdirected the latter was thought to be. Instead, the impressionable youngster without sufficient moral judgment might seek out famous outlaws as attractive and desirable companions while rejecting them as suitable role models. Within the parameters of contemporary gender ideology, the hardened gangster's hyper-masculinity and his familiarity with the seamier side of urban life ultimately placed all those awestruck youngsters who wished to share the gangster's company at risk and vulnerable to his perverse seduction. As conventionally understood, the typical wish of the fan was not to be the star, but only to be with the star.

Similar to the repeated insistence that Valentino's fans were always women, continually expressed concerns about copycat crimes which were supposed to have resulted from the mass media's favorable attention to dangerous male criminals and their violent acts was actually a strategy for normalizing potentially deviant mass cultural receptions. By representing mimicry and identification as the only possible ways for young male delinquents to enjoy criminality in the media, social commentators could pretend that the only attraction such criminals held for boys and young men were their ill-gotten power, social status, and enviable wealth. Because every celebrity implied the existence of an audience, and because every audience implied a particular star-audience relation, the film audience (as well as the star) could be effectively regulated by controlling the representation of that relation.

In similar fashion, it is also clear that the expressed concerns about Valentino's gender deviance and its influence upon an entire generation of young men

were only partially accounted for by the fear of an epidemic of Valentino imita-
tors. While Valentino's popularity with men might have indicated that some men
saw themselves as Valentino types, there was also the possibility that there existed a number of men who found themselves charmed by the actor's undeniable
grace, beauty, and sex appeal. In fact, it is precisely such men who have been
thoroughly erased from the dominant representation of the cult of Valentino. At
a public exhibition of Valentino memorabilia at the 1979 Berlin Film Festival,
Kenneth Anger told the audience about "the little known attraction the star held
for men, and, Anger clarified, he meant by this decidedly masculine men."[64] In
the 1920s and 1930s, the existence of this decidedly masculine fandom for Valentino would have been easily recognizable within an urban working-class milieu
as described by Chauncey's historical research. Part of this fandom would have
been comprised, of course, of Italian American men who took pride in the fact
that one of their own had become so successful and popular. Yet another part
would have been apparently "normal" men who held a sexual attraction for the
star. One of the most troubling aspects of these latter types of men was that
they—unlike impressionable youths or emotionally weak young men—were
thought to be strong and independent individuals and, therefore, not vulnerable
to any easy seduction by a glamorous celebrity. From a sexological point of view
of an enlightened middle class, such men either freely chose their deviance or
were constitutionally perverse, indiscriminate, and, therefore, possibly criminal.
The fact that this fandom is more difficult to consider today speaks to the deformation and partial destruction of working-class experience and working-class
social and sexual categories under the continuing advancements of bourgeois
cultural hegemony with its reliance on a stable set of gender expectations to police sexuality and enforce heteronormalcy. The trap of gender conformity and
the erasure of sexual diversity is revealed succinctly in the false dilemma as-
serted by the *Tribune*'s powder puff editorialist(s), "Better a rule by masculine
women that by effeminate men."

The question of Valentino's queerness considered within the context of American mass culture is not, then, about his individual sexual identity, but about the
types of sexualities his stardom made possible, gratified, or otherwise indulged.
Yet this larger cultural context is narrowed or foreclosed by those film historians
and celebrity biographers who rely on dominant narratives about sexuality and
subjectivity to determine the star's historical reception. Appeals to empirical evidence about Valentino's true sexuality—or, as in the case of Morris, appeals to
the lack thereof—work against any consideration of Valentino as a site of social
divisions and multiple contestations of power. The demand to find the real Valentino behind all the innuendo and gossip effectively removes Valentino from
the field of American social and cultural history where innuendo and gossip played
crucial roles. Alternately, the historiographical work of Foucault, in particular,

has made possible a new way of refusing the coherency of such historical truths by concentrating on discontinuities in the accepted narratives about the past and by reading any gaps, omissions, and contradictions in historical accounts as the effects of social and political struggles over the production of knowledge and the means of representing the world. The goal of this new historiography is not to produce an alternative historical account that is adequate in itself and restores some lost subjectivities to the fullness of an authentic past.[65] These different ways of actively refusing the coherence of historical narrative have been described by cultural historian Jennifer Terry as "deviant historiography." For Terry, deviant historiography depends on Foucault's notion of an "effective history," where the archivist

> traces the conditions whereby marginal subjects apprehend possibilities for expression and self-representation in a field of contest. Effective history allows us to theorize a counterdiscursive position of history-telling which neither fashions a new coherence, nor provides a more inclusive resolution of contradicting "events." It is *not* an alternative narrative with its own tumescence peopled by previously elided but now recuperated Others. Effective history exposes not the events and actors elided by traditional history, but instead lays bare the *processes* and *operations* by which these elisions occurred.[66]

In political terms, effective history puts history up for grabs once again. It is not the magical return from the dead of all those who have been silenced and forgotten by official history, yet it is the recognition that such a return is still possible.[67] Effective history opens up spaces in what had been a previously full historical account, and it is not impatient to have those spaces filled once again. It is always dissatisfied and is never finished. Effective history is an insubordinate act of waiting for the past.

Foucault's work has been important to queer theorists such as Sedgwick and Terry, in part, because of its attention to the always unsettled nature of sexual identity and the ways that knowledge about identities is produced through diverse and active discursive fields of power relations. This acknowledgment of an untidy and dynamic multiplicity of social identities resists the easy reduction of subjectivity to a set of knowable and verifiable categories of experience defined by a particular dominate order, and, at the same time, it begins to map out possible deviant subject positions that were (or are) possible (or even probable) at a given historical conjuncture. Throughout this chapter, I have attempted to review some of the standard narratives of Valentino's stardom in order to unsettle some of the meanings of his biography's most recurring elements, meanings that have been so often taken for granted. My symptomatic reading of the powder puff editorial's authorship, for instance, was not aimed at establishing some authentic queer authorship or at locating some verifiable queer audience for the newspaper editorial or the resulting scandal. Instead, I have sought to question the very transparency of the editorial's bigotry that so many commentators have simply assumed. I have also sought to put into doubt the very meaning and significance that the editorial is usually thought to have held for both Valentino and his public. I have, thereby, created a critical space for a more diversified historical audience and for more heterogeneous receptions.

While I have used Chauncey's historical research on gay urban life in the 1920s to give a more complicated picture of masculine sexuality in that era, I am not interested in restoring particular segments of American society to our understanding of an emerging mass audience, or, at least, I do not think that the most useful project suggested by Chauncey's findings is one of historical recovery. Chauncey's work demonstrates the visibility, diversity, and sheer breadth of gay male life in New York during the early part of this century, and, at the same time, it reveals how *gay identity was always an open question*: how complex codes of recognition and announcement had to be negotiated on the street; how the identification of the homosexual depended on conflicting notions of gender characteristics and behaviors that did not always translate across class or ethnic lines; and, most importantly for any consideration of a queer mass culture, how homosexuality often revealed itself openly through strategies of ambiguous (ad)dress and double entendre. I term gay identity in the 1920s an open question as opposed to an open secret precisely because what was definitive about its articulation in the mass media was its destabilizing effect rather than its knowledge effect.

Valentino was (and still is) a sort of sexual enigma, especially given the tensions between his obvious gender deviance and the stature he achieved as a romantic leading man within the heteronormative Hollywood star system. While raffish pansies and other effeminate men had, from the very beginning, appeared in American films in roles that catered to pervasive stereotypes of the male homosexual, very few men who could be easily (mis)taken for queer had achieved such fame, recognition, and popular adoration as had Valentino.[68] It was not that Valentino represented a radically new type of man, but that he was able to represent, in a new way, several familiar types of men and some of the relations that were possible between them, relations that sometimes revolved around the erotic exchange of looks. Valentino posed a problem of identity to middle-class culture to the extent that he was popular and to the extent that his sex appeal had mass appeal. This is why Valentino was a radically queer star.

In order to get a sense of Valentino's challenge to traditional standards of middle-class masculinity and heterosexuality, one can compare his stardom to those often-celebrated film actors of the early sound period who enjoyed a brief period of popularity as pansies in motion pictures and on the Broadway stage. What Chauncey and others have called the "pansy craze" of the early 1930s marked a dramatic rise in urban middle-class enthusiasm for nightclub performers and other entertainers who used pansy humor or who cultivated pansy personalities. The vogue for pansies appears to have begun in New York nightclubs in the late 1920s, though it quickly spread to other cities including Los Angeles and Hollywood.[69] During this period, several character actors in motion pictures (such as the perennially bashful Edward Everett Horton and the persnickety Franklin Pangborn) benefited from the increasing popularity of the pansy figure, and widely admired film and vaudeville entertainers (such as Eddie Cantor) incorporated much pansy humor into their routines. Chauncey points out that while the pansy craze often drew on or reproduced the most demeaning stereotypes of male homosexuals, it did, at times, provide a space for some gay performers to speak about, to resist, and even to counter heterosexist presumptions about fairies and other queers. Similarly, in his work on queer representations in the films of the early 1930s, film historian David Lugowski has found that the proliferation of pansies on the movie screen during this period helped foster an irrepressible subversion of the sexual status quo. For Lugowski, this proliferation was made possible by the industry's conversion to sound. "Queer characters were common enough in silent film, but the means of presenting queerness in live performance often rested on innuendo in dialogue and vocal intonation. Thus, when sound film came in, urban audiences in particular were culturally primed for pansies, sissies, and lesbians. In terms of both mass dispersion and on-screen performance, sound gave queerness a new voice."[70] Lugowski emphasizes urban audiences' familiarity with pansies and he locates that familiarity in the speech of the live performer previously seen on the floor of the nightclub or on the theatrical stage. We might say, following Foucault, that with the sound film homosexuality began to speak its own name within mass culture.

Lugowski's work suggests that an important shift in the cinematic representation of queerness occurred in the early 1930s. While it is important to be cautious about an easy reliance on the entrenched historical divide between the silent and sound cinemas, Lugowski's investigation does suggest that recorded speech was a new and significant element for facilitating the easy recognition of familiar queer types at the cinema. Furthermore, the presence of the pansy's voice in early sound film together with the types of roles these performers were typically assigned would have called upon a theatrical tradition that supported the more distanced and less dynamic relations between audience and performer that were more typical of the Broadway stage and the nightclub floor than the motion picture screen. In other words, these new screen representations relied on a previous elaboration of queer identity within a fairly regulated entertainment context that was defined by the pansy's theatrical display and his specular-aural objectification by a fascinated audience relatively assured of its own sexual and class uniformity. As Chauncey has observed, the pansy craze was, in this respect, somewhat similar to the immediately prior enthusiasm that middle-class white audiences had expressed for certain Black entertainers:

> both fads allowed members of the dominant culture to shore up their identities by contrasting themselves with the otherness of the African American and the homosexual. At a time of bitter white ethnic rivalries, which resulted in the resurgence of anti-Semitism and the passage of the exclusionary immigration laws in the early 1920s, the spectacle of black "primitivism" allowed whites to express their solidarity with other whites by distinguishing themselves from blacks. At a time when the culture of speakeasies and the 1920s celebration of affluence and consumption might have undermined conventional sources of masculine identity, the spectacle of the pansy allowed men to confirm their manliness and solidarity with other men by distinguishing themselves from pansies.[71]

What Chauncey points to as the ultimate historical basis for the brief, spectacular ascendancy of blacks and queers into the American cultural limelight are the upheavals to traditional communities, populations, and urban topographies wrought by rapid urbanization and the general massification of modern society and social life. The rise of the cities and the consolidation of the mass-culture industries brought previously segregated groups into very close proximity for the first time. As a mass public sphere was being established, it was important for privileged social groups to maintain the integrity of their identities and, thus, their right and ability to exercise power. One of the more effective strategies for maintaining this subjective integrity was the objectification, commodification, and consumption of those who might possibly attempt to share in the traditional social privileges that had formerly accrued only to, or primarily to, the dominant social groups. While mass culture had made the liquidation of traditional identities a possibility, it also made possible the rapid reification and mass dispersal of social identities. Thus, visibility for subaltern groups often came, as it still does today, with a minoritizing price tag.

This is not to suggest that the pansy craze or its Hollywood manifestations functioned only to reaffirm white, middle-class male privilege. Indeed, Lugowski shows how the pansy figure, as stereotyped and as confined to the narrative margins as he usually was, increasingly became more threatening to "normal" masculinity as the Depression deepened. With such a large number of men visibly out of work, it had become a priority for New Deal ideology to represent them, especially the white, working-class unemployed, as deserving of respect and assistance despite their unfortunate circumstances. Pansies just called attention to the terrifying prospect of a sweeping feminization of American society, a prospect made evident by all those "failed" masculinities on display at the country's many bread lines, soup kitchens, and relief stores. Part of the Production Code Administration's (PCA) purpose in attempting to censor film references to "perverts" after 1934 was, as the 1930 code had put it, to raise "the whole standard of a nation."[72] The pansy was, then, an identity that could be and was easily recognized, known, and safely quarantined. Valentino's relation to fairies was never so simple or so easily determined. More importantly, Valentino was granted a sophisticated and complex eroticism that was pretty much denied to the pansies of the early sound era. The textually implied audience for the pansy figure, a figure who more often than not functioned as comic relief for the more central heterosexual romance, had been fairly homogenous and unproblematic until, ironically, post-1933 PCA censorship required the use of more subtle codings which, in turn, suggested that there was a portion of the audience who knew the queer codes and a portion who did not know them.[73]

The implied audience for Valentino, in both his filmic and his extra-filmic manifestations, was so difficult to locate because of the star's radical indeterminacy and his essential inauthenticity. Valentino's masquerade implied that any number of different social, political, and sexual interests might attach themselves to his stardom. These possible interests departed from the assumed interests of the white, middle-class female audience for Valentino that was so often insisted upon. These "new" diverse interests, which included deviant male sexualities, were made cogent and palpable by the racial, ethnic, and sexual hybridity associated with the melting pot of the urban working classes. Of all of Valentino's masquerades, it was his class masquerade that subtended the mass reception of his ethnic and sexual ambiguity and which challenged bourgeois hegemony over mass culture. Valentino had been so thoroughly objectified and commodified that he threatened to publicly reveal the class basis of the commodity and of commodity culture. Unlike the proliferation of pansies in the early 1930s, Valentino's star persona was far too available and could not be safely regulated within the terms of middle-class experience. One might say that the ideological supply of Valentino was outstripping middle-class ideological demand. What could be, and ultimately was, regulated about Valentino were the representations of his market audiences, a project of social control whose success can be measured by the dismissive treatment of those very audiences by present-day historians such as Morris.

What Valentino's stardom finally signified were the changes in modern American society brought about not only by the country's experience of the First World War, but also by the emergence of an autonomous working class who now, after the Russian Revolution of 1917, posed a significant new problem in the United States and elsewhere in the industrialized West. The successful founding of the Soviet Union provided labor movements around the world with an accomplished example of a worker's state. The Bolshevik victory in the Russian civil war together with the founding in 1919 of the international Comintern to support revolutions throughout Europe led to an escalated assault on the trade-unionist movement and on political radicalism in the United States. The Red Scare era that began in the spring of 1919 culminated in early 1920 with the arrest or deportation of some 10,000 individuals considered to be the enemies of America.[74] Yet the detainment of suspected communists and the passage of restrictive immigration laws to exclude unwanted foreigners were only part of a much larger pacification of America's growing worker and new immigrant populations. This pacification effort not only sought to discredit and destroy the intellectual vanguards of the worker's movement, it also transformed the very social conditions necessary for the development of the type of class leadership on which Bolshevism depended for its political organization. Such a transformation of social conditions was accomplished through the wide-scale application of factory organization to all sectors of American society. Taylorist and Fordist techniques for the de-skilling of the American worker and for the rationalization and depersonalization of the labor process were extended to as many aspects of social and cultural life as possible, including working-class leisure.

While such a transformation of cultural life had been underway for some time, its acceleration after 1919 was intimately tied to the need for capitalist expansion and control in the face of a newly invigorated and confident labor movement. The political theorist Antonio Negri has discussed how the capitalist strategy of social massification in the 1920s was only a temporary response to much larger structural imbalances.

> It is precisely here, however, that the qualitatively new situation after 1917 imposed limits. The possibilities for recomposition of the labor force in the phase of postwar reconversion certainly existed in the short run, but the capitalist class soon realized that this reorganization would open up an even more threatening situation in the long term. Not only would capital have to contend with the enlarged reproduction of the class that these changes would inevitably bring about; it would have to face its immediate *political* recomposition at a higher level of massification and socialization of the work force. The October Revolution had once and for all introduced a political quality of subversion into the material needs and struggles of the working class, a specter that could not be exorcised. Given this situation, the technological solution would backfire in the end. It would only relaunch the political recomposition of the class at a higher level. . . . The admission of working-class autonomy had to be accompanied by the ability to control it politically.[75]

The postwar construction of a modern mass society produced qualitatively new collectives—the new masses—whose political power and subversive potential were both created by and revealed through the sheer leveling of traditional social forms and by the rationalization of cultural authority. What was revealed by the liquidation of older forms of social organization was the possibility of a new and powerful political bloc. Valentino, whose stardom was virtually co-extensive with the period between the postwar repression of the labor movement and the collapse of the stock market in 1929, was one of the most popular and visible manifestations of these new masses. To the extent that his identity was figured as a dangerous subterfuge, Valentino was, indeed, the specter of an autonomous working class that haunted even the most confident celebrations of postwar consumer capitalism. Disguised in the unconvincing finery of mass-cultural fame, Valentino's inauthenticity made him available for the multiple and, finally, unregulated receptions of a vast public, and it also made him, more than any other film star of the period, a special representative for the experiences of the new urban working classes—especially the millions of new white-collar technical and clerical workers—and their vertiginous experiences with the processes of rapid social transformation itself.

That such a violent transformation could be represented as pleasurable and exciting should not be surprising since Valentino's status as a mass cultural icon was inextricably tied to working-class forms of sensuality. The great star's eroticism was often conveyed in the fan magazines and in the newspapers by an attention to his past servitude and his humiliation at the hands of middle-class employers.[76] For example, the possibility of Valentino's homosexuality was sometimes insinuated in reports on his own ambivalence about his class and ethnic background. Valentino seemed to alternate between pride and shame about his early years in America, and he was sometimes portrayed as having a past that, he felt, would just as well be kept a secret. Consider one of the few incidents of the 1923 tango tour that was enthusiastically reported by the press. Carl Fischer, the proprietor of a Detroit ballroom where Valentino and Rambova were engaged to perform, became indignant when Valentino refused Fischer admittance to one of the hotel suites that Fischer had arranged for the couple. Attacking Valentino's pretensions to the press, Fischer claimed Valentino was "the biggest snob I have ever seen. Several years ago I was the guest of Mr. and Mrs. Cornelius Bliss at their great country estate on Long Island. And who do you think was the bird who polished our golf clubs? None other than Rudolph Valentino, the assistant gardener." Valentino's angry reaction to the public remarks of Fischer, whose business establishment Valentino called a "third-rate dance-hall," also made good newspaper copy. When asked about the truth of Fischer's claim that the out-of-work film star could only attract "flappers and dissatisfied married women," Valentino quickly reminded the press that his public was the masses who could not be defined by gender or social type. "I need refer only to performances in Philadelphia where the police reserves were called out to handle the crowds that flocked to see me." Valentino, more interested in responding to Fischer's attacks on his past than defending his current career, quickly added, "And as for polishing golf clubs—no, never!" For some reason, Valentino felt compelled to reiterate this particular denial, and the press gladly reported it: "I was not the assistant gardener at Mr. Bliss's home, but the head landscape gardener. I never polished Fischer's golf clubs. I am not ashamed to admit that I was once poor. This country has been made by immigrants who started from the very bottom."[77] Valentino's unsuccessful attempt to construe his life as a Progressive-era success story required, in this instance, both his denial of ever having to work in such a degraded position as an "assistant gardener" and his urgent correction of the detail about "polish[ing] Fischer's golf clubs," a detail that clearly took on a sexual significance by virtue of the consternation it appeared to have caused the star.

As much as he might try, Valentino was never able to adequately represent his life as if he were the hero of a Horatio Alger novel in which his Hollywood stardom was the miraculous reward for those prized middle-class virtues of hard work, determination, common sense, and moderation. If the younger Valentino was the boy adrift in the city, he was also always the dark immigrant whose motives were as dubious as his means. In his study of film representations of the American labor movement during the silent period, Steven J. Ross has shown how Hollywood filmmakers, even in purportedly pro-worker films, used ethnicity and gender deviance to signify leftist radicals. As an example, Ross describes the film *Dangerous Hours* (Thomas Ince, 1920):

> Casting instructions for a strike scene in *Dangerous Hours* call for the director to use "very good specimens of American workmen" to play unorganized workers, and actors who are "slightly foreign in appearance" as the "rag-tag army of the I.W.W. [International Workers of the World]." Progressive reformers, contemptuously referred to as Parlor Bolsheviks, are played by men and women who are "pale and anemic" and have "a general air of unhealthiness both mentally and physically about the majority of them."[78]

While many biographers and historians have noted that, due to his "obvious foreignness," Valentino was often the victim of the rampant xenophobia of the period, no one has discussed the way Valentino's star image participated in a fairly well-established set of conventions in the early 1920s for representing an angry, deceitful, and politically dangerous sector of the urban working class. Of course, Valentino was not decidedly dangerous or deviant, only *possibly* so. There was always so much that *might have been possible* when it came to Valentino, and that is why he was a figure who elicited so much gossip and innuendo. His duplicity went far beyond the industry's typical mystification of star personalities and, while he did not represent the working classes directly, the apparent randomness of his stardom served the interests of the working classes by helping them understand who they were and who they might become through the new social conditions that they now faced. If the hero "of a bunch of Clark Street faggots" could become a matinée idol, then one might well ask, "Are pink powder puffs and parlor pinks in any way related?"

The attempt to rescue the public memory of Valentino from the taint of rumors continues today. One strategy has been to limit the discussion of Valentino's stardom to only his film works and to dispense with any analysis of the historical context for his star reception by denigrating as unreliable almost all biographical testimony and all media publicity concerning Valentino. This "rigorous" formalist approach has been most recently pursued by Brian Taves, who curated the Valentino film series screened in February and March of 1999 in Washington, DC, at the Library of Congress' Mary Pickford Theater. Taves begins his series description in the theater's program guide by posing Valentino as an historical problem yet to be solved: "Most impressions of his life have been based on half-truth and gossip, or the 1951 and 1977 biographical movies, and much work remains to be done to accurately chronicle both the story of his life and the films. Such a reassessment of Valentino properly begins with a look back beyond the legend to his actual work for the screen."[79] While it might not be surprising that a film archivist such as Taves would privilege the films over other kinds of texts representing Valentino, his subsequent reportage on this same film series to the Society for Cinema Studies reveals that Taves seeks to use the Valentino's films as a corrective to the historical damage done by the screen biographies and other popular sources of Valentino mythology: "Incredibly fictive 1951 and 1977 biopics have helped confirm a legend that is often either without basis in fact or demonstrably false; fortunately the bulk of Valentino's screen work survives to provide a more accurate account of his films and their use in generating what has become an enduring celluloid myth."[80] By making the surviving films the basis of a careful reevaluation of Valentino, Taves hopes to avoid an inclusion of what cannot be proven in the public remembrance of the great film star.

By way of countering Taves' confidence that we will only be sure to find the truth about Valentino if we begin our investigation by limiting ourselves to a consideration of his film performances, I would like to conclude this chapter by taking a closer look at two of Valentino's feature films which have received only scant attention from film historians and Valentino biographers. The films are *Cobra* (Ritz-Carlton Pictures, 1925) and *Moran of Lady Letty* (Famous Players-Lasky, 1922). My purpose in discussing these films is twofold: to show that Valentino's queerness is also textually inscribed in his motion picture work and to demonstrate how that textual inscription is, of necessity, always pointing to the insufficiency of the film text in settling questions of identity. In other words, these films use textual ambivalences to signify Valentino's intertextual and extra-diegetic queerness, here understood as a performative inability or refusal on the part of Valentino to play a role completely straight. Gender deviance is one of the central characteristics of Valentino's roles and performances in these films. Both films depart from the star's more well-known costume spectacles by being set in modern Western environments, and, unlike the historical romances and costume pictures with which Valentino is most often associated, the films' modern-day stories and familiar settings prompted audiences to relate the depicted events and characters to their own experience and knowledge of the world.

Some historians have lauded Valentino's final film, *The Son of the Sheik* (Feature Productions, 1926), for its humorous self-reflexivity and for Valentino's evident ability "to step outside of his manufactured image, analyze the Valentino mystique with tongue firmly in cheek, and still give the public what it desired."[81] Valentino had, though, already appeared in a motion picture which not only relied on a distanced critical awareness of its star's public reputation for being sexually provocative, but which also seemed to respond to the rumors about his sexual perversity. Like *The Son of the Sheik*, *Cobra* was made at the end of Valentino's short film career, but unlike any of his other starring roles, Valentino was asked to perform a character in *Cobra* that had some autobiographical relation with his own life and career: Rodrigo Torriani, an Italian immigrant in America. Even though Rodrigo is a count from the Neapolitan aristocracy, he comes to America penniless and uses his aristocratic identity and his refined manners to make his way in America society. The film's plot begins with Rodrigo still in Italy where he is the decadent descendant of a debt-ridden noble family. Besides his financial troubles, Rodrigo constantly finds himself in various imbroglios because of an insatiable interest in beautiful women and because of their mutual fondness for him. With self-mocking reference to Valentino's career of playing libertines and the irresistible rascals of historical romance pictures, this modern-day Don Juan is shown to have inherited his penchant for sex scandals from a distant sixteenth-century ancestor (also played by Valentino) who we see, in an historical flashback, frantically attempting to hide a young woman in his chambers after her husband pays Rodrigo an unexpected visit. Though the husband searches Rodrigo's quarters, he is only able to find, hiding behind a curtain, a second woman who neither he nor the film audience has seen before.

Rodrigo is tormented by this inherited inability to find any single woman with whom he can be satisfied, and he finally seeks help from an American businessman, Jack Dorning (Casson Ferguson). Jack is an art collector and a dealer in fine antiques who has inadvertently and unknowingly helped Rodrigo in his flight from the angry guardian of one of his more recent conquests. For assisting in this escape, Rodrigo invites Jack back to the Torriani palace where he complains to his new companion, "Women—always women! If only I could get away from them all." Jack is in Italy on a buying tour for his business, and when he witnesses how Rodrigo attempts to finagle his way out of yet another romantic entanglement by offering the offended parent a rare antique chalice to cover the damages, he proposes that Rodrigo take a job in America as an art and antiques appraiser. Jack vows to Rodrigo, "I will keep you too busy to think of women."

Rodrigo and Jack sail to New York and the two live together in grand style at Jack's lavish apartment. Rodrigo proves himself quite useful in the Dorning antiques gallery, particularly with appraising and authenticating valuable artifacts for Jack's female clients who are utterly charmed by Rodrigo's European manners and aristocratic title. And so begins what ultimately becomes a story about the strength of male loyalties as Rodrigo tries to remain true to his friend Jack by staying away from women, even though he continually disappoints. On one occasion, when a woman comes to the apartment demanding that Rodrigo live up to all he has promised her, Jack buys the woman's silence by giving her a thousand dollars, saying to his friend, "Rod, you're a puzzle to me. You're one of the best fellows I've ever known, but. . . ." Rodrigo interrupts by placing his hand on Jack's shoulder and, looking steadfastly into his friend's eyes, confessing, "I know what you're going to say. The worst of it is, it's true." For many members of the audience, moments such as these undoubtedly called to mind rumors about Valentino's secret and "unspeakable" sexuality. The film continually builds to moments that, sometimes comically, suggest Rodrigo's or Jack's homosexuality. For instance, Rodrigo tells his friend how lucky Jack is to only consider women his "pals." At the very least, such moments register and provide a commentary on Valentino's reputation as a fake; the fact that Valentino's duplicity was often discussed as a disparity between his screen reputation as a lady-killer and his off-screen disinterest in women suggests that *Cobra* is as complex and sophisticated in its intertextuality and self-reflexivity as *The Son of the Sheik.*

Besides Rodrigo's national identity and his attempt to earn a living by charming and ingratiating himself to American women of the genteel middle class, there are numerous references in *Cobra* to other events of Valentino's life that would have been familiar to American cinema audiences of the period. First, Jack's tour of Italy and Rodrigo's connoisseurship of fine European antiques recall the three-month trip that Valentino and Rambova made to Europe the previous year, after Valentino had completed his contractual obligations to Famous Players-Lasky. Valentino and Rambova had already taken an extended vacation in Europe during the second half of 1923 and the extravagance of this second trip was justified by their need to study European architectural design and to purchase period furniture and other items for use in a historical adventure picture they were planning to make. Valentino and Rambova were also purchasing *objets d'art* with which to decorate the sixteen rooms of the mansion on their new Beverley Hills estate, Falcon Lair.[82] The narrative premises of *Cobra*, then, bore more than a passing resemblance to Valentino's real-life interests and activities. Also, Jack—as an American entrepreneur who sells rare and eclectic European cultural artifacts to wealthy collectors and status-seeking social climbers—is very much the fictional counterpart of the Hollywood producers who exploited Valentino's exotic ethnicity and sensuality. Like the producers and promoters of

Valentino's star career, Jack is ultimately willing to pay for Rodrigo's indiscretions and extravagances because he realizes the Latin lover's value in attracting customers and in lending to his business enterprise a romantic aura. Additionally, Rodrigo's almost supernatural ability to seduce any woman he chooses mimicked the prevalent representations of Valentino's star power and sex appeal. Finally, Rodrigo's troubles with women, as well as his inability to be satisfied with any of them, resonated with Valentino's then current marriage difficulties (he and Rambova had separated by the time *Cobra* was released); with his 1921 trial for divorce from actress Jean Acker in which it was revealed that their marriage had never been consummated; and with the bigamy charge Valentino faced when he failed to wait the required length of time after his divorce from Acker before marrying Rambova.[83]

In *Cobra*, women are portrayed as predatory, with the film's serpentine and phallic title serving as a key metaphor in the film's misogynist representations of feminine sexuality, greed, and treachery. The major narrative conflict develops when an ambitious young socialite, Elsie Van Zile (played by Nita Naldi, who had co-starred with Valentino in two previous pictures), sets her sights on the young Italian count until she learns that he has no money to his name. She then pursues Jack, and the two of them quickly marry, much to Rodrigo's chagrin. Within a short period of time, the vile Van Zile begins to find her husband boring and sexually unfulfilling, and she attempts to begin an adulterous affair with Rodrigo. At first, Rodrigo resists her advances, partially out of respect for his friend Jack, partially out of a nascent moral sensibility, and partially because he has fallen in love with Jack's secretary, Mary Drake (Gertrude Olmstead), whose virginal purity is conveyed by her almost maternal devotion to her employer, her self-modesty, and her whiteness. Though Rodrigo enjoys Mary's friendship and company, he does not act on his passion. He seems to respect Mary's moral integrity, and he is ashamed of his own salacious desires and his past indulgences. His feeling for Mary is described in one intertitle as the "one, pure clean love he had ever known."[84] Rodrigo finally agrees to go to a hotel with the ever-persistent Elsie, though, at the very last minute, he has a change of heart and leaves; he cannot betray his friend Jack in such a manner.

At this point in the narrative Elsie is punished for her transgressions as she perishes in a devastating fire at the hotel where she has telephoned another man to take Rodrigo's place in her room. The two bodies cannot be identified. When Jack searches for his wife the next day, Rodrigo cannot bring himself to tell his friend all that he knows and what has transpired. A doctor warns Mary and Rodrigo that Jack's mental health is quite poor because of his wife's disappearance and that any shock may have serious consequences. Sometime later, after Jack has slowly improved, Mary commends Rodrigo on the manner in which he has nursed Jack back to emotional health. Jack now tells Rodrigo that he has found and read his wife's letters and that he knows about his wife's infidelities and about Rodrigo's loyalty to him. Rodrigo returns to Italy for a short stay, and when he returns he finds Jack much improved through the auspices of Mary's tender care. She has replaced Rodrigo in his role as Jack's constant companion and affectionate confidant. Since Jack has become so taken with Mary, Rodrigo decides to return to Italy, turning his back on the woman he loves so that his best friend might continue to enjoy happiness and health.

Undoubtedly, one of the purposes of *Cobra* was to refigure Valentino's stardom by combining what was thought to be true about the star with a plot that emphasized Valentino's homosocial commitments and his respect for proper white womanhood, despite his previous screen reputation as an unscrupulous seducer. Certainly the film's ending, with Valentino's character returning to Naples and leaving the American heterosexual couple intact, would have been something of a reassurance to anyone who was threatened by Valentino's "dark" ethnicity and his popularity with white female fans. In this instance, the dark foreign woman played by Nita Naldi is given to the white man, but she is punished for her deceit and her uncontrollable sexuality; the sexually pure white woman is spared her anticipated deflowering at the hands of the dark Rodrigo, and she is returned to her proper place at the side of the white American businessman. At the level of its overall narrative, *Cobra* performs "the traffic in women" that so often cements patriarchal power through male homosocial bonding and the exchange of women.[85] At the level of performance and image, however, the film so emphasizes the physical and emotional closeness of Jack and Rodrigo that *Cobra*'s reassuring ending is unable to completely deny the connotations of male homosexuality that have defined their relationship from their very first meeting in Naples. This is not to imply that the film's visual and intertextual registers in anyway subvert the ideological project of the film's narrative. Instead, we might say that male authority is affirmed in *Cobra* precisely by its construction of male homosexual desire through Valentino's star persona, or, as Sedgwick has pointed out, "the status of women, and the whole question of arrangements between genders, is deeply and inescapably inscribed in the structure even of relationships that seem to exclude women—even in male homosocial/homosexual relationships."[86]

Cobra eschews those displays of extreme sexual passions that were often an anticipated part of Valentino's film performances. Such passions were often conveyed through Valentino's intense stare at his chosen libidinal object. Miriam Hansen has termed this particular look of Valentino's an "undomesticated gaze," and she proposes that such a look destabilizes the traditionally gendered looking relations of classical cinema to the extent that Valentino "seems to become paralyzed rather than aggressive or menacing." For Hansen, Valentino's frozen stare produces an "oscillation" in the visual field between active and passive forms of looking, an ambivalence that, for Hansen, ultimately verges on masochism to the extent that not only is Valentino on display in the reciprocation of looks that his momentary paralysis allows, but his body is at risk of physical harm while he is so entranced. At these moments, Valentino's character looses mastery over the visual field and is unable to protect himself from his enemies. For Hansen, Valentino's eroticism was intimately bound up with the death drive.[87] The smoldering Valentino stare is, however, conspicuously absent in *Cobra* as Rodrigo spends most of his time expressing either boredom with women or remorse at his own inability to control his sexual behavior. When he is not exhibiting the mildly vacant stare of ennui, Valentino's glance in *Cobra* is most often cast downward in shame. The one other significant look employed by Valentino in this film is one of suppressed sadness and mourning in which his eyes are completely closed. Valentino uses this expression throughout the end of the film to express a bittersweet regret over Jack's and Mary's newfound happiness and his exclusion from their lives. Valentino's look in this film is a look that goes nowhere.

Instead of the look, *Cobra* uses framing, the spatial relation between performers, and touching to convey passion, concern, and intimacy between characters. Because Rodrigo is attempting to keep his heterosexual desire in check, he is often turned away from the many women he encounters, and, throughout most of the film, he is shown standing or sitting at some distance away from both Elsie and Mary. Whenever Valentino appears in a scene with either Naldi or Olmstead, the camera typically maintains a distant framing, emphasizing the absence or fading of desire rather than its ecstatic expression. There is never a dramatic circumstance that would lead to the type of close-up used for the "undomesticated gaze" about which Hansen writes. However, when Valentino is on the screen with Casson Ferguson, the two are often standing or sitting together, facing one another in close proximity. The camera's framing on the two men is noticeably tighter than it is on Valentino and the actresses in the film. Rodrigo and Jack are often seen in scenes of confession to one another, and the camera placement at these moments usually emphasizes their physical closeness as they touch one another and hold hands. It is not such moments, though, which ultimately represent Valentino or his character as queer, though such scenes were and still are available for gay appropriations.

What lends a more radical queerness to Valentino/Rodrigo in *Cobra*'s textual system is the narrative trajectory of the story together with Valentino's frustrated performance. Rodrigo is a young man unable to change his deviant sexuality. Even though he wishes to devote his full attention to his new friend Jack, he finds that he cannot break free from the ways of his past. Try as he might, he is cursed with a sexuality identical to that of his distant ancestors from whom he has inherited his pathology. Rodrigo is more or less a case of arrested development and Valentino's performance is marked by the stasis of distracted introspection and psychic struggle. The flow of *Cobra*'s narrative is considerably slowed and some-times even blocked during moments when Valentino looks away from the other actors in shame or when he closes his eyes in concealed sorrow. While certainly not the ambivalent gaze of erotic ecstasy which Hansen analyzes, these dead looks by Valentino in *Cobra* similarly place him in a type of paralysis. Rodrigo's body is forever in danger of being ravished by sexually predatory women (or conceivably even men), and he is also constantly at risk of blackmail because of his lack of discretion and control. Rodrigo cannot change. Despite the momentary possibil-ity that he might be transformed at the end of the picture, Rodrigo is different from Jack who begins the film with only his warm regard for Rodrigo, then de-cides to marry the dark and calculating Elsie who will cause him grief, and, in the end, learns to appreciate and love the beautiful and loyal white woman, Mary, who had been under his nose and in his employ the whole time. It is the American businessman who is able to make the necessary changes and adjustments in order for the story to come to completion and for a satisfactory union to take place. There is no place of permanence in the modern world for a chronic deviant such as Rodrigo, whose queer appearance in the metropolis is cause for curiosity, con-cern, and the remembrance of a primal sexual past that must be transcended.

Valentino's performance in *Cobra* is consistent with his construction in fan magazines and studio publicity as possessed of a primitive sexuality which was considered to be more or less of a challenge to the supposedly over-civilized pas-sions of white, middle-class American men. These representations of Valentino's sexuality obviously carried racial implications (which I discuss in Chapter 4), but they also corresponded to widespread cultural notions about sexual perversity that were buttressed by sexological concepts and popular discourses about the place of sexual pleasure within marriage. In his work on the construction of sexual abnormality in the early twentieth century, queer theorist and critical historian Julian Carter, has discussed the ways in which marriage manuals of the period and sexological science both employed evolutionary schemata to represent sex-ual desire and sexual pleasure as important and necessary components of human life, components which had properly evolved toward heterosexual coitus, their final civilized expression. According to this paradigm, sexual relations for mod-ern heterosexual couples will normally involve archaic modes of sexuality that are recapitulated or recalled from earlier moments in human evolutionary his-tory and which might involve several auxiliary forms of physical arousal such as, for example, oral stimulation. However, despite the importance of these other forms of sexual gratification, the point of closure to normal sexual relations must always be heterosexual genital coupling and reproduction. Sexual perversity in an otherwise normal and civilized individual was thus explained as either the premature halting at some early or intermediate point in the recapitulation of the evolutionary history of sex or the too rapid and incoherent expression of that history. The idea that a grand narrative of phylogenic development was continually retold or remembered with each individual sexual episode was a widely accepted idea and determining of many definitions of *degeneracy* in the early century: inverts and other sex perverts were more or less stuck at some (pre)historically earlier moment of human evolution.[88]

Reviewing the sociological commentaries and sexological works of Edward Carpenter, Maurice Chideckel, Havelock Ellis, Charlotte Perkins Gilman, and several other influential writers, Carter finds that sexual inversion was commonly thought to be atavistic in nature. More importantly, the homosexual's abnormality was not only understood as a failure to exhibit or perform the gender behaviors and appearances appropriate to her or his anatomical sex, but the condition was also regularly described "as a problem of perception and interpretation of reality."[89] While Hansen does not discuss Valentino in terms of degeneration, she does interpret the actor's trademark stare in psychoanalytic terms as a "psychogenic disturbance of vision" in which the survival instinct and the reality principal are significantly compromised. Likewise, my own reading of Valentino's vacant look in *Cobra* suggests that disrupted or impaired eyesight was a central component of the actor's performance style. Buttressed by his publicized interest in the spirit world and the practices of the occult, the repetition of a visually and psychically disoriented Valentino helped underwrite a popular reception of the star as a degenerate exhibiting the more emotional and unorganized mentality believed to be characteristic of so-called primitive peoples.[90] While such a mentality was considered well-suited to a particular stage or moment of evolutionary development, disorientation and perversion could result when the less-developed individual was placed in a more sophisticated social context or environment. Carter examines how the early sexologists, by continually pointing out that homosexuality existed among indiscriminate savages, were attempting to counter the masculinist Progressive-era argument that the causes of male decadence, effeminacy, and homosexuality were the feminizing influences of an over-abundance of culture and civilization. Carter cites Ellis's inclusion of the opinions of a physician in his 1897 study, *Sexual Inversion*.

> Similarly, an American doctor wrote to Ellis that inversion was "far more prevalent" among "American negroes . . . than among white people of any nation." While Ellis's correspondent believed that homosexuality was obviously atavistic—a survival of ancient undifferentiation of sex—he also considered the possibility that it was a degeneration caused by disruption of the normal sequence and pace of development. He thought that homosexuality in the American Negro might result from the fact that "his civilization had been thrust upon him, and not acquired through the long throes of evolution." In this view, sexual perversion was a consequence of either halting or overaccelerating development; in either case, Negroes were predisposed to sex perversion, and sex perverts predisposed to racial primitivism.[91]

Essentially, Carter's argument is that sexual abnormality was being increasingly understood and represented as a chaotic disruption of the grand narratives of natural evolution and the rise of civilization. Inversion was a regressive response on the part of underdeveloped or constitutionally abnormal individuals to the demands of the modern world; it was quite literally a flight back to an archaic mode of existence in which the differentiation between the sexes had yet to be fully accomplished.[92]

As mentioned in Chapter 1, a common criticism of Hollywood during the period of the early star scandals was that the industry placed in positions of great renown those who were ill-prepared to appreciate their fame and it gave great wealth to those who were incapable of handling large sums of money. Some people believed that because many of the new Hollywood stars had been taken from the lower ranks of society, they inevitably fell into vice and moral depravity. Hays himself explained Hollywood's early problems as the result of the "too rapid" development of a modern industry.[93] More than any other star of the period, Valentino embodied the arbitrariness of the Hollywood star system. His contractual disputes with the studios, his reputation for being a pretentious fake, the rumors that circulated about his sexuality—all contributed to a reception of the star as the latest manifestation of a primitive and potentially disruptive force within the heart of mass society. Whether one celebrated, feared, or was indifferent to Valentino, that force was associated with an archaic sexuality and with the irrationality of the mob. The centrality accorded to the riots in front of Campbell's Funeral Church by Valentino's biographers has only provided a final means for representing the cult of Valentino as a regressive expression of chaos, as a primal force that was only interesting in its spectacular confirmation of Valentino's animal appeal and the crowd's inability to meaningfully participate in modern mass society. An Italian immigrant who finds himself out of place and out of time in 1920s America, like most of the star's screen roles, Valentino's performance in *Cobra* was only one of many dress rehearsals for his funeral.

Valentino's 1922 performance of Ramon Laredo in *Moran of the Lady Letty* is an earlier example of the way modern settings tended to throw Valentino's queerness into stark relief. Based on a seafaring novel by Frank Norris, most critics have quickly dismissed the film as a failed attempt to cast Valentino in a more traditional, manly role. Studlar sees the film as an uninteresting variant of the Fairbanksian mollycoddle narrative in which a pampered weakling is transformed into an athletic hero. However, the story of *Moran* is fairly complicated despite the fact that the characters do not actually undergo any radical transformations.[94] Ramon is a wealthy society fop in San Francisco who is bored with his "almost fiancée," Josephine Herrick (Maude Wayne), and with his entire social milieu. An intertitle tells us that Ramon, "his temperament inherited from Spanish ancestors, spends his time dancing and in similar useful pastimes." One way he enjoys spending his time is in wandering around the docks of San Francisco where he first sets eyes on Moran (Dorothy Dalton), the strapping daughter of a Norwegian fisherman who sails the *Lady Letty*. Dalton plays the part of Moran extremely butch. She walks with a manly swagger, wears men's clothes throughout most of the picture, and inhabits all-male social spaces with supreme confidence. We are first introduced to Moran as she bids farewell to several young women at her home port by heartily shaking each of their hands. When Moran is in San Francisco and sees Ramon walking along the pier in his spiffy yachting outfit, she makes light of him by pointing out to her father the inappropriateness of the seaside dandy's clothes. Ramon, however, does not seem to notice her mockery and is momentarily transfixed by Moran's unusual appearance. He does not take his eyes off of her until she and her father have left the scene. We are told during the opening titles that, despite their being born on opposite sides of the world, Moran and Ramon are soul mates. The logic of their fated coupling is that they are "two of a kind" in their gender peculiarities. Even their names are anagrams for one another. The film's narrative only minimally supports the familiar mollycoddle scenario wherein Ramon is destined to transform himself through an adventure of physical adversity and finally win the hand of the Moran. While the script for *Moran* is loosely structured by such a narrative trajectory, the performances of Valentino and Dalton, the framing of the scenes, and the information provided by the intertitles tell an altogether different story about a queer romance. Like *Cobra*, much of the early exposition of *Moran* is highly suggestive about the possible homosexuality of Valentino's character. An early intertitle explains Ramon's interest in strolling along the docks: "No quarter of the most picturesque cities in the world has more interest for Ramon than the waterfront. More than once he had talked with loungers on the wharves." We see Ramon talking to one of these "loungers," a rugged older man who appears to be a sailor of some sort. Ramon points to a distant ship, the *Lady Letty* from which Moran had come ashore, and the sailor responds, "Yes, siree—sonny—ships from every port in the world an' some queer creatures on 'em too, I reckon." The old sailor then offers to buy Ramon a drink and the two go to a wharf-side tavern where they purchase drinks (Ramon orders a "mild manhattan") and retire to a private room in the back of the tavern after a knowing wink from the barkeep. We never find out if Ramon intends to have a sexual adventure since the older man quickly drugs Ramon and drags his limp body through a trap door in the floor. The old sailor then takes Ramon aboard a pirate ship, the *Heart of China*.

The ship on which Ramon finds himself smuggles contraband liquor and drugs. There is also the suggestion that the *Heart of China* is involved in the white-slave traffic, a suggestion that is confirmed later in the film. Ramon comes

FIGURE 6. While strolling along the wharf, Ramon is picked up by an old sailor who treats him to a drink and a private room at a nearby tavern. Production still from *Moran of Lady Letty*. Collection of the author.

to consciousness on the ship's deck in front of the entire crew, who present a haggard but rough-hewn assortment of seafaring types. Ramon awakes and stands at the center of this group of men, a shot that in its framing and composition recalls an earlier shot of Ramon at an afternoon tea. In that earlier shot, he sits in the midst of a group of women who are talking, sipping tea, and exchanging pleasantries. Ramon is depicted as comfortably belonging to this group of society women. On board the deck of the pirate ship and surrounded by the all-male crew, Ramon is separated from the group by their collective gaze at him; he doesn't belong here, and he is in grave physical danger. Kitchell (Walter Long), the ship's captain, pokes fun at Ramon's dress and manners just as Moran had done earlier in the day. He calls Ramon a "dance master" and tells the crew that their new captive probably still dotes on his mother. Ramon soon comes to understand that he has been shanghaied to labor as an additional deckhand, but when he protests his mistreatment and the crew's mockery, Kitchell knocks him to the boards. The sole person to come to Ramon's aid is "Chopstick" Charlie (George Kuwa), the only Asian crew member of the *Heart of China*.

Ramon's adventures at sea are intended to provide the types of experience that can transform him into a "regular fellow," and while he does become an able seaman admired by his shipmates and the captain alike, Valentino's star status confers upon Ramon an undeniable difference. We see Ramon swabbing the deck with other deckhands who cheer when he successfully defends himself against a hulking sailor attempting to intimidate him. The scene is reminiscent of Ramon's first encounter with the crew in that it is set up to emphasize Ramon's relationship to the group. While he now wears clothes of a more practical nature and he is no longer the object of ridicule, all eyes are still on him, and his clothes differ from those of the other seaman in color (Ramon wears a white undershirt while the others are dressed in dark colors) and in their form-fitting snugness. Ramon's trim physique is on display for the sailors in this shot as is Valentino's for the members of the film's audience. By cutting from this scene to a scene aboard the *Lady Letty*, another parallel is established between Moran and Ramon, as each is able to find his or her place at sea by performing a tough and self-confident version of masculinity.

The *Lady Letty* accidentally catches fire, and Moran and her father are overcome by the smoke and fumes as the rest of the crew abandons the ship in a lifeboat. Soon afterwards, Captain Kitchell spies the smoldering vessel and assumes it to be completely deserted. Hoping to loot the *Lady Letty* of its cargo, he takes Ramon and several other men aboard where they find a sailor, Moran, unconscious but still breathing, though the ship's captain, Moran's father, is dead. Ramon recognizes Moran from their brief encounter in San Francisco and he decides to rescue her just as the raiding party is forced to return to their own boat because of the increasing precariousness of the still-burning ship. Safely back on board the *Heart of China*, Ramon takes Moran below deck where Charlie helps him tend to her and where he finally realizes that the unconscious sailor is a woman. Upon regaining consciousness, Moran also remembers Ramon, and there is a flashback to their brief dock-side encounter. Charlie promises Ramon not to tell the others about Moran's true identity, but Kitchell soon finds out that the rescued sailor is a woman. He threatens Moran with rape, though she remains well protected by Ramon, Charlie, and the rest of the crew, presumably in deference to Ramon's wishes. However, it is Moran's own unflinching self-confidence in the face of his aggression that seems to effectively deter Kitchell from following up on his threats. He refers to Moran as "a rugged wench."

Kitchell anchors the *Heart of China* somewhere off the coast of Mexico where he goes ashore to meet a confederate group of smugglers. In the meantime, Ramon and Moran also go ashore where they run on the beach and leisurely explore a cove. Alone together by the seaside, Ramon tells Moran, "I've never known a girl like you. You have no idea how different you are from the kind of girl I've known." The visible difference of Moran from other girls is, of course, that she is like a man and Ramon says as much. This love scene is intercut with the meeting between Kitchell and a band of his fellow smugglers. These outlaws are a mixed assortment of coarse racial stereotypes, primarily comprised of Mexican *banditos* who wear large sombreros and Chinese opium smugglers in coolie hats. Kitchell confers with the group's apparent leader, Pancho, with whom he devises a plan to attack Ramon (who he calls "the dandy") and the rest of his crew members, so that he might capture Moran and sell her to Pancho. Back on the beach, Ramon confesses to Moran, "Well, I might as well say it. I love you more than I imagined I could ever love a girl." Moran's reply to this pronouncement is every bit as astonishing: "Believe me, it's all wasted. I never could love a man. I'm not made for men." The subsequent intertitle, which at first appears to have been included in order to disclaim the lesbianism implied by Moran's last remarks, does absolutely nothing to normalize her sexuality or her gender identity. Moran continues, "No, nor for women either. At all events, mate, I'm not a girl. I'm just Moran of *Lady Letty.*"

This exchange between Moran and Ramon is given in alternating medium shots. Then, after Moran's disclosure of being sexually unique, a full-shot abruptly shifts the mise-en-scène to the deep space of a highly atmospheric shot where the couple occupies the mid-ground. Moran gets up and walks from the shadows of the cove into the luminous distance while Ramon sits in silhouette, his head cast pensively downward. Moran returns to give Ramon a slap on the back, and, after getting to his feet, Ramon runs off with Moran into the eerily lit distance of an alien world. Many of the shots at the cove seem jarringly artificial in their abstractness, especially when placed in the midst of a series of naturalistic shots taken at what appears to be an actual beach and coming after so much location footage taken aboard the sea vessels. While these atmospheric shots may have been included to lyrically convey the emotional tenor of such an oddly intimate scene, their undeniable alterity only heightens the scene's queerness and the film's overall preoccupation with gender deviance.[95]

At this point, Charlie appears on the beach, telling the couple that he has overheard Kitchell plotting to kidnap Moran and warning them about the captain's plan to attack his own ship with a band of outlaws. Moran, Ramon, and Charlie quickly return to the ship to apprise the crew of the mounting danger. Armed against the surprise attack but fearing defeat nonetheless, Moran asks Ramon, "Are we not a strange pair to die together, my friend?" Significantly, Moran answers her own question, "But we can do that better than we could have lived together." Ramon and Moran are a couple who have no place in the present world and have no foreseeable future. Up to this point in the story neither character has done much to advance the narrative of *Moran*, and what agency they do

FIGURE 7. A strange landscape for an equally strange romance. Valentino and Dalton in *Moran of Lady Letty*. Digital frame enlargement.

possess is almost entirely defensive against the forces that seek to annihilate them. When Kitchell and the outlaws finally attack, they are able to board the ship despite heavy fire from the guns of Moran, Ramon, and the rest of the crew of the *Heart of China*. In the melee that follows, Kitchell is injured and Charlie is fatally wounded. The attackers are finally repulsed, but Ramon, who had stopped in the midst of the battle to gaze passionately upon Moran firing her revolver, must finally calm Moran who is still in such a frenzy of physical violence that she does not, at first, even recognize Ramon or realize that the conflict is over. The ship now is in the control of Moran and Ramon and the two sit together on deck watching the sunset. Matching close-ups with iris mattes emphasize their un- canny physical resemblance. The film then provides a coda that allows Ramon to distinguish himself in more traditionally masculine terms. Returning to San Francisco to visit his old society friends and to explain his sudden disappear- ance, Ramon leaves Moran aboard the ship while he is ashore. Finding his friends at a formal debutante ball, Ramon tells his "almost fiancée" that he can no longer stay in the social world that he had known before and that he must return to the sea. Predictably, he goes back to the boat just in time to rescue Moran from an attack by a reinvigorated Kitchell who has been recuperating in the hold. The film ends with Moran and Ramon in a warm embrace aboard the deck of the *Heart of China* while the ship's crew turn their heads to afford the couple a moment of privacy.

Despite the ending's attempt to normalize what had been a relationship founded on perverse narcissistic desire, Moran and Ramon remain outsiders to modern society. Unable to live happily on land, they prefer the vastness of the wide-open ocean where they are free from society's expectations and judgments. Whether they will discover any new lands in uncharted waters is highly doubtful, though there is a fantastical utopian quality about *Moran*'s ending. The film was less successful than many of Valentino's other pictures for Famous Players-Lasky, though it was certainly not a complete failure. Box office was fair, but critics complained about the unbelievability of the romance and the poor casting of Valentino in the role of Ramon. A critic at the *New York Times* wrote that Valentino was "too slick. He doesn't impress one as the kind of youth who would be attracted to Moran, except momentarily, or attractive to her. In some scenes he is persuasive, but in others it seems a pity he ever left the ballroom. And it is through his character too that the story becomes just movie stuff."[96] Interestingly, the critic responds to the film by repeating the film's own intertextual cues to Valentino's popular star identity and his earlier career as a ballroom dancer. Indeed, it is difficult to determine if the "he," in the critic's phrase, "he should have never left the ballroom," refers to Valentino the actor or to Ramon the fictional character. What Valentino brings to the film, then, is a "slick" personality that introduces into the realism of this sea adventure an incongruent artificiality that turns the entire story into just so much "movie stuff." Yet this is precisely how the narration of *Moran* works. In the playing of a character who unhappily inhabits a rigidly gendered world, Valentino's presence in the film drew on his reputation for dissembling machismo in order to succeed in life. The types of exaggerated masculinities assumed by Valentino in both his film roles and in his public appearances were often recognized (and indulged in) as belonging to the world of make-believe. *Moran* is able to tell the story that it does because it re-enacts Valentino's failure to convince anyone, and it productively exploits the contradiction between his star identity and the type of generic story in which Ramon appears as a character. In this early starring role, Valentino is already thoroughly convincing that he, as Ramon, and this strange creature, Moran, do not really belong in this modern-day world where romance is a story that must develop along conventional lines. If we look to the films of Valentino to find the truth of the man and the actor, as Brian Taves has suggested, we find that the "truth" of Valentino is, in fact, his falsity.

Charles William Elliot, the former president of Harvard College, passed away on August 22, 1926, a day before Valentino's death. Elliot was ninety-two years of age, Valentino only thirty-one. During his forty years as Harvard's president (1869–1909), Elliot had become renowned for his progressive views on education and culture. At the time of his death he was most widely remembered as the editor of the Harvard Classics, fifty-one works first published by Collier's as a series for the mass market in 1909 and considered to be a foundation for informed and intelligent discussion. A few commentators saw in the deaths of these two men a chance to point out the harm caused to American society by the Hollywood star system and its mass audience. Juxtaposing the relative lack of media attention given to the passing of the influential man of letters and the widespread outpouring of unruly emotions that met the news of the matinée idol's death, writers lamented the evident erosion of social purpose and progressive ideals in contemporary American society. For example, an editorial distributed by the Preston News Service appeared on the front page of *the New York Amsterdam News*, the African American news weekly published in New York City. Several prominent African Americans received their degrees at Harvard while Elliot was president, including W.E.B. DuBois (1890), William Monroe Trotter (1895), and Alain Locke (1907). The author of the editorial observed, "Thus the rank and file of America mourns over the objective of the clicking camera, while a few bereaved will assuage their grief over the builder of ideals. It is just beyond the pale of the first group that the mob abides. Thus we see what the black man of America is constantly facing—the psychology of the crowd, not the staid judgment of real thinking men and woman in America."[97] The stories of the riots at Valentino's funeral were here made terrifying by being implicitly linked to racist violence and to vigilante practices such as lynching. Valentino's legacy had nothing to offer projects of racial uplift and social transformation, with the star's appeal itself viewed as a social problem in need of reform. Conversely, Elliot is remembered as a progressive who successfully advanced the causes of uplift and racial justice, and whose life might still offer inspiration to anyone working to improve the race.

The largest front-page headline in that issue of *the New York Amsterdam News*, however, concerned an issue of more local importance, the murder of a Harlem resident by a white police officer: "Actor Dies from Blows of Central Park Officer." The first paragraph of the story provides the essential details:

> When Clinton De Forest, 42 years old, a female impersonator, left his residence at 256 West 130th street, last Tuesday evening to pay tribute at the bier of Rudolph Valentino, his friend, it was with no thought that death would shortly claim him, too. This was about 9:15 p.m. By 1 o'clock Wednesday morning, De Forest was lying on a white cot in the emergency ward of Metropolitan Hospital with a black eye, a broken jaw, a fractured skull, and internal injuries from which he never recovered.[98]

De Forest is here emphatically linked with Valentino in both life and death, almost as if they were tied together by fate. Unlike the syndicated editorial, Valentino is here acknowledged as having real importance for the paper's readership beyond the facts of the story, since the movie star is posed as having some powerfully formative relation for at least one of the members of a public about whom the paper's readership is critically concerned. The story goes on to tell of how a white policeman claimed to have beaten De Forest with his fists after encountering him in the dark in Central Park and ordering De Forest to move along. The officer was subsequently arrested on a murder charge after De Forest died, but neither the patrolman nor his captain would explain why De Forest was not arrested for disobeying a police order. De Forest had been found unconscious by a taxi driver in another part of the park from where the assault occurred. De Forest's mother was called from her home in Boston "to identify her son by his hands as his face was too badly mutilated to be recognizable."[99] The news report did not state whether De Forest was in drag at the time of the assault.

4

Black Valentino

Consciousness of the body is solely a negating activity.
—FRANZ FANON, *BLACK SKIN, WHITE MASKS*

In an interview in 1985, Lorenzo Tucker, the African American matinee idol of the 1920s and 1930s, commented on Oscar Micheaux's strategy of billing him as the "colored Valentino," a promotional label that supposedly occurred to Micheaux while encountering publicity for Rudolph Valentino's *The Son of the Sheik* in 1926. Tucker remembers,

> Yeah, it worked. And I kind of looked like Valentino, too. But I never got any white press at all, and very few people outside the black community ever heard of me. But I want to make one thing straight: these historians today always say that I was called "The Black Valentino." Well, I never was that because we never used the word "black" like that in those days. Micheaux only called me "The Colored Valentino," nothing else. In fact, if you really want to know, I was even lighter than Valentino himself.[1]

Tucker's comments suggest that, at least sometimes, "blackness" was primarily a factor of skin color, while being "colored" had more to do with social life and with personal identifications to a racial community. Hence, Tucker's identity as a colored performer insured the segregation of him and his film work from white audiences. Tucker also implies that, in some important sense, Valentino, while not colored, was already "black," and that if, indeed, there were to have been a "Black Valentino," it would more likely have been Rudolph Valentino and not Tucker himself.[2]

Writing about the same film that inspired Micheaux to exploit the Valentino name, Richard Dyer notes that the spectator of *The Son of the Sheik* sees the film's heroine, Vilma Banky as Yasmin, well before seeing Valentino as Ahmed, the young sheik introduced when Yasmin remembers him in a flashback. As Dyer points out, Ahmed is "already located in her dreams, a spiritual realm of desire." Dyer concludes his symptomatic reading of the film, however, by suggesting a somewhat naïve and decidedly anti-modern mode of reception by a mass audience presumably bereft of any nuanced notion of an unconscious:

> The most curious aspect of the film is the relation between the setting and the characters. All act as stock Arab figures, such as sheiks and belly-dancers; they act out a rather stark drama of sexual morality. Yet most of the main characters are not Arabs but Europeans (English and French) who live as Arabs. In this way *The Son of the Sheik* comes to feel like the "secret life" of contemporary western society, an exploration of the otherwise unspeakable subjects of female desire, rape and father-son conflict. The audience could take it two ways. Shocked by the sexual explicitness, it could dismiss the depicted events "anthropologically" as foreign behavior. Drawn into the characters, however, it could welcome the film as a sunlit dream of sexuality. In a period not yet saturated in Freudian ideas, such dreams were still possible.[3]

Dyer demonstrates here, as I have in Chapter 3, that Valentino's image was strongly associated with memory and with the ideological crossing of sexual desire and an exotic distant past. Yet Dyer's representation of contemporary film audiences as existing in some sort of state of innocence with respect to the vicissitudes of sexuality assumes a rather rigid and uncomplicated set of binaries at work in the mass reception of Hollywood movies and movie stars: fantasy/reality, object/subject, other/self, projection/identification. Furthermore, he interprets the understanding of such binaries by a mass audience to be uninformed by any modern theoretical or scientific discourse (this is how I understand the quotation marks around the word *anthropologically* in the quote above). In this chapter I again take up the stardom of Rudolph Valentino, this time to investigate how contemporaneous representations of the relations between the famous film star and his public both relied on and promulgated modern sociological and ethnographic ideas about racial identity and the ultimate instability of such categories of self and other. Dyer's suggestion that cinema audiences of the period were either unwilling or incapable of intimately relating "the anthropological" to their own subjective lives and experiences does not necessary follow from *The Son of the Sheik*'s narrative premise that "Europeans [could] live as Arabs." In fact, a widespread fascination with ethnic disguise in the popular romantic fiction and in the films of this era would suggest a rather extensive investment in scrutinizing who might or might not qualify as European or as Arab, since these identities no longer seem so obvious.[4] I am primarily concerned here with the way that both Hollywood cinema of the 1920s and the human sciences of the period were informed by specific narratives about racial transience and miscegenation, and with the way that these narratives about race were simultaneously a conspicuous part of popular and scientific representations of modernity and modern life.

Sociology's academic ascendancy in the 1920s occurred at the very moment that the mass media made possible a full-blown consumerist culture in the United States. This meant that sociological inquiry was often tied to document-ing and explaining the role mass media played in the rapid social transforma-tions occurring among the various ethnic cultural communities in America's largest cities. The researchers of the highly influential Chicago school of urban sociology were particularly interested in mass communications since newspa-pers, national magazines, movies, and radio programs were all occupying more and more of people's leisure time. As mass-produced entertainment came to re-place the traditional cultures of new immigrant populations, as well as those of the many long-established ethnic and racial communities of the United States, members of these groups came to understand themselves and their relation to others primarily through mass-media representations and no longer only through their own traditions and indigenous social practices. Social identity was now susceptible to a much wider and more dynamic field of influence. The sociologist Robert B. Park explained the lure of the metropolis in 1925:

> Transportation and communication have effected, among other silent but far-reaching changes, what I have called the "mobilization of the individual man" [sic]. They have multiplied the opportunities of the individual man for contact and asso-ciation with his fellows, but they have made these contacts and associations more transitory and less stable. A very large part of the populations of great cities, includ-ing those who make their homes in tenements and apartment houses, live much as people do in some grand hotel, meeting but not knowing one another....
>
> Under these circumstances the individual's status is determined to a consider-able degree by conventional signs—by fashion and "front"—and the art of life is largely reduced to skating on thin surfaces and a scrupulous study of style and manners....
>
> This makes it possible for individuals to pass quickly and easily from one moral milieu to another, and encourages the fascinating but dangerous experiment of living at the same time in several different contiguous, but otherwise widely sepa-rated, worlds.[5]

The possible anonymity provided by big-city life led to a flattening out of per-sonal identity, and with the dissolution of small-town familiarity the possibility of leading a secret double life now gave rise to a number of possible deviant iden-tities: the drug addict, the delinquent, the queer. As discussed in Chapter 2, *per-sonality* was one of the key terms of the period, designating both a fascinating object of scientific investigation and a very important media commodity. More-over, in both the laboratory and in the marketplace, personality was, as Park says, "determined to a considerable degree by conventional signs"—*determined* both in the sense of coming to know something through familiarity or inquiry (as in the sentence, "she finally determined just what type of person he really was") and in the sense of being a sufficient cause. In other words, an individual's personality within mass industrial society was determined by the sum total of her or his participation in an increasing number of new lifestyles available in the modern city, only some of which still required sustained and intimate group socialization for inclusion. Many of these new identities were defined simply through the temporary adoption of particular fashions, behaviors, or attitudes. By the beginning of the 1920s, the mass media were widely regarded in the United States as some of the most significant sources for moral instruction and knowledge about the world. While personality was still an expression of a particular life history, the rise of a consumer culture and the fragmentation of social life meant that personalities were being much more easily and quickly refashioned by new social forces such as advertising and mass entertainment. This refashioning, as we shall see, even extended to ethnic and racial identity.

CASTING FOR TYPE IN THE URBAN DANCE HALL

Gaylyn Studlar situates Valentino's stardom in relation to the growth and popularity of ethnic dance in the 1910s, and she has suggested how Valentino's status as an ethnic other along with his female fandom complicated the star's reception by tapping into whites' anxieties about the maintenance of racial purity. Studlar observes how "racial purity was clearly a lost cause if the 'new woman' did not restrain her contact with the dark 'new immigrant,' whose stereotypical association with barbarous sexual desires and decadent 'Oriental' passion did not require an imaginative projection of the fears of a black/white miscegenation but excited sufficient paranoia in and of itself."[6]

Considering the Valentino phenomenon in relation to a set of social concerns about race, ethnicity, and urban dance halls in the 1920s, I continue this inquiry into Valentino's problematic ethnicity. Unlike Studlar, however, I argue that black/white miscegenation was indeed involved in Valentino's reception, though not as some "imaginative projection" of nativist fears. Instead, blackness was structurally a part of Valentino's popular identity and appeal. In this particular case, miscegenation narratives were not only the paranoid responses of committed white supremacists, but were available to a much wider public as a way of understanding Valentino's relationship with his white female audience, as well as a way of representing that relationship as a form of social deviance. While these miscegenation narratives sometimes traded on various racial hierarchies inherited from nineteenth-century scientific theories about the racial body, theories which understood race as more or less brute facts about genetics and evolutionary development, these new narratives more often than not articulated racial and ethnic identity as determined by dynamic (dis)functional relations between different cultural groups interacting within the same or adjacent social environments. Such a potentially non-essentialized understanding of ethnicity and race is most dramatically evident in the emerging discourse of urban sociology in the 1920s.

Studlar's subsequent work on Valentino has sought to draw connections between the star's appeal and the emergence of an exotic and orientalist dance culture typified by the popular success of the Ballets Russes in the United States of the 1910s. Moreover, she has proposed that during this era of "dance madness" the figure of the "tango pirate"—an exotic and often foreign-born male dancer who makes his living by dancing with white middle-class women at "tango teas"—was an important cultural predecessor to Valentino who had, himself, worked as a dancer for hire before becoming a movie matinée idol.[7] While the tango pirate was surely a recognizable personality to quite a number of Americans, he, like "the new woman" who sometimes kept company with him, was primarily the creation of a genteel middle class for whom tango teas posed such an exhilarating threat. Valentino's stardom, however, was anything but a phenomenon of the genteel classes, and the cult of the star was certainly not the result of some sort of trickle-down effect where Valentino became the Nijinsky of the masses. To account for Valentino as a mass phenomenon means taking up a mass-cultural perspective and considering the ways in which this star's ambiguous identity enabled film audiences to recognize the terms of their own sociality.

Public perceptions of popular dance as a social problem in the 1920s were most often attuned to the proliferation of cheap public dance halls in America's urban centers, especially those dance halls that provided young female dancers for hire and were usually closed to all but male patrons.[8] These halls were known variously as dime-a-dance halls, monkey hops, closed halls, and taxi-dance halls. In such establishments, men would hire female dancers on a dance-by-dance basis, exchanging for each dance one of the several tickets that had to be purchased upon entering the hall. The young women who worked in these dance halls were sometimes called teachers or instructresses, but they were more popularly known as taxi-dancers or dime-dancers. Because of the perceived connection between these commercial establishments and prostitution, these businesses were often the primary targets of social reformers and of municipal legislatures concerned with regulating dance as commercial recreation. For example, the Commissioner of Licenses of New York City, with the assistance of various social reform groups, undertook a study on the conditions of dancing establishments at the end of 1923. The study, which was widely cited in newspapers and magazines around the country, concluded that the most "immoral" conditions were to be found in the city's closed dance halls where, as the New York Times reported, "[o]nly men are admitted and most of them are 'socially undesirable' Orientals."[9] Such places provided one of the very few ways in which foreign men could make the acquaintance of young, white American women.

In 1929, sociologist Paul Cressey wrote his master's thesis on Chicago's "closed dance halls," and he published a more extensive monograph on the subject in 1932 entitled simply, *The Taxi-Dance Hall*.[10] Cressey was a student of Robert Park and Ernest Burgess in the Department of Sociology at the University of Chicago, and he later taught at the Payne School of Education at New York University. Along with his colleague Frank Thrasher he was to have co-authored *Boys, Movies, and City Streets*, one of the two unpublished volumes of the Payne Fund studies on cinema audiences.[11] Continually seeking to carve out a place for modern sociology, Burgess, in his introduction to Cressey's study, laments the general public's lack of familiarity with the social dynamics of the closed dance hall and suggests that real social reform should proceed from an informed and thorough understanding of the dance hall's patterns of development and growth as an urban social institution.

The largest part of Cressey's study is devoted to the social development and personality of the taxi-dancer and the way the closed dance hall constitutes a unique social world for her. Examining several case histories, he discerns a patterned life cycle in the careers of taxi-dancers, who are almost always young, working-class white women, very often the daughters of recent immigrants from Western Europe. Cressey finds that most of these young women come from unstable family situations and seek the world of the dance hall as a way to achieve some degree of autonomy as well as to find a type of social prestige that being a successful and sought-after dancer confers.

However, Cressey finds that when a taxi-dancer cannot maintain her popularity and standing within the dance hall, then she can no longer afford the luxury of choosing her dance partners, and she is forced to dance with the many non-white patrons who frequent these establishments, typically Filipino men in the dance halls that Cressey studied. Cressey points out, though, that the Filipino patron holds a special attraction for many taxi-dancers "in preference to other Oriental groups, [and this] is explained by such factors as his Occidental culture, represented in the Spanish influence in the Philippine Islands; his suave manners, dapper dressing, and politeness; and the romantic Spanish lover rôle that it is possible for him to play."[12]

While not the innovator of the cultural role of "the romantic Spanish lover," Valentino could have certainly laid claim to being that role's most significant interpreter in the 1920s. What was definitive of this role was not the specificity of any ascertainable Spanish heritage, but rather the very hybridity that such ethnic and racial role-playing produced: the mannered Westerner living out intense orientalist passions and the colonized Other exhibiting a polished European gentility. Cressey makes it clear that he believes the taxi-dancers do not just find

the Filipino patrons acceptable because of their "old world" manners, presumably derived from a colonial-era Mediterranean heritage, but are attracted to
their extraordinary combination of a (presumably misrecognized) racial identity
and glamorous posturing. He illustrates this attraction by quoting the testimony
of a taxi-dancer, Case No. 19: "I didn't know much when I started at the hall. I
didn't even know what a Filipino was. I thought they were movie actors or something. They were always well dressed, and treated me nicely; I fell for them hard."[13]
This young woman demonstrates, unwittingly perhaps, the adoption of the sociological perspective in everyday life. She is presented as commenting on her past
from a more experienced position where she understands her earlier career and
emotional life to be determined by the movies and the arbitrary character of her
vocation. Cressey, too, sees the closed dance hall as a socially disorganized space
in that the dance hall brings together individuals, patrons, and dancers who presumably have little or no organic social relation or shared cultural interests.

From a modern sociological point of view the closed dance hall existed primarily as an economic institution in which socially distant individuals sought to
fulfill traditional psychological and social needs that had been disrupted through
changes brought by urbanization and modern industrial expansion. In many respects, the cinema was a similar institution, especially when the cultural exchanges
taking place there involved a quite a number of white Anglo Americans purchasing tickets to see a heavily exoticized foreigner like Valentino. Consistent with
Chicago school sociology, Cressey also conceived of the closed dance hall, like all
disorganized spaces, as a place where new social forms develop and take shape,
and in this way the taxi-dancer and her patron could be seen as pioneering new
organic social institutions and exchanges. Both the dance hall and the cinema
could be and were considered as ambivalent social spaces that simultaneously
signified disaster and progress, two of the most important and pervasive tropes
of modernity.

Cressey, however, ultimately hypothesized that the taxi-dancer's life cycle
formed a downward spiral in which the less successful dancers become more and
more incapable of choosing or sometimes even distinguishing the ethnicity or
race of their dancing partners, until, finally, they were forced to leave the halls to
work in racially nonsegregated establishments. Drawing on the familiar narrative of the "falling star," Cressey writes:

> A failure to make satisfactory adjustments in the world of Orientals may bring the
> girl to a fourth cycle, which is begun when she centers her interests upon the social
> world which in Chicago has been associated with "black-and-tan" cabarets. She
> usually comes into contact with these groups through her association with Orien-
> tals. With the Negroes she again achieves temporarily the prestige accorded the
> novitiate. But here, too, she is doomed to a decline in status, and this seems very
> frequently to lead to prostitution in the Black Belt.[14]

As one of Cressey's investigators reported, this last stage of the taxi-dancer's life was popularly referred to as "going African," a phrase quite ideologically commensurate with Cressey's understanding of the taxi-dancer's career as a retrogressive "behavior sequence."[15] Cressey's motivation for including the investigator's report of this popular phrase was the way the phrase helped clarify his hypothesis about the life cycle of the taxi-dancer. The phrase also demonstrates the similarity between the sociological representation of the taxi-dancer and her popular identity. Africa, here, is both a destination and a destiny, a magnetic force that becomes operative for whites, especially white working-class women, when they embark upon certain cultural exchanges with other ethnicities. As the terminal point in this process, blackness is accorded the powers of both attraction and disintegration. The non-segregated club represents the chaos of undifferentiated racial identities and the annihilation of white cultural integrity. This particular narrative about the taxi-dancer's work represents the urban dance hall as the site of miscegenation, where the mixing of races threatens to destroy not blood purity, but the very identity of racial society itself. In this way, sociology, in both its scientific and popular forms, indirectly helped to rationalize the policies of racial segregation in America. Despite Burgess's claim about the public's ignorance of the social world of the closed dance hall, the taxi-dancer was already a well-known social identity whose personality was understood precisely in terms of her economic exploitation and the disorganized social experiences that the conditions of her labor entailed. Consider, for example, *The Nickel Hopper*, a three-reel comedy that Mabel Normand made for Hal Roach in 1926. Mabel works as a taxi-dancer to support her antisocial father, and we see that, even within the space of a few minutes of a single evening at the dance hall, Mabel must dance with an exhausting number of decidedly uninteresting men. While the men who exchange tickets for dances with her vary wildly in age, body size, sobriety, and dancing ability, it is clear that these disorienting bodily and behavioral differences emphatically stand in for and signal ethnic and racial differences for an urban cinema audience of the 1920s.

Likewise, Ruth Etting's popular 1930 recording of the Rodgers and Hart song, "Ten Cents a Dance," portrays the work of the taxi-dancer as given over to a rapid serialization of male dance partners whose ethnic and class differences are here signaled by differences in occupations: "Fighters and sailors and bow-legged tailors / can pay for their ticket and rent me. Butchers and barbers and rats from the harbor / Are sweethearts my good luck has sent me."[16] The taxi-dancer was a compelling popular figure in the 1920s and early 1930s, heroic in her efforts to be an independent modern woman, but ultimately tragic because of the precariousness of her fate and because of the presumed cultural and racial alienation she experienced as a dancer for hire.

FIGURE 8. Anatomical difference signals ethnic difference as Mabel is forced to dance with a strange assortment of men. Digital frame enlargement from *The Nickel Hopper*.

The vast white, female audiences who were presumed to adore Valentino and who were, by falling under the star's spell, promoting radically new standards for male beauty, certainly came under attack for abandoning their duty to their own race. Racist, masculinist, and sexist portrayals of Valentino and his fans were common enough media events.[17] Often, however, these portrayals shared with more sympathetic representations of the star an emphasis on the way his identity, in its ethnic fluidity and indeterminacy, allowed for the proliferation of a diverse array of other ethnicities. This was true not only because of the many varied roles Valentino performed in his films but, more importantly, because of his determining relation to the appearance of several other film performers who were also strongly marked as non-white. Writing in the September 1923 issue of *Photoplay*, columnist Herbert Howe gives, with racist humor, the following account of the Valentino phenomenon under the title, "Sheiks of Hollywood":

There are more sheiks in Hollywood than in Sahara. They slink the Boulevard, droopy of eye and of cigarette, complexions ranging from oleomargarine to deepest anthracite. While seated in a Hollywood barber chair I happened to remark to a casting agent, who was waiting his turn, that Lillian Gish wanted a leading man of the Latin type. Instantly, my chair was whirled violently around, and the barber hissed, "Look at the man in the second chair." Confronting me was a dark, lowering individual who looked as though he might have tied his peanut roaster outside. "If he won't do," whispered the barber, "I have another customer—dark, slick hair, sexy—who will be in for a shave in a few days." No wonder producers have so many Valentino successors when you can get one with every hair-cut![18]

The recognizable model of a racial continuum here—"complexions ranging from oleomargarine to deep anthracite"—and the infiltration of the barber shop's white male social space by these new types of patrons are tied by Howe to the industrial serialization of Valentino types. This column is accompanied by a cartoon of a barbershop which has a sign on the wall reading: "Valentinos while you wait." The need to restrain Valentino's influence on the standards of male stardom had been voiced in *Photoplay* a year earlier by a reader who asked, "why will people persist in comparing him with Wallace Reid, Thomas Meighan, et al. [*sic*] He is a distinctly different type from these American men. . . . To me he is perfection of *his* type, but that does not stop me from sincerely admiring other stars, especially the likable Thomas Meighan."[19] Valentino's celebrity was so disturbing and exciting not because he represented a particularly successful version of the romantic Latin-lover type, but because he was complicating the utility of historically dominant racial and ethnic categories.

Representations of Valentino as a disruptive influence on traditional racial and ethnic boundaries were ubiquitous during 1923, the year he was absent from the screen after walking out on his contract with Famous Players-Lasky. While the studio prevented him from working in the industry while it held onto his contract, he and Natacha Rambova toured the United States with a tango performance. The popular press gave some notice to this exhibition tour, but much more coverage was given over to Valentino's absence from the screen and the implications of his absence for cinema audiences. For example, *Vanity Fair*'s coverage from June 1923 is a page of seven portraits entitled "Saint Valentino's Day." Because of the prominence and direct gaze of Valentino's countenance at the center one might, on first glance, assume that the smaller profiles surrounding this image represent different roles the actor has performed. On closer inspection, we come to realize that all these portraits are of other men who bear some relation to Valentino: they are all his protégés—even the director, Rex Ingram, whose Irish identity allows him to be counted as one of the these "seven dark horses," is represented as in some way derivative of Valentino and under the star's influence.

The arrangement of the profiles of the six protégés sets up a circuit of looks between these men, a circuit that circulates around the returned gaze of Valentino's image at the center of the page. Repeated representations comparing Valentino to other male stars articulated his erotic power over other men by placing them in such close proximity to Valentino within the space of glamour

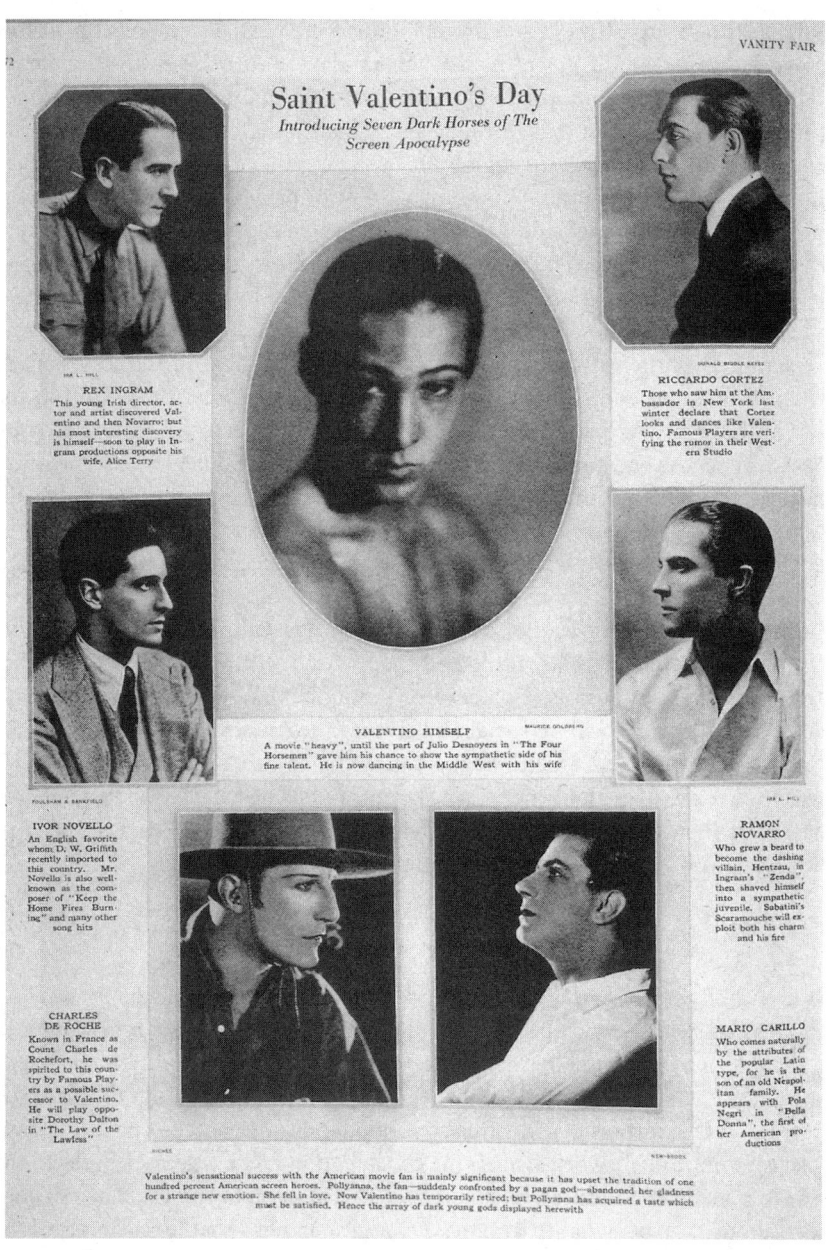

Saint Valentino's Day
Introducing Seven Dark Horses of The Screen Apocalypse

REX INGRAM
This young Irish director, actor and artist discovered Valentino and then Novarro; but his most interesting discovery is himself—soon to play in Ingram productions opposite his wife, Alice Terry

RICCARDO CORTEZ
Those who saw him at the Ambassador in New York last winter declare that Cortez looks and dances like Valentino. Famous Players are verifying the rumor in their Western Studio

VALENTINO HIMSELF
A movie "heavy", until the part of Julio Desnoyers in "The Four Horsemen" gave him his chance to show the sympathetic side of his fine talent. He is now dancing in the Middle West with his wife

IVOR NOVELLO
An English favorite whom D. W. Griffith recently imported to this country. Mr. Novello is also well-known as the composer of "Keep the Home Fires Burning" and many other song hits

RAMON NOVARRO
Who grew a beard to become the dashing villain, Hentzau, in Ingram's "Zenda", then shaved himself into a sympathetic juvenile. Sabatini's Scaramouche will exploit both his charm and his fire

CHARLES DE ROCHE
Known in France as Count Charles de Rochefort, he was spirited to this country by Famous Players as a possible successor to Valentino. He will play opposite Dorothy Dalton in "The Law of the Lawless"

MARIO CARILLO
Who comes naturally by the attributes of the popular Latin type, for he is the son of an old Neapolitan family. He appears with Pola Negri in "Bella Donna", the first of her American productions

Valentino's sensational success with the American movie fan is mainly significant because it has upset the tradition of one hundred percent American screen heroes. Pollyanna, the fan—suddenly confronted by a pagan god—abandoned her gladness for a strange new emotion. She fell in love. Now Valentino has temporarily retired; but Pollyanna has acquired a taste which must be satisfied. Hence the array of dark young gods displayed herewith

FIGURE 9. Valentino as industrial prototype. *Vanity Fair*'s coverage of the star's absence from the screen in 1923 emphasized the serialization of Valentino types.

and objectified sexuality. Such representations were partially responsible for the disavowed reception of Valentino as a sexual deviant (discussed in Chapter 3), and these representations also help explain the continuously repeated insistence that the cult of Valentino was incontestably female, that it was white women who were thought to be at risk through their contact with Valentino's almost supernatural powers of attraction. However, what is of principal importance for the analysis of Valentino's relation to social scientific conceptions of racial identity is the way in which *Vanity Fair* figures Valentino's ethnic identity as a structuring absence determining an assumed white female desire for dark skin. As the text accompanying the portraits states, "Now Valentino has retired; but Pollyanna has acquired a taste which must be satisfied." The oval framing and soft-focus of Valentino's image contrast with the other portraits to confer on Valentino the aura of the absent or distant loved one. His nudity and his frozen, returned stare mark him as the entranced and entrancing primitive who occupies some other space and some other time. While the other portraits seek to illustratively supplement the biographies, the image of Valentino, we are told, is "Valentino himself."[20] Valentino is here figured as precisely an *image*, as present in his very absence: a master signifier of race, one who organizes a taxonomy of ethnic differences and supposedly puts into motion a series of "dark" masculinities for display on the motion picture screen. If Valentino had simply been an ethnic star like any other ethnic star such as Sessue Hayakawa or Antonio Moreno, he would not have posed such a threat to white social and cultural hegemony. But he brings all his friends along with him, and he creates a growing demand and an increasing desire for dark skin. As an iconic image, Valentino had become the industrial prototype for the desegregation of the cinema, a cinema that he was helping turn into just another type of taxi-dance hall.

THE VALENTINO SKIN TEST

As inscribed in the *Vanity Fair* portrait, Valentino's status as a media personality who was completely subsumed by his photographic image was a recurring idea in the mid-1920s, helping to support the cult value of his stardom as well as activating the racial vertigo that I have been describing thus far. Significantly, the almost total reification of Valentino's visual identity did not, as one might suppose, simultaneously work against his construction as a cult object. Indeed, the very terms of this reification relied on a set of ethnographic and sociological notions about race, personality, and mass communications that formed part of the necessary material conditions for the establishment of a mass cult. In "The Work of Art in the Age of Its Technological Reproducibility," Walter Benjamin proposed that, in the past, the cult value of an object and its aura depended primarily on that object's unique existence and its ritual function. By contrast, the work of art under industrial relations of production is chiefly defined by its exhibition value; that is, the very reproducibility and transmission of the work of art made possible by modern photographic processes and communication technologies produce a qualitative change in the social function and effects of art works. While Benjamin defines cult value and exhibition value as polarities, and while he sees the latter as historically displacing the former, he also implicitly argues for their co-presence and dialectical oscillation in almost every artwork.[21]

Writing at a moment in European history when the successive modern art movements of cubism, expressionism, and surrealism had each taken an interest in the "primitive" and ritualistic art practices of non-European cultures—especially African cultures—Benjamin's theorization of the loss of aura and of the technological diminution of the work of art's cult value is actually premised on, historically and theoretically, the rather abrupt (re)appearance and return of the primitive.[22] Not only is his ability to indicate a new distracted mode of mass reception made possible through that reception's juxtaposition with prior modes and practices, but those earlier modes and practices are themselves now circumscribed and rendered strange, contributing significantly to that sense of historical discontinuity and disruption that Benjamin so highly valued. Even if past modes of perception are now uninhabitable, they are not unknowable, and while he sees the culture industry's attempts to attribute quasi-auratic qualities for mass-produced commodities (often, interestingly, by exploiting the iconography of orientalism) as a reactionary response "to the shriveling of the aura," cult value does persist for Benjamin, traveling through time to haunt modernity:

> But cult value does not give way without resistance. It falls back to a last entrenchment: the human countenance. It is no accident that the portrait is central to early photography. In the cult of remembrance of dead or absent loved ones, absent or dead, the cult vale of the image finds its last refuge. In the fleeting expression of the human face, the aura beckons from early photographs for the last time. This is what gives them their melancholy and incomparable beauty.[23]

The comment about "the last time" notwithstanding, it is aura's waxing and waning, its continual disappearing act that ultimately defines mass culture for Benjamin and allows him to employ a binaristic language marked as well by racial history and ethnography: prehistory/history, shaman/engineer, magic/science.

Another of Benjamin's theoretical concepts in which a racial basis for mass cultural reception is evidenced is in his notion of "testing." Drawing on theoretical work by Soviet filmmakers regarding the screen actor's performance and on Bertolt Brecht's dramaturgy, Benjamin notes that under the conditions of visual and aural montage now constituted by the social and technological arrangement of the cinema, the performance of an actor is no longer experienced as the unique duration of an integrated body or personality. Instead, the actor is subjected to a series of segmental tests by the camera in which the viewer's role is not empathetic identification with the personality of the actor/character, but critical evaluation of the highlighted segment or the detail. The film spectator occupies the position of the camera and performs along with the camera the function of objectively testing reality. Benjamin calls the new film spectator an "expert," and he points to the increasing wide-scale adoption of emerging bureaucratic and scientific-management methods, such as the standardized aptitude test, as an index of this new form of social organization and consciousness. Yet the cinematic examples that Benjamin chooses have just as much to do with observing anatomical bodies and physiological behaviors as with quantifying intellectual and vocational skills.[24] Similarly, the Hungarian film theorist Béla Balázs observed in 1923: "A few more years of film art and our scholars will discover that cinematography enables them to compile encyclopædias of facial expression, movement and gesture, such as have long existed for words in the shape of dictionaries. The public, however, need not wait for the gesture encyclopædia and grammar of future academies: it can go to the pictures and learn it there."[25] Balázs explicitly defines modern Europe as having lost the richness of "[t]he gesturing of primitive peoples," and, like Benjamin, Balázs regards mass culture as the site of the prescient (re)discovery of new forms of knowledge and expertise about bodies and behaviors.[26] Both Balázs and Benjamin suggest that the cinema is anticipating or even directing the future discoveries of the traditional sciences and is, therefore, the most historically advanced site for the production of new knowledge.

One of the most repeated and conspicuous manifestations of "testing" in Valentino's early stardom was the attention given to the relative darkness of his skin. Both in his films and in studio publicity materials, occasions were invented so that Valentino's face, arms, and hands could be visually compared with the lighter skin of his female co-stars. While almost every romantic embrace ostensibly afforded audiences an opportunity to make such comparisons, the contrasting skin tones of Valentino and his leading ladies were very often emphatically presented through the photographic or cinematographic selection of an anatomical detail, with a difference in skin color being a significant pictorial element within the graphic composition of both Valentino's publicity stills and specific shots within his films. For instance, a production still from *Blood and Sand* (Famous Players-Lasky, 1922) shows Valentino in a passionate embrace with Nita Naldi, a film star who was, herself, marketed as a dark *femme fatale* and as "one of the most popular actresses . . . playing vampire roles."[27] While their passionate kiss is the occasion for this publicity image, the most visually prominent elements of the composition are Valentino's two hands against Naldi's bare shoulder and back. His hands stand out starkly against Naldi's lighter skin,

FIGURE 10. The Valentino Skin Test. Valentino in a signature pose with (*left to right*) Nita Naldi in *Blood and Sand* (1922), Gloria Swanson in *Beyond the Rocks* (1922), Naldi again in *Cobra* (1925), and Vilma Banky in *The Son of the Sheik* (1926).

and they are visually connected to one another by the dark strap of her dress. This arrangement of graphic elements pushes the viewer's attention downwards, along Naldi's body—from the couple's lips, down Naldi's left shoulder to Valentino's left hand, and continuing down her back along the strap of her dress, finally halting at Valentino's right hand clutching the actress's lower back where the contrast in skin tones is most dramatic. This particular pose, with its almost signature emphasis on the darkness of Valentino's hands, was used over and over with other leading ladies throughout his star career. While it was common practice within the classical Hollywood cinema to photograph a romantic couple with the woman more brightly lit than the man in order to emphasize her whiteness and thus her desirability, the fetishistic attention and sheer repetition of these images of Valentino's hands on women's white backs went beyond any institutional coding of the conventional romantic couple.

Such graphic differences in skin color also played a significant role in the narration of the dramatic events in *The Sheik* (Famous Players-Lasky, 1922). Once again, it is Valentino's hands that function as an optical skin test. In this film based on novelist E. M. Hull's hugely successful popular romance of 1919, Valentino plays Ahmed Ben Hassan, a young and powerful sheik of the Sahara who becomes enraptured with and who then abducts a young Englishwoman named Diana Mayo, played in the film by Agnes Ayers. The two first meet in the city of Briska where "the new civilization rubs elbows with the old." Diana, motivated both by an adventurous ethnographic curiosity as well as by a mounting erotic fascination, disguises herself as a young Arab woman and attends a marriage auction presided over by Ahmed Ben Hassan. As fate would have it, Diana is soon chosen to be put up for sale and told to perform a dance for the benefit of the male patrons and spectators at the auction. When she resists, the Sheik approaches her and, taking hold of her hand, compares her skin to his own by way of a close visual inspection. We can see that Ahmed's hand is significantly darker than hers, and he remarks that she has "[t]he pale hand and the golden hair of the white woman." He then asks her to leave, presumably because the auction is forbidden to all non-Arabs, but also because, as we soon learn, he plans on keeping Diana for himself. This incident, in which the comparison of hands forms an important moment of truth and discovery, initiates the film's central motifs of sexual humiliation, miscegenation, and racial (mis)recognition, the same motifs that underlay both the sociological and popular versions of the taxi-dancer's experiences.

As has often been noted, miscegenation is neatly avoided in *The Sheik* by the last-minute revelation that Ahmed is not really an Arab at all, but rather the aristocratic son of an English father and a Spanish mother who found themselves stranded in the Sahara and who, after being assisted by the elder Ben Hassan, allowed their son to "[grow] to manhood as an Arab." Yet it is significant that the earlier comparison of hands is recapitulated at the end of *The Sheik* and that this final revelation of Ahmed's true racial and ethnic identity is also initiated and verified by the visual analysis of a bodily detail. He and his men have rescued Diana from the desert bandit Omair who has abducted her with the intention of rape and enslavement. During the rescue Ahmed is severely injured. In the next scene we see him lying unconscious in his tent with his head bandaged while outside the men of his "tribe" pray and await news of his condition. Diana, now helplessly in love with the wounded Sheik, kneels by his bed and, holding his hand in hers, remarks, "His hand is so large for an Arab." Despite the new emphasis on the size of Ahmed's hand instead of its color, the image once again highlights a brown hand against white skin, with Diana's eyeline strongly cueing us to make such a comparison for ourselves. It is at this point that Ahmed's European friend, Raoul de Saint Hubert (Adolphe Menjou), reveals to Diana the Sheik's true parentage. While at the beginning of the film it was Ahmed who recognized Diana's racial identity through the close analysis of morphological difference (skin color and hair), now, at the end of *The Sheik*, it is Diana who calls Ahmed's Arabness into question through her close observation of a portion of his body. Saint Hubert's explanation of Ahmed's true identity, while working to resolve what has been the ongoing scandal of miscegenation in the film's narrative, is now doubly required since Diana's new observation about the largeness of Ahmed's hand in no way entails a white or hybrid European ethnicity. In fact, given the preoccupation with myths about the monstrous bodies and genitalia of blacks within the popular white American imagination,[28] the relative largeness of Ahmed's hands could have easily implied that the sheik was descendent from Africans rather than Europeans. Even if the proportions of Ahmed's hands only ambiguously stand in here for the size of Valentino's penis, the sheer amount of investigative scrutiny given to Ahmed's body suggests that the discovery and

mapping of blackness is an ulterior aim. Frantz Fanon has written about the ex-
istential moment of this particular visual logic within the context of colonialism:
"I am being dissected under white eyes. I am *fixed*. Having adjusted their micro-
tomes, they objectively cut away slices of my reality. I am laid bare. I feel, I see in
those white faces that it is not a new man who has come in, but a new kind of
man, a new genus. Why, it's a Negro!"[29]

THE RETURN TO THE DESERT

Probably one of the most significant contributors to the rising importance of
popular ethnography in the United States was *National Geographic*, the monthly
magazine of the National Geographic Society which began publication in 1888.
In their study of the magazine's representational practices, Catherine Lutz and
Jane Collins have pointed out that in the first decades of the twentieth century,
the National Geographic Society's "main role [was] popularizing and glamorizing geographic and anthropological knowledge." They also note that, alterna-
tively, the society supported just enough of what was then perceived as serious
expeditionary research to maintain the mantle of a legitimate and valuable scientific organization, a perception that was also aided by *National Geographic*'s
editorial policy of keeping its advertising pages completely separate from the
scientific articles.[30] Nevertheless, *National Geographic* participated in an ever-
increasing overlap between the presentation of ethnographic knowledge and
popular entertainment that was then taking place.[31] Such an overlap was at times
so great that writers for scientific journals sometimes felt the need to construct
their own authority by employing a rhetoric of having to correct the mass media's distortions of scientific methods and facts, or, as in the case of Cressey's
study of dance halls, of having to educate a public who is pronounced entirely
ignorant about a particular subject, despite that subject's conspicuous ubiquity
within mass culture.

Writing about his 1924 expedition across the Libyan desert in *National Geographic*, A. M. Hassanein Bey, identified at the outset of the article as a "graduate
of Oxford University and now First Secretary of the Egyptian Legation in Washington," makes the following clarification about Bedouin Arabs at the very beginning of the account of his journey into an area "unknown to civilized man":

> After leaving Siwa I put aside my khaki clothes and assumed desert garments, trav-
> eling as a Bedouin sheik. I find that in America *sheik* means something very terri-
> ble and fascinating; but 90 per cent of the sheiks in the desert are as little likely to
> run away with a beautiful woman as the same per cent of the sedate bankers of
> America! The word "sheik" in Arabic means "an old man," and it has come in time
> to mean the oldest man of the tribe—that is, its chief, or the head of the region, or
> the head of a caravan.[32]

IN THE COSTUME OF THE DESERT

At Siwa the author put aside his khaki uniform and assumed the garb of a Bedouin sheik (see text, page 237).

WITH THE THEODOLITE IN THE DESERT

The Bedouins were extremely suspicious of this surveyor's instrument. They were told it was a type of camera which *attracted* pictures from a distance (see text, page 247).

FIGURE 11. A. M. Hassanein Bey's performance of a sheik. Popular science gets into the act but needs to distinguish itself from both mass-cultural deception and existing desert cultures. Photographs from *National Geographic*.

While "sheik" imagery and other orientalist motifs were, by the mid-1910s, already a recognizable part of mass culture in general and Hollywood in particular,[33] Hassanein Bey is clearly responding to the way that the word sheik had so quickly became a part of popular speech in America after the immense commercial success of Valentino's film in 1921. It is interesting that even while Hassanein Bey maintains that authentic sheiks have more in common with "sedate" American bankers than they do with the fabrications of Hollywood, he himself has no difficulty "traveling as a Bedouin sheik." The magazine article even provides readers with a full-length photograph of Hassanein Bey "in the costume of the desert" despite the fact that he also appears in at least three other photographs in full shot, donning the same or a similar outfit. In one of these, he is shown standing in the desert with a tripod and theodolite, an instrument used to make topographical maps. This photograph's caption reads: "The Bedouins were extremely suspicious of the surveyor's instrument. They were told it was a type of camera which *attracted* pictures from a distance." In this instance, the ethnographer's own performance of a sheik is shown to be superior to that of actual Bedouins, whose lack of technological sophistication makes them incapable of adequate self-representation. The ethnographer's portrayal of a Bedouin sheik is also far superior to the performances of Hollywood actors, whose fanciful renditions lack any informative relation to reality.

Popular ethnography's need to authenticate itself against both its objects of study as well as mass-cultural appropriations of those objects had much to do with the merger of art and science that the social and technological bases of mass culture entailed at that historical moment. It is perhaps no accident that Hassanein Bey's "magical" explanation of the surveyor's instrument which he gives to pacify the Bedouins—a "camera which attracted pictures from a distance"—is precisely Benjamin's scientific description of the spectator/camera of the cinema, a cinema that was, for him, materially at the forefront of the transformations of mass consciousness within industrial society. Citing the French essayist and poet Paul Valéry, Benjamin used the model of public utilities—"water, gas, and electricity are brought into our houses from far off"—to describe the speed and delivery of a rationally planned mass communications industry whose products are consumed through "the desire of the present-day masses to 'get closer' to things spatially and humanly, and their equally passionate concern for overcoming each thing's uniqueness by assimilating it as a reproduction."[34]

In the years immediately following the box office success and media sensation of *The Sheik*, U.S. cinema audiences were treated to such films as *Arabian Love* (Fox Film Corporation, 1922); *The Sheik of Araby* (Robertson-Cole, 1922), a re-release of *The Man Who Turned White* (Jesse D. Hampton Productions, 1919); *When the Desert Calls* (Pyramid Pictures, 1922); *Burning Sands* (Famous Players-Lasky, 1922); *The Tents of Allah* (Encore Pictures, 1923); *A Son of the Sahara* (Edwin Carewe Productions, 1924); *The Desert Sheik* (Truart Film Corporation, 1924); *The Arab* (Metro-Goldwyn Pictures, 1924); and *A Cafe in Cairo* (Hunt Stromberg Productions, 1924). While the film industry's preoccupation with images of Arabs during the early to mid-1920s was certainly first and foremost a marketing strategy which successfully exoticized the mise-en-scène of conventional melodrama, Hollywood's repeated returns to the desert were also often construed as a laudable and instructive interest in geographic and ethnographic realism. For example, in a brief photo spread on the production of the film *Burning Sands*, *Photoplay* playfully lamented the industry's continuing exploitation of "Arab" themes and "[t]he procession of 'Sheiks'" coming out of Hollywood. However, the primary point of this coverage was to promote the technical achievements of the director and the four hundred workers who made this particular film on location in the California desert. One of the stills reproduced in *Photoplay*'s coverage is a panoramic view of a desert oasis that runs horizontally across the top of the page. With an aspect ratio of 3.33:1, this photograph is intentionally out of place in a popular motion picture magazine like *Photoplay*, though such panoramic views were often encountered in the travel literature of the period and in magazines such as *National Geographic*, where the unusually high number of six such panoramic landscapes accompanied Hassanein Bey's account of his journey through Libya and the Sudan. *Photoplay* used the conventions of travel photography to enhance the geographic authenticity of the Hollywood film's locales: "This little oasis in the Arabian desert was built by hand, with specially imported palms. When you see it on screen you'll never guess it's within a few hundred miles of Hollywood—unless you read this."[35] Benjamin's insight into the cinema's ability to substitute a reproduction of reality as equal to reality itself is here figured as the film industry's ability to substitute a Hollywood reproduction of a desert landscape as equal to a *scientific reproduction* of a desert landscape.

The desert lent itself so readily to fantasies of infinite reproducibility, in part, because of the role that images of the desert and desert cultures played in nineteenth-century colonial projects of Western imperialism.[36] As post-colonial theorist and cultural historian Ella Shohat points out, the mass media inherited many of these colonialist images and ways of viewing the world and made them their own.

> The popular image-making of the orient internalizes the codes of male-oriented travel narratives. Strong continuities link Hollywood's ethnography with Hollywood's pornography, which often latently inscribes harems and despots even in texts not set in the orient. What might be called "harem structures," in fact, permeate Western mass-mediated culture. Busby Berkeley's production numbers, for example, project a harem-like structure reminiscent of Hollywood's mythical orient; like the other harem, they house a multitude of women serving, as Lucy Fischer suggests, as signifiers of male power over infinitely substitutable females.[37]

While Shohat emphasizes the control, rationality, and visual mastery entailed by an infinite substitutability of gendered and racialized bodies within a unified visual field, the harem structure that underpins the serial manufacture of cultural commodities—what I have been describing as the racial basis of mechanical reproduction—must also threaten confusion and regression whenever the visual mastery of the spectator in some way fails or is called into question. Just like the taxi-dance hall where the serialized nature of the taxi-dancer's work diminishes her ability to recognize and distinguish ethnic and racial differences, the undifferentiated vastness of the desert is a fantasy site of misrecognition, racial disguise, and sexual violation despite its promise of a clear and unobstructed view without coordinates.

The gods and heroes of ancient times were born in the desert, and the desert remains a liminal space within Western representation and philosophical thought. The French anthropological theorist Georges Bataille understood the desert as that space where the dynamic and ambivalent interrelation of the sacred and the profane was most violently manifest: "In the ideally dark void, there is chaos—to the point of revealing the absence of chaos (there everything is desert, cold, in closed night, while at the same time being a painful brilliance, inducing fever); life opens itself up to death."[38] The desert is the place for the transformation of all categories and values, where darkness becomes light and life embraces death. If the desert is the mise-en-scène of the violent rupturing of identity which is so important for Bataille and which he sees as most profoundly expressed in the culture of so-called primitive societies, the most important remnant of authentic violation in modern society is, for him, the bullfight. Significantly, the other role with which Valentino was and still is most closely associated beside the desert sheik is his performance of the toreador Juan Gallardo in *Blood and Sand*. Almost a decade into the fully developed Hollywood star system, Valentino represented a radically new type of star precisely because he had such an intense and intimate relation to the auratic. In films like *Blood and Sand* and *The Sheik*, the young screen idol's star image was carefully constructed in relation to archaic ritual and to the desert as a space of transgression, violence, and death.[39]

Constructed from the beginning of his star career as an appearance of the distant and exotic cultural Other who appears and disappears within the midst of modernity itself, Valentino enacted throughout his career the atavistic principles on which the mass-cultural commodity depends. Even before his disappearance from the screen became quite literal after his death in August of 1926, the paradoxical use of absence to construct Valentino's appeal and identity was both an integral part of his press coverage throughout the early 1920s as well as a significant component of his film work. In *The Four Horsemen of the Apocalypse* (Metro, 1921), the film most often cited as initiating Valentino's popular stardom, Valentino plays Julio Desnoyes, a decadent libertine born in Argentina to a Spanish mother and a French father. The film begins long before Julio's birth with a shot of Madariaga, Julio's grandfather (Pomeroy Cannon). The framing, space, and overall narration of this shot are entirely ethnographic, with Madariaga depicted as a kind of centaur amongst his cattle that dot the distant mountain vista behind him. The entire opening sequence works more as a representation of a way of life than as an exposition of character. An intertitle tells us, "While in the new world, boundless space offers a haven to the alien, and ancient hatreds are forgotten." This film, which begins in pastoral South America and in a space and time outside of European history, will end with Madariaga's grandson, Julio, returning to Europe to die on the battlefields of World War I, the apocalypse of modernity here figured as the pull and collision of two worlds on one individual and transcended only through his death. At the end of the film Julio appears as a specter to Margarite Laurier (Alice Terry), the married woman with whom he had been having an illicit love affair before his enlistment. He tells her of his own death on the battlefield, and he urges her to remain and care for her war-wounded husband. While Julio's death at the end of *Four Horseman of the Apocalypse* works to affirm his restoration to dutiful and proper manhood, this patriarchal legacy is complicated by the way Julio's disappearance and death at the end of the story relates to the time before his arrival and his birth at the film's beginning.

After the shot of Madariaga tending his cattle, the film's images narrate a story about miscegenation, rape, and colonial exploitation. A scene of Madariaga whipping an idle worker is preceded by the intertitle, "Many of the hybrid youths of Madariaga's employ bore a striking resemblance to the Spaniard." The film then introduces his legitimate children: two daughters, one of whom is married to a German while the other has married a Frenchman. In a surprising application of Lamarckian theory, the three sons born to the German son-in-law all don wire-rimmed spectacles and exhibit Wilhelmite militaristic behaviors: spontaneously marching everywhere, playing war, and striking statesman-like poses.[40] The grandfather despises these three children and anxiously awaits the day when his daughter who is married to the Frenchman will have a child. When that day arrives and an intertitle tells us that the child is "A Boy!," we see a brief shot of a native woman smiling and applauding followed by a close-up of a white cockatoo crowing. After the fade, the next sequence opens on the famous and much-discussed dance-hall scene in which Valentino appears in the film for the first time and dances the tango. While the final two images of the expository sequence work formally, dramatically, and ideologically to justify European colonialism by portraying the colonized as a creature of nature who celebrates the continuation of her economic and sexual subjugation, these images also work to mark Julio's birth as a ritual event.

As the scene in the Buenos Aries dance hall will demonstrate, Julio shares his grandfather's appreciation for coarse physical pleasures, and the two spend their time together pursuing licentious amusements. In many ways then, Julio becomes the son that Madariaga never had, but he is also one of the many sons that Madariaga has already had and who bear such "a striking resemblance" to their father. Julio is thus related to his many half-aunts and half-uncles through his lived appreciation and acceptance of the local customs of the Argentine; yet he is also different from them in that he must return to the "old world" of Paris as a type of exotic spectacle, where, predictably, he becomes a *décadent* painter of female nudes and a tango instructor. However, this transplanted flower cannot survive as an authentic presence in the land of technology, and Julio is finally destroyed by his stoic acceptance of the simultaneous stupidity and inevitability of modern war.

This particular reading of *The Four Horsemen of the Apocalypse* agrees with the common observation that the film was crucial in launching Valentino's stardom and in setting out the particular terms of his subsequent career. These terms, within the larger context of mass culture, take on specific relations and produce specific effects beyond Valentino's problematic foreignness as a matinée idol. His associations with sartorial excesses, ethnic dance, and decadent sexuality are sometimes presumed to have presented a challenge to normative white masculinity. However, in *The Four Horsemen of the Apocalypse,* as elsewhere, these particular components of Valentino's persona are depicted and ordered so as to re-enact a set of imagined racial histories that underpinned both popular and social scientific constructions of modernity: an evolutionary atavism that helped explain the reappearance of cult value within the midst of the metropolis. With his presumed appeal to a vast, white, female audience who worshiped his image by consuming it, Valentino's dark and exotic masculinity helped to make sense of and to legitimate the disruptions of traditional social relations caused by the new economic and social conditions of monopoly capitalism and bureaucratization.[41]

Like much of mass culture, Valentino's stardom was more or less a demonstration that the seeming alienation of modern life was also full of surprises: disorienting and dangerous, but also offering previously impossible and undreamt of experiences and encounters, very often through the venues of commercialized leisure.[42] What was specific about his stardom was the way it so thoroughly relied on scientific concepts of race and social development that were then in ascendancy elsewhere in American society. Chicago school sociologists and the mass media of the period both portrayed the geographical dislocation and social hybridity of rapid urbanization as a type of cultural disintegration always threatening to produce an attendant (though often only temporary) regression to psychological primitivism, at least for certain groups of susceptible workers or consumers and for pathological individuals. Within the limits of my analysis these workers and consumers have been taxi-dancers and Valentino's fans, but a similar logic would also apply to other modes of work and other modes of consumption evident in the seemingly infinite retail positions that appeared in the employment advertisements of major newspapers and in the proliferation of cheap amusements which had become an almost unremarkable part of urban life. The modern story of the taxi-dancer is a lesson about the social basis of personality and of individual identity; the life cycle of the taxi-dancer tells us that who we are depends on how we are socially and psychically related to others. This modern insight was often evident in both the human sciences and the mass media of the 1920s as an interest in the possible social transformations brought about by new inter-ethnic and inter-racial cultural exchanges made possible under the conditions of mass culture. Rather than seeing Valentino's ethnic otherness as a primarily disruptive or potentially controversial quality, we can understand how his stardom was a privileged site for demonstrating the power of the cinema to transform modern life and identity, where identity itself was understood to be a historical effect of the dynamic and organic social processes of modernity. Valentino is privileged in this respect precisely because of his relation to emerging social scientific understandings of racial identity and because of his celebrity's almost flawless adherence to the structure of the commodity, especially the racial meanings subtending the cultural and scientific significance of the cinematic commodity as it was analyzed by Benjamin and other cultural critics.

"ALL I KNOW IS JUST WHAT I READ IN THE PAPERS"

At the beginning of a chapter on Valentino and his female fans, Miriam Hansen places the following epigram taken from a 1922 Cleveland newspaper:

> One is Rudolph Valentino—he is of penciled eyebrow and the patent leather hair; the symmetrical chin and nose and cheek; the deep, hypnotic, subtle and alluring eye. . . .
>
> The other is Will Rogers, Ugly Will. With the eyebrows nature gave him; Will of the rough, ill-fitting clothes, and deep-lined face, and frank eyes in which you read no musings of hidden romance. Cowpuncher Will—who probably never spent so much as a dollar on a manicure in his life, and thinks of a beauty parlor as a place for women only.[43]

Hansen convincingly argues that such comparisons were not only masculinist attacks on Valentino, but on his fans as well. Furthermore, these attacks, as well as the anxieties which motivated them, support her argument that the popular matinée idol constituted, however tentatively, an alternative public sphere for women. Despite the commercial exploitation attendant on the collective and ritualized consumption of his screen personality, Hansen sees the female cult of Valentino as providing some temporary space for the expression of women's mutual interests in excess of the cinema's institutional solicitation of their desire. By way of concluding my own analysis of the social and political implications of Valentino's reception, I will extend and somewhat revise Hansen's arguments about the representation of his female audience.

While my own investigations agree that the representation of the cult of Valentino in the media "gave public expression to a force specific to relations *among* women,"[44] I want to stress that these relations were first and foremost understood and represented as socioeconomic relations (the female consumer as producer) and that the collective experience embodied in the cult was not only a matter of proto-political expression, but of knowledge production (women actively involved in determining just who Valentino might be). This means that the threat posed by the cult of Valentino to traditional white patriarchy (and the social identities and classifications of race and gender that it supported and maintained) was in no way in excess of its commodity form but more or less identical with it. In short, the historical appearance of a women's public sphere in relation to Valentino depended on the star's appearing as a commodity and emphatically registering the racial meanings that underlie the commodity as cultural artifact.

The comparison of Valentino to Will Rogers is a case in point. By 1922 Rogers was a widely recognized media personality whose celebrity stature was significant enough to contrast with Valentino's. Rogers was the sort of commonsense humorist whose pithy aphorisms and cowpoke identity were the latest manifestation of a longstanding populist and critical patriotism that extended back at least to Benjamin Franklin's *Poor Richard's Almanac*. An accomplished vaudeville performer, political commentator, and movie star, Rogers exhibited the simple and rough-hewn wisdom of the All-American male, the inheritor of the myth of the frontier and of the history of America's western expansion into the prairies and beyond. He was, then, a perfect foil to the obviously manufactured veneer of a recent immigrant like Valentino, whose past was considered sufficiently shady and decidedly unheroic. Interestingly though, Rogers' claim to representative Americanness was made, in part, by the pride he took in his Native American ancestry. Cherokees and Europeans of varying ethnicities had been intermarrying in North America since the early eighteenth century, and their descendants who assimilated European social practices and cultural traditions were commonly referred to as "white Indians." Rogers' mother was one-quarter Cherokee and his father claimed native ancestry on both sides of his family. Born in Indian Territory in 1879, Will Rogers occasionally spoke from the position of a Native American as he did in 1926 when he addressed the Ladies Auxiliary of the Old Trail Drivers in San Antonio by congratulating them on so successfully "stealing *our* cattle in the Indian Nation."[45]

Rogers actually played Rudolph Valentino in a short film he made for Hal Roach in 1923 called *Uncensored Movies*. This two-reel comedy satirized the sensationalized representations of the Hollywood colony that were then to be found in the reports of tabloid journalists and in the rhetoric of industry reformers. Performing multiple roles, Rogers first appears as Lem Skagwillow, a "retired bartender commissioned by the Cleaner Screen League." Skagwillow seeks to expose "what's wrong with the movies" by screening short films of the private lives of movie stars. A poster at the beginning of the film announces: "See Motion Picture Stars in their Homes and in Public. Secrets of the Screen Laid Bare. Nothing Concealed. Uncensored Movies." Addressing the assembled members of the Cleaner Screen League, Skagwillow assures them that everything they have heard about Hollywood's inhabitants is absolutely true. He then proceeds to lecture on the sins of the film colony, providing evidence for his claims by screening seven short films that candidly feature prominent movie stars of the day. The films avoid any direct references to actual Hollywood scandals or to controversial stars such as Mabel Normand or Juanita Hansen. In fact, the stars who are the subjects of these exposés were, for the most part, relatively immune to suspicions of vice and immorality. The films make reference to veteran actor of westerns William S. Hart, director D. W. Griffith, Douglas Fairbanks and Mary Pickford, cowboy star Tom Mix, Rudolph Valentino, and Will Rogers himself.

With the exception of the Valentino film, each of these mock exposés parodies media sensationalism by showing—against the wild claims of moralists and reformers—just how pedestrian the stars' lives actually are. For example, Skagwillow reveals that William S. Hart has been seen "in a public thoroughfare as late as 10:00 PM." Some of the other "incriminating" films reference topical events as well. The public aloofness of Fairbanks and Pickford during this period is the basis for showing "Doug and Mary in the Covered Wagon."[46] This film shows only an extreme long shot of a covered wagon crossing a ridge and is followed by the intertitle, "Too bad they didn't drive over this way—They were on the inside." The film within the film in which Rogers plays Rudolph Valentino alludes to the beauty pageants for which Valentino had recently served as a judge. The contests were conducted by The Beauty Foundation of America in conjunction with Valentino's transcontinental tango tour with Rambova. However, unlike the other six films shown in *Uncensored Movies*, this one, instead of undercutting an expectation of shocking and scandalous behavior, exaggerates Valentino's imagined transgressions. Purporting to catch Valentino at home, the film shows Rogers/Valentino dressed in sheik's attire and languidly smoking a cigarette. A large and muscular manservant named Selimi, whose skin has obviously been artificially blackened for this role, parades three dancing women in succession before Valentino for his approval. The three women all wear Arab costume, and Valentino quickly dismisses each dancer, telling the last one to "take a number." Since the movie star shows little signs of interest in these women, Selimi returns with a blonde woman in feminine Western attire. At the sight of this white woman, Rogers gives a pop-eyed leer in grotesque imitation of Valentino's hypnotic stare, and he then instructs Selimi to "[s]ave this one and drown the other three."

Aggressively racist and violently misogynist, this Valentino parody "safely" deploys the harem structure of infinite substitution (and, in this case, infinite annihilation) to represent only Arab women. Yet the media events to which the film alludes involved Valentino judging only young, white women representing eighty-eight different cities in the United States and Canada. The parody, however, shows the white woman as uniquely desirable against the background of the undifferentiated Arabs, and while miscegenation is represented as the threat of rape here, the "greater" threat posed by Valentino to categories of white cultural integrity is neatly avoided, or at least nearly so. Unlike the previous films screened in *Uncensored Movies*, the Valentino episode cuts away to show the responses of the assembled members of the Cleaner Screen League. As in most representations of Valentino's film audiences, the men look away from the screen in disgust while women in the audience take great interest in the film and its star. One man even pulls his hat over his head before the film begins. When the star appears on the screen, a woman in the front row exclaims to her friend, "It's him; it's Rudy. He sent me his picture." While on the screen Valentino peruses the women paraded in front of him, the two women in the front row retrieve lockets from their blouses and, looking rapidly back and forth from lockets to screen, compare their two photographs of Valentino and each to the image on the screen. One of the women concludes, "I'd recognize him anywhere." The joke here is about the hypocrisy of motion picture reformers and the delusions of Valentino's female fans. The vastness of the cult of Valentino is such that it has even recruited prudish women reformers who are shown to be already under the star's spell. These women foolishly covet the mass-produced image of the matinée idol as if it constituted an intimate relationship between fan and star: "He sent me his picture." Yet what we actually see are two women involved in a comparative investigation of Valentino images.[47] *Uncensored Movies* attempts to mock these women's expertise in evaluating the media when one of them declares, "It's him." They have, obviously, mistaken Rogers for Valentino, a grotesque impossibility according to the film. Yet this mockery presumes that Valentino is something beyond his reproducible image, that his identity lies in the physical body of a performer and cannot be authentically copied and circulated.

The rhetoric of this film's joke insists that these women, oblivious as they are to the violation of white womanhood taking place on the screen, are engaged in the meaningless and ultimately destructive consumption of Valentino images. Like their urban working-class sisters who work in commercial dance halls and who often mistake Filipinos for movie stars, these fans in the cult of Valentino are losing their ability to make accurate and meaningful distinctions between different ethnic and racial identities, so inundated are these women by mass-cultural images of the foreign and exotic. Such practices approximate the regressive "behavior sequence" that Cressey describes in his study of taxi-dancers.

How did mass audiences of the period understand their own activity through such representations? What these representations will not allow and what constitutes the real scandal of the cult of Valentino is that the "pathological" film audience of *Uncensored Movies* who equates the identity of Valentino with his reproducible image might be right after all. Such a possibility represents the radical limit of the cult of Valentino. Yet it is not difficult to imagine that film audiences glimpsed the political possibilities of such an alternative star reception, even in such satirical representations of the "regressive" cult of Valentino as we find in a short comedy like *Uncensored Movies*. By searching for similarity rather than difference in the flow of mass media images, the renegade women of the Cleaner

Screen League challenged the entrenched ideas about the relative permanence and stability of racial identity, and they thereby threaten the social policies of enforced segregation that those ideas underwrote. The most effective deterrent to any such challenge to the color line was social science's claims that such a reception was, if not delusional, at least self-destructive, and that while the masses were certainly the object of sociological study and sometimes the students of the sociological point of view, they could never, by themselves, be practitioners of science.

5
———

Mabel Normand and
the Ends of Error

Psychologist casuistry.—*This individual is an expert in the knowledge of men: for what end is he actually studying men? He wants to get some little advantages over them, or even some great advantages—he is politicus! . . . That [other] individual is also an expert in the knowledge of men, and you say he wants nothing for himself thereby, he is one of the grand "impersonal." Look at him more carefully! Perhaps he even wants a more reprehensible advantage: to feel himself superior to men, to be allowed to look down on them, not to confound himself with them any longer. This "impersonal one" is a despiser of men; the former is a more humane species, whatever appearances may indicate. He at least places himself on an equality with men, he places himself among them.*

—FRIEDRICH NIETZSCHE, *TWILIGHT OF THE IDOLS*[1]

In the summer of 1918, as part of an attempt to refashion her stardom and broaden the range of dramatic roles she might pursue, *Photoplay* magazine reported on Mabel Normand's personal library. When visiting the former slapstick comedienne at her New York apartment, journalist Randolph Bartlett reported that he found within her bookcase an "array of authors as unusual as it was fascinating. There were Gautier, Strindberg, Turgeneff, Stevenson, Walter Pater, Kipling, Oscar Wilde, Shaw, Ibsen, John Evelyn, J. M. Barrie, Francois Coppé, Bret Harte. Of superficial best sellers there was not a single sample. Nor was there to be found in the room a copy of any of the cheap, current fiction magazines."[2] Bartlett goes on to assure the reader that the motion picture star has actually read these important works and that she is possessed of a genuine interest in literary culture and an enthusiasm for new ideas. With the exception of Evelyn, Normand's library apparently consisted of late nineteenth- and early twentieth-century novelists and playwrights, all of whom would have been recognized at that time as aesthetically progressive writers. Without being too radical or experimental, these authors helped define what could be broadly characterized as a modern literary and dramatic sensibility. Normand's up-to-date artistic tastes are verified in the *Photoplay* article by the conspicuous absence of any classical works that might cast her in the role of the boring scholar who is out of touch with her times. Indeed, even the manner of her reading, we are informed, shuns the contemplative stance of the highbrow. As Bartlett attests, Normand "does not take her reading like a sponge, but like an electric motor."

While the unstated purpose for this particular piece of publicity was the promotion of Normand's new position as a glamorous feature-film star for the Goldwyn company, such articles in the fan magazines were also part of Hollywood's broader attempt to court genteel middle-class patronage and to increase the industry's prestige by emphasizing the refinement and good taste of its creative talent. Normand's regular appearance with Fatty Arbuckle in a popular series of slapstick farces for Keystone just a couple of years before is referred to by Bartlett as an apprenticeship in a previous era of filmmaking in which the actress' "mind was developing toward something more important." In this way, as was often the case when the early stars were still considered to be privileged representatives of Hollywood, Normand's career and private life synecdochically stood in for the film industry's own history of improvement and increasing cultural refinement. However, not only the film industry benefited from the star's aesthetic education. By giving the public a glimpse into the film star's consumption of important modern authors, *Photoplay* was also offering motion picture audiences indirect access to these same authors and the cultural capital they represented. The very attention that audiences paid to the career and personality of Mabel Normand was a means to self-improvement.

There was nothing necessarily class-specific about the content of this educational address of the early star system. For instance, the *Photoplay* article on Mabel Normand's library does not seek a middle-class audience by emphasizing her knowledge of literature or even by naming particular authors such as Stevenson, Kipling, or Turgenev. Members of different social classes, including significant numbers of the urban and regional working classes, would have recognized these authors and the cultural values they represented. What guarantees Normand's embodiment of middle-class values and what places her squarely within the dominant paradigm of middle-class uplift and reform is the article's promise that no cheap or popular literature existed alongside these more serious works of art. A modern literary canon was being established in the article on Normand's reading habits, and cultural and social hierarchies were being respected in the process. Stardom was beneficent because its educational effects apparently lead to a particular refinement of taste and to the acceptance of bourgeois standards of evaluation.

By 1918, veteran women stars such as Mary Pickford and Mabel Normand were central in the film industry's ability to represent itself as an organic corporate community involved in the industrial production of refined culture. The "colony" called "Hollywood" had embarked on a grand social experiment in which the talents of various artisans, performers, and executives were finding their perfect realization in a progressively efficient social arrangement where the very divisions between business and art were magically dissolved. All one needed to transform a studio into a home was a woman's touch. In the December 1916 issue of *Motion Picture Magazine,* for example, Pearl Gaddis described the newly built studio of the Mabel Normand Feature Film Company as "having ever so many feminine touches that make it artistic as well as businesslike, comfortable as well as efficient."[3] Normand readily admits that the men of the studio tease her about her "woman's touch," but she points out how eager they are to go to work in the morning and how reluctant they are leave once the workday is over. The star-producer explains: "You see I have a hobby that dovetails beautifully with my work here. It's studio housekeeping, or, rather, studio homekeeping. . . . Efficiency comes first of course, but I didn't see why a studio should be a huge, unlovely barn of wood. So I planned for comfort and beauty, as well as efficiency. That explains the rugs downstairs, the adorable balcony, and the attractive dressing rooms."[4]

By making domestic labor an enjoyable hobby, the women of Hollywood were transforming the very nature of industrial work and, in the process, making mass culture itself more refined, more respectable. Though, according to the article, the idea of studio boss as homemaker had long been a dream of Mabel Normand's, she assured those readers of *Motion Picture Magazine* who might be skeptical of her matronly qualifications to run a reputable household that she had "worked so hard and planned so hard to attain just this end." Gaddis reviews Normand's career struggles from artist's model to world-renowned comedienne in order to represent her new executive position as a further step in a process of creative self-improvement. She concludes the piece by noting, "The finest work of Mabel Normand's career is blossoming forth under the stimulus of her own company."

During the early 1910s, even before the formation of the movie colony in southern California, the film industry had constructed its public face by thoroughly identifying itself with its beautiful stars. It was the seemingly identical interests of the stars and the studios that originally defined the early star system and which would eventually subtend the representations of Hollywood as a progressive corporate community in the late 1910s. By the early 1920s it seemed as if the industry was paying a very high price for such intimacy. The early Hollywood scandals had a way of sticking to everything, haunting those who were named in connection with them, and calling into question the social utility of Hollywood itself. After the scandals, star publicity and industry public relations would never again completely overlap or fit together quite so easily. Norman's industrial status as a good housekeeper would be shattered when her involvement with many of the early scandals led to the public demand for the studios to seek hired help in "cleaning house."

By the 1920s, Normand's stardom was complicated by more than her relation to scandal. As a working-class woman and movie star, her claim to new forms of cultural authority in the 1910s was rapidly attenuated by the implementation of regulatory discourses about motion pictures and other products of mass culture, making those products subject to various forms of verification and institutional certification. After the 1920 to 1924 period, film stars would never again have the kind of appeal they had in the early star system because the field of that appeal was largely reduced to popular amusement. A better sense of the enormity of Normand's public command can be glimpsed in the now unlikely comparison of her celebrity to that of director Lois Weber, her Hollywood contemporary. In an analysis of Weber's *Shoes* (Universal, 1916), film historian Shelley Stamp describes how the filmmaker was widely promoted and appreciated as a social worker committed to moral reform.[5] Like other filmmakers of the Progressive era, Weber often found narrative inspiration in the same social problems that were on the minds of sociologists, journalists, reformers, religious leaders, and politicians of the day. Yet Weber saw her films as more than topical dramas, and Stamp points out that Weber's publicity often positioned her as a sort of editorialist who used the cinema as a means of social intervention. The first few shots of *Shoes*—a film about a young woman who cannot afford to replace her worn-out shoes because of the paltry wages she is paid as a retail clerk—present images of Jane Addams' 1914 book, *A New Conscience and an Ancient Evil*, thereby positing the film's source in the famed reformer's study of prostitution. If *Shoes* presented itself as a sort of case study exemplifying in cinematic form the observations and arguments of Jane Addams, Stamp notes that Weber often made her own experiences the basis of the social reform perspectives of her motion pictures. In one interview, Weber connected many of her films, including *Shoes*, with her earlier background in missionary work among the urban poor. For Stamp, such attributions worked to promote Weber's own authority as a voice of reform: "By occulting her script's genealogy in Jane Addams's mission, pointing instead toward its origins in her own lived experience and her own recollections, Weber fashioned a particular vision of the filmmaker as social worker, literally substituting her own gaze in place of Addams's fieldwork."[6] Of course, such occlusions are never complete, and Weber's life experiences certainly gained in value through propping themselves on the citation of Addams' sociological text at the beginning of *Shoes*.

Weber's relation to the book is relevant to the celebrity of Mabel Normand. What is at stake in both is the place of cinema in the production of knowledge, as opposed to its production of pleasure. To the extent that the cinema sought only to duplicate the knowledge of the world produced by sanctioned sources elsewhere, the cinema posed no threats to traditional authorities. What was censorable in the cinema during the late Progressive era was either the production of certain forms of unwholesome pleasure or the *failure to duplicate accepted wisdom* about the state of the world: displaying risqué images or letting a crime remain unpunished, for example. That the cinema could be enlisted toward educational ends or could even participate in debates on social policy was not typically a controversial proposition. Stamp's work on *Shoes* is quite important because she uses the film to indicate an emerging tension about what motion pictures might add to their visual reiteration of accepted knowledge, an addition that Stamp locates in the newly offered pleasures of an emerging cinematic language that increasingly facilitates psychological identification with individual characters, particularly through the elaboration of point of view. Despite the fact that Weber emphasized her commitments to social realism while downplaying her creative role in innovating or even using these new forms of visual pleasure, Stamp argues that *Shoes*, unlike Addams' published fieldwork, forced its middle-class audiences to share the heroine's perspective and participate in feelings of empathy with her situation. Such emotional identification with the poor was not only uncharacteristic of most middle-class reform discourse, but also fairly at odds with the ethnographic project of sociological case studies. Instead of assuming classical narration to be the expression of a bourgeois worldview, Stamp rightly sees that the addition of these identification structures to the causes of reform signaled a potentially "more radical role" for the cinema's ability to participate in the social production of knowledge.[7]

The public availability of Normand's reading habits similarly constituted a potentially radical addition to the pleasures offered by the expanding star system. Coverage of the hobbies and recreations of film stars were commonplace by the late 1910s, and the private pursuits of the stars often provided the public with information on how to experience and understand contemporaneity. They were, indeed, idols of consumption, but Normand's library was neither a reflection nor a simple appropriation of established canons of literary culture. The *Photoplay* article credits Normand herself with being able to construct that canon, to authorize it through her unique celebrity. The piece concludes by making Normand's studio work and her leisure all of a piece. "But no matter what she does— romping through a picture and lifting it out of the commonplace, or reading Strindberg, Shaw, or Ibsen after a hard day's work at the studio, Mabel Normand stands all by herself."[8] Distinctions between expert and amateur, scholar and dilettante are at least partially elided by the unique personality of the star herself. Here the pleasures of star promotion and reception have become a vehicle for the production and dissemination of literary knowledge. If Weber was adding the cinematic pleasure of identification to the practice of sociological investigation in the mid-1910s, then we might also think of Normand as adding cultural criticism to the pleasures of her star reception. Where Weber assumed the role of social reformer through an act of substituting her own life in place of a recognized authority, Normand assumed the role of a *belle des lettres* by making her library just another unremarkable part of her life. Both women demonstrated the possibility of effective improvements through the fairly effortless task of being themselves.

The *Photoplay* article on Normand's library begins with the interviewer asking the star whether she rented her New York apartment furnished or whether its furnishings belong to her. "This was the only important thing I asked Mabel Normand." Establishing the library as Normand's personal collection was a crucial requirement for this particular instantiation of contemporary literary value, even if the *Photoplay* writer also felt obliged to assure readers that the actress had "a thorough knowledge of what is contained between the handsome covers" of her books. Walter Benjamin has noted the central importance of book ownership to the conferral of cultural values. Even though scornful of the cult of Hollywood stars as mystifying the revolutionary conditions of the new mass medium, Benjamin's figure of the book collector applies to Mabel Normand.

> For a collector's attitude toward his possessions stems from an owner's feeling of responsibility toward his property. Thus it is, in the highest sense, the attitude of an heir, and the most distinguished trait of the collection will always be its heritability [. . .] the phenomenon of collecting loses its meaning when it loses it subject. Even though public collections may be less objectionable socially and more useful academically than private collections, the objects get their due only in the latter.[9]

While the collector disappears through the rapid erosion of the traditional preserves of culture wrought by the increasing rationalization of society and the development of mass communications, Hollywood's star system provided a new situation for individual ownership and for the emergence of new mass cultural preserves. Transmission was now instantaneous and the heir the public itself. Yet whether we wish to consider Normand's library an attempt to mystify a contemporary cultural crisis or whether we view her collection as an authentic form of cultural stewardship, it is the film star's personal attachment to her books that made the book's authors newly interesting and worthwhile. Normand's very ownership of these books defined that attachment.[10] The answer to the piquant title of the *Photoplay* article on Normand's library—"Would You Ever Suspect It?"—turns out to be "yes."

Normand's book collection also represented the very apparatus for her self-directed intellectual refinement, while Weber's lived past is responsible for the correction of present social injustices. The different contexts for the effectiveness of their respective personalities—self-improvement and social uplift—are a result of their differing class positions, as well as the presumed class positions and affinities of their respective publics. However, the instrumentality of Normand's library was downplayed as the explanation for its existence: "Miss Normand's collection of books has, probably, done little toward making her successful, but they are an index of that intelligence without which there can be no success."[11] Like Weber's past experience with missionary work, the actress's books are just part of her life. Film scholar Ann Morey has documented the ways in which the cinema and its ancillary institutions emerged in the 1910s as sites for the discourses of self-fashioning, discourses that worked through tensions between creativity and standardization, individualization and collective effort, work and play, knowledge and pleasure. In her analyses of juvenile serial fiction and the Palmer Photoplay correspondence courses, Morey reveals the multiple ways that affect, personal experience, and consumption were increasingly refigured as the basis of socially useful knowledge and as salable merchandise.[12] From the point of view of political economy, such enterprises were attempts to create new consumer markets through the sham enfranchisement of members of the public. Yet, as a cultural discourse, the threat posed to established social authority by the commodification of personality, particularly in the form of a non-laboring personality, ultimately resulted in the curtailment of the progressive use of the cinema for social change and self transformation. This curtailment was achieved through institutionalized censorship and through the newspapers' denunciation of film celebrities as fakes. Weber's fortunes suffered in the 1920s because of the former, Normand's because of the latter.[13]

The star culture promulgated by the fan magazines offered readers access to these new personalities, to the orientations to the world these stars pioneered and, most importantly, to the very mass cultural conditions that make the creation of stars, their circulation, and their publics possible. Gaylyn Studlar was one of the first to suggest that the highly reified personalities on display between the covers of fan magazines were presented with a double perspective in which the women readers in particular were simultaneously encouraged to engage with details of the stars' lives through affective fantasies, and to hold both the stars as well as their fantasies about the stars at some critical distance. Studlar adopts the psychoanalytic concept of masquerade to describe this address as a "play of identities," a relatively new cultural possibility with rising importance for "many women in the 1920s who were themselves engaged in an attempt to resituate themselves in relation to changing concepts of female social and sexual identity."[14] This double perspective of fan magazines was achieved partially through the contradictory presentation of stars as both affectively close and distant from the fan, as well as by a growing refusal of the magazines to uphold an easy conflation between the off-screen lives of the stars and their appearances in motion pictures. In other words, publicity functioned in the motion picture magazines by revealing the work of publicity and by suggesting its possibilities for the fan's pleasure, knowledge, and self-transformation. Studlar notes that as the industry sought to control the damaged caused by the various star scandals of the early 1920s, the fan magazines grew increasingly insistent on the distinction between the actual performer and her or his star persona. To push beyond the seemingly intractable problem of female spectatorship as it had been defined through feminist psychoanalytic theory, Studlar seeks to give theories of masquerade a historical grounding in the practices of the fan magazines and their women readers during the silent period. However, the post-scandal insistence on a gap of credulity in star publicity, while perhaps making available to women a means of founding their subjective lives on a critical distance from the star image, was also the means for curtailing an earlier form of star promotion and reception that was not truth-functional. This earlier mass cultural address figured star personality as a series of inscriptions that were not determined by any considerations of veracity and verifiability. A subsequent jazz age valorization of ballyhoo worked to discipline mass audiences by dividing them into those who were fooled or taken in by Hollywood fakery (and thus in need of protection), and those who could achieve the proper fracturing of belief. While in retrospect this earlier condition of star reception might appear to be only a form of naive fascination, the early star system was making possible a situation in which the effective distinctions between pleasure and knowledge would no longer be fully operational for the public.[15] The growing preoccupation with the truth or falsity of star promotion at work in multiple regulatory discourses functioned just as much to discipline a mass audience as it did to protect the interests of particular social institutions or capital investments. And this is why Mabel Normand's library haunts her during the Taylor scandal of 1922 and after. The continued press attention to her literary interests was not simply a means of attacking her as a fake; Normand's library was one of the important targets of those regulatory discourses that sought a continuation of particular cultural distinctions, as well as the maintenance of the class and gender divisions underwritten by those distinctions.

The central importance of cultural canons in the construction and maintenance of early motion picture stars can be seen in the scandal that engulfed Normand three-and-a-half years after *Photoplay*'s discussion of her reading habits. Normand's involvement in one of the major Hollywood scandals of the early 1920s so compromised her ability to be represented as a discriminating producer and consumer of culture that her career never fully recovered. When William Desmond Taylor, a well-known film director for Famous Players-Lasky, was found murdered in his Hollywood bungalow in February 1922, Normand was an early suspect in the case because she was the last known person to see Taylor alive and because she had a plausible motive for murdering Taylor—she purportedly held a jealous rivalry with actress Mary Miles Minter for the affections of the debonair director. While the suspicions against her eventually subsided, the harm done to Normand's career was more than the result of being involved in a notorious murder case. When asked by the police and the press about her visit to Taylor's residence on the evening before the discovery of his corpse, Normand explained how she had been returning some books that Taylor had loaned her. According to the actress, she and the film director had a mutual interest in modern philosophy, and the press continually mentioned Taylor's schooling of the young star in the works of Nietzsche and Freud. More significantly, it was also reported that Normand claimed to have stopped on the way to Taylor's house to buy herself bags of roasted peanuts and a copy of the *Police Gazette,* a publication whose bathing beauties, boxing news, and other "vulgar amusements" were usually thought to pander to the interests of uncultivated, lower-class men. In one of her first statements to the police after the murder, Normand purportedly testified that Taylor had teased her about eating roasted peanuts and reading the *Police Gazette*: "He put me in the car and as he saw the peanut shells and the pile of books he laughed and said, 'Here you are with Nietzsche under one arm and Freud under the other and the *Police Gazette* close by. You certainly are going in for heavy reading this winter.' "[16] The press had a field day appropriating Taylor's joke and poking fun at the supposed incongruity of post-Enlightenment theory and working-class culture. For example, a writer in a Detroit paper had this to say about the whole affair:

> Magazines devoted to motion picture plays and players do a great deal of harm by the nauseating drivel that they print. The silly prattle that is put into the mouths of screen players who are "interviewed" for these magazines and then pen pictures drawn of them are beyond reason. Rex Ingram, a scholar, is not given any better "boost" than the former salesgirl who has suddenly become a headliner. The same superlatives that are used to discuss Ingram are used to describe the brainless cutie whose face is her fortune and whose brain is still in the kindergarten age.
>
> It is a long jump from paperbound novels and chewing gum to Plato and Thoreau, but the facile writer of the screen monthlies blithely makes the leap. It must have been with pain and anguish that the screen fans read how Mabel Normand, pictured as a devotee of Voltaire and Nietzsche, testified that on her way to William Taylor's house on the fatal night she stopped at a newsstand to buy a bag of peanuts and a copy of the *Police Gazette*.[17]

Employing the now long-familiar gendering of high and low cultures, this editorialist represents the problem of star promotion as Hollywood's inability or refusal to discriminate culturally important works and authors from mere popular ephemera. While this writer blames the fan magazines for liquidating these traditional distinctions, other newspapers blamed the actress herself for the destructive mixing and merging of different cultural values. Referring to reports of

Normand's weakened state after the Taylor murder, one journalist commented, "Between old Mister Nietzsche and the *Police Gazette* it's no wonder that Mabel is nervous and confined to her bed."[18]

Normand biographer Betty Harper Fussell relates that, after columnist Louella Parsons inquired as to how many of the books in Normand's library had the actress actually read, Normand jokingly replied, "Not a one, but I've read the reviews."[19] Such flippancy was part of Normand's appeal, but by the early 1920s she would have to insist on the genuineness of her literary studies. Fussell's biography is premised on the impossibility of ever recovering the truth of Normand's life since the actress "embodies the mystery of memory, of identity, of truth even to herself."[20] Even so, Fussell often attributes a deep-seated and unfulfilled need for love and respect as the emotional basis for much of Normand's behavior and life decisions. When writing about the star's growing interests in books and intellectual culture, Fussell moves quickly from the terrain of the political to the realm of romance. Briefly noting Chaplin's claim that his intellectualism was "a defense against the world's contempt for the ignorant," Fussell ends her chapter on Goldwyn's refashioning of the star by reducing Normand's library to a term within her romantic entanglement with her studio bosses. "That she cut through Pierre Louys's *Aphrodite* and Olive Wadsley's *Sand* at the same speed was irrelevant. Mabel's point was that neither Mack [Sennett] nor Sam [Godwyn] had read anything at all."[21] In many ways, Fussell correctly marks out the inappropriateness of the traditional biographical mode to Mabel Normand's life. A modern personality at odds with the "truth of identity," Normand does not so neatly embody the mysteries of memory, truth, and identity as much as she enacts a failure to escape from the imposition of biographical truth. Even while the "mystery" attributed to Normand by Fussell is a further mystification of the star and of our interest in her, it also describes the continued success of a psychologizing imperative that still subtends our historical inquiries. No longer just a publicity set-up for a star witticism, Louella Parsons's question about the number of books Normand had actually read seems irresistibly to shape our own interest in the star's library.[22]

In her work on the late silent-era film star Louise Brooks, film and media scholar Amelie Hastie has documented the types of complications introduced into the cultural field by the intellectual female star.[23] Brooks emerged as a celebrity just after Normand's eclipse from prominence, and while she never became as popular or well-known as Normand had been, Brooks did enjoy a successful, if short, career as a motion picture star in Europe. Indeed, as Hastie points out, it was Brooks's association with European modernism, particularly through her performance of Lulu in *Die Büchse der Pandora* [Pandora's Box, 1929], that later provided the basis for her post-World War II resurrection as a critical voice on modernism, film history, and stardom. Hastie argues that Brooks's own essays on the film cultures of Hollywood and Germany demonstrate how the film star simultaneously produced herself through biographical revelation, even while she denied the possibility of ever producing an authentic account of her true self. Hastie is therefore concerned with Brooks as a witness to and participant in the international modernism of the early twentieth century, but she also examines the differing authority accorded to Brooks's testimony by those cultural critics, archivists, and film theorists who have continually turned to Brooks as a source for thinking through many of their own important projects. While Normand's authority was rapidly foreclosed after the scandals, and while she never lived long enough to provide a critical retrospective account of her Hollywood life, her difficult status as an intellectual is clarified by Hastie's work on Brooks.[24]

As a star, Brooks may have been more successful at becoming a producer of cultural knowledge than Normand because, as Hastie shows, much of Brooks's authority rested on questions of sexuality and sexual definition. As Richard deCordova's work suggests, the star system functioned most effectively as a system of knowledge based on the continual interrogation and revelation of identity. Thus, the type of testimonial privilege granted to Brooks, while unusual, did not seriously call into question the epistemological basis of the star system itself. What was more disruptive about Brooks's performances and her critical writings—and where they intersect with the difficulties of Normand's stardom—was their subversion of truth functionality, or what Hastie terms Brooks's ability to perform and negotiate "the deceptiveness of truth."[25] It was the very rejection of truth functionality that founded Brooks's "intelligence," and I would suggest that a similar rejection was behind Normand's cultural authority. Ironically, it was also this rejection that allowed Normand's intelligence to be called into question. Hastie concludes her chapter on Brooks by quoting film historian Lotte Eisner's expression of skepticism upon finding Brooks reading a volume of Schopenhauer on the set of *Das Tagebuch einer Verlorenen* [Diary of a Lost Girl, 1929]. Eisner had initially dismissed the occasion as a staged publicity event, but she then claims to have reached a fuller appreciation of the actress' relation to Schopenhauer as integral to who Brooks was and who she projected herself to be.[26] As was the case with Normand, Brooks's relation to intellectual culture was continually deniable only by ignoring its basis in a process of self-fashioning and by insisting on criteria of veracity and verification. In other words, the story about Brooks reading post-Romantic German philosophy has to be made true or false by yet another witness, in this case Eisner. Interestingly, Hastie shows how much of what was said by others about Brooks originated with the actress herself, sometimes appearing as a form of de-authorization obfuscating Brooks as the original source of the information. Similarly, we have seen how the first person to publicly comment on the apparent incongruity of Nietzsche and the *Police Gazette* was Normand, as she bore witness to the murdered director's playful chiding of her tastes and habits. She thereby claimed a comfortable familiarity with the very cultural distinctions that she refused to enact but that her fiercest critics would claim were beyond her grasp and, therefore, an indication of a dangerous pretense.

In response to threatened bans on her films by local censoring bodies and by regional exhibitor organizations after the Taylor murder, Normand claimed to have been the victim of cruel circumstance. The actress saw herself as only guilty of being in the wrong place at the wrong time, and this has been a fairly standard biographical explanation of Normand's moribund career after 1921. However, the way the Taylor murder scandal unfolded in the press left the actress open to charges of holding dangerous intellectual pretensions and of claiming a false cultural authority. What was ultimately at stake for Normand was the perception that her popularity and her star appeal rested on what Pierre Bourdieu describes as "illegitimate culture." Bourdieu distinguishes illegitimate culture from the authentic knowledge of the cultural aristocracy:

> The reader of the popular science monthly *Science et Vie* who talks about the genetic code or the incest taboo exposes himself to ridicule as soon as he ventures outside his circle of peers, whereas Claude Lévi-Strauss or Jacques Monod can only derive additional prestige from their excursions into the field of music or philosophy. Illegitimate extra-curricular culture, whether it be the accumulated knowledge by the self-taught or the "experience" acquired in and through practice, outside the control of the institution specifically mandated to inculcate it and officially sanction its acquisition, like the art of cooking or herbal medicine, craftsmen's skill or the stand-in's irreplaceable knowledge, is only valorized to the strict extent of its technical efficiency, without any social added-value, and is exposed to legal sanctions (like the illegal practice of medicine) whenever it emerges from the domestic universe to compete with authorized competences.[27]

Normand's stardom failed precisely when her literary interests emerged "from the domestic universe to compete with authorized competences." The Taylor scandal facilitated this emergence but it was not the cause of the protracted attacks on Normand in the press. The scandal moved Normand's personality out of the fan magazines and the entertainment pages and onto the front pages of the nation's most authoritative newspapers, where Normand's participation in elite culture could no longer be shielded from the guardians of that culture. Even Normand's most mundane traits, such as her love of roasted peanuts, became damning evidence when mentioned on the front page.[28] Since Normand's longstanding interest in literature and philosophy was intractably inscribed in the details of the sensational murder case and in her relation to the murdered director, that interest exceeded its function as an index of Normand's fascinating personality and became a factor in understanding what was wrong with Hollywood. While the so-called sins of Hollywood might have been on the lips of reformers throughout the country, a deeper question about the authoritative role motion pictures had assumed in mass society was a more vexing problem for bourgeois cultural hegemony. Hollywood had offered itself as an ideal model for a modern and efficient means to self-improvement. The star system presented the public with the opportunity to participate in various types of personal transformations and ways of being in the world. If the star system was the film industry's chief means of demonstrating the power of movies to develop compelling and interesting personalities, then it was also one of the key points of attack for those wishing to forestall mass culture's perceived liquidation of traditional institutions and the social divisions those institutions upheld. In this conservative project, Mabel Normand provided a particularly useful means for unmasking Hollywood's image of itself as the arbiter of the new and beautiful not only because she had been in the wrong place at the wrong time, but because Mabel Normand's personality—which included her claim to a European tradition of intellectual thought—had been developed through the non-accredited school of the early studio system and because her glamorized identity as an instructor in cultural knowledge had been made too easily available to the public through star publicity and through the press coverage of the scandal.

While many of the jokes made about Normand's cultural pretensions sought to expose the star's long-purported interests in highbrow culture as nothing more than a publicity sham, these jokes also betrayed a deep-seated uneasiness about the possibility that one might, indeed, read Freud and the *Police Gazette* as similarly interesting expressions of modern times.[29] The press effectively contained this threat to traditional intellectual hierarchies by portraying the actress as suffering from a pathological condition in which she was too mentally immature to appreciate significant cultural distinctions ("[Her] brain is still in the kindergarten age") or in which she was suffering from some sort of mental disturbance due to her free and indiscriminate consumption of texts ("[She is] nervous and confined to her bed"). Normand's deviance was further confirmed by journalists' assumptions that the news reports of the star's purchase of the *Police Gazette* had been received by her public "with pain and anguish." It was no coincidence that at the height of her popular stardom in 1918, Normand had been associated with a canon of mostly English, French, and American novelists, playwrights, and literary essayists, while at the time of the Taylor murder scandal her name was connected to Nietzsche and Freud, two German intellectuals popularly represented as having radically questioned traditional Christian morality and whose books were believed to pose serious dangers to individuals whose minds were unprepared or unable to read them properly.[30] As covered in Chapter 2, the reading of both Nietzsche and Freud would be repeatedly mentioned as corrupting influences on Leopold and Loeb during their trial in 1924. As an idol of consumption and a suspect in a murder case, Mabel Normand posed many dangers to an impressionable public, but it was her reading habits that were attracting the most ink in February 1922.

Normand's immediate response to this state of affairs was to deny the newspapers' charges of inauthenticity and cultural pretension by telling her fans that her longstanding love of books was entirely genuine. In a series of articles for *Movie Weekly* appearing less than three weeks after the Taylor murder, Normand advised young women on how to prepare for careers as screen actresses in Hollywood.[31] Given that these lengthy pieces appeared immediately following the Taylor murder when Normand was widely reported to have been suffering from exhaustion and influenza, these articles were likely ghostwritten by a publicist. Of course, it was not entirely unusual for a star to have an advice column ghostwritten for her or him by someone entrusted to sympathetically represent that star's perspective. For example, Hollywood historian Cari Beauchamp has discussed how Mary Pickford employed Frances Marion to write Pickford's advice column, *Daily Talks*, during the mid-1910s.[32] In his bibliographical research on Normand, William Sherman has suggested that the delegated authorship of Normand's advice articles in early 1922 had a precedent in her statements to the *Los Angeles Times* in 1916. At that time, she claimed to be receiving so many letters from young women seeking career advice that she turned the task of responding to these inquiries over to her secretary who "knows just what my opinions are and just how I would personally answer almost any question."[33] Whatever the nature of the authorship of these later advice articles, they represent a distinct shift to a defensive position in which the terrain on which Normand could construct herself as an intellectual had shifted to a question of proof, requiring her to insist on the depth, sincerity, and hard work of her scholarly pursuits. Normand was no longer a cultural authority; she had now become a struggling student.

Throughout the ten *Movie Weekly* articles, Normand makes casual references to poets, short-story writers, and well-known playwrights such as Chekhov. In the fourth installment, on developing personality, she emphatically tells her readers that she "abhor[s] artificiality. A poseur to me is impossible. I could never pretend to be something that I am not because I so detest pretense in others." Normand urges her readers to "read, read, read" so that they might "develop something within" themselves, and she proposes that rather than simply identifying with characters in novels, readers should "strive to understand a character, its motives and mental processes."[34] In a subsequent installment Normand urges would-be starlets to keep a diary of their ideas and their observations of human nature. She also reminds them once again to read as much as possible. "I read a great deal, and I like to remember what I read. In fact, I have a special contempt for people who can't remember what they read. It shows a lack of appreciation or concentration. And you need both to be an artist or an educated human being."[35] Along with advice to young women about budgeting their money and making ends meet while looking for work, these narratives of cultural self-improvement suggest a narrative of class mobility and disguise that did little to alleviate Normand's public-relations difficulties. In the face of attacks on her stardom as a sham, Normand continued to offer herself as a model for emulation, apparently without comprehending the nature of the threat she posed to cultural order. Her love of literature and philosophy was not simply an alibi that explained why she had been in the wrong place at the wrong time; the crime for which she stood accused in the newspapers was precisely her claim to a cultural capital at odds with her class standing and her gender.

The types of film roles that Normand pursued after the scandal continued her penchant for characters from socially marginal backgrounds who suddenly find themselves cast among the swells of high society. The disruption of class and gender boundaries had been an important part of Normand's appeal since her Keystone days. Entirely comfortable in her new upper-class surroundings, the typical Normand character, because of her spontaneous enthusiasm for adventure and because of her love of life's many pleasures, inadvertently pokes fun at the decorum of the wealthy and the rigidity of their manners. While these film stories had previously served Normand's stardom by showing her possessed of an irrepressible and dynamic personality, the social transgressions of these characters now supported an investigation into the star's possible criminality. Three weeks after the Taylor murder, a writer in the *Cincinnati Commercial Tribune* jokingly asked, "Why did Mabel have a copy of *The Police Gazette* with her when she called on the slain director? Did this indicate that she had been to a barber shop immediately before? And if so, could she have taken a copy of *The Police Gazette* without slaying the barber?"[36] Here the ideological link between Normand's inappropriate cultural appropriations and criminal violence is finally forged, and the important lesson for Normand's fans and for those young would-be Hollywood starlets is not to believe everything you read about the movies.

In his insightful history of the Keystone Film Company, Rob King argues that Normand's early success with that company during the period 1912 to 1915 rested principally on her innovative combination of beauty and daring physicality, a version of women's modernity that was grounded in working-class culture and that resonated with the experiences of many working-class women. For King, Normand's keen ability at disturbing genteel gender expectations was significantly diminished after 1916 as the star seemingly began her process of cultural refinement in earnest. He cites as evidence of this transformation the new premium placed on pathos and sentiment in Normand's performance of the title character in *Mickey* (1918), the first feature-length film Normand produced after leaving Keystone. Unlike her earlier characters, Mickey is a waif of the countryside and is romantically identified with nature, thereby, according to King, undercutting Normand's associations with the milieus of the urban working classes.

Any rise in Mickey's social station or any deflation of petit-bourgeois pretension by her was now far less relevant to contemporary social antagonisms than had been the case with the knockabout Mabel of her Keystone days. King also sees a simultaneous fading of the political dimensions of Keystone's product as Sennett compensates for Normand's absence by launching the Bathing Beauties as a central attraction of Keystone motion pictures. This bevy of young women, fashionably clad in the latest sportswear, became the company's newest version of the compelling modern woman, but one that was now removed from the violent action and confrontations of physical comedy. Instead, the Bathing Beauties more or less occupied the sidelines of these comedies as visual spectacle. Commenting on the increasing serialization of women's bodies at Keystone during this period, King observes how "the Bathing Beauties take on the structure of commodities, shedding their qualitative differences and freezing into quantifiable, interchangeable 'things' to be grouped within the film frame—an orderly and static mass of bodies quite unlike the distinctly *dis*orderly mass movements of the earlier Keystone Kops."[37] Ultimately, King sees this reification of Keystone women as tied to the successful penetration of consumerist forms into working-class leisure and amusements; in other words, as tied to the founding of a consumerist mass culture.

Interestingly, King discusses some of the publicity strategies Keystone used in promoting individual Bathing Beauties to film exhibitors and to the public, and he shows how elaborate biographies about world-class athletic achievements and elite college educations were manufactured for these young women by the studio's publicity department.[38] According to King, the continuing abstraction of these young women away from any recognizable social reality is tied to the sheer falsity of the sorts of claims made about their remarkable achievements. Yet, as I have made clear in the previous chapters on Valentino, the commodification of a performer's identity, at least in instances of star reception during the period, in no way guaranteed the impossibility of a social or political use value. In fact, it is the very loosening of the commodified star from a delimited social context that allows for the freer circulation of that star, who might then belong to any number of social contexts and cultural projects. Furthermore, commodification can never fully erase the bodily disposition of the performer whose relation to social class as a laborer always remains evident, even in the very instance of her appearing as an advertising image or posing for a monumental statue. Normand had first appeared within mass culture as an artist's model a decade earlier, lending her image to the sale of various mass-produced goods, and her subsequent stardom at Keystone surely benefited from what was known about her work in advertising.[39] If star biography is only so much ballyhoo, insisting on the sincerity of a star biography so as to preserve some authentic notion of social class is a decidedly anti-modern endeavor, though not necessarily a retrograde one.

The star system became a system of knowledge for the masses after the First World War, and the star scandals that erupted in the early 1920s were only the more dramatic expressions of a larger state of emergency with respect to the production and control of cultural knowledge and scientific thinking. As I indicated at the end of Chapter 2, the mutuality of star-audience relations was a means for understanding modern personality as developmental and socially conditioned, an understanding strongly suggesting that film audiences were participating in the production of new values and new identities. The impact of the new social forces of mass production and of the mass media on different American communities quickly became the concern of politicians, reformers, and social scientists.[40] One of the most vexing influences for the defenders of tradition was the media celebrity who represented—no matter what set of values she or he embodied, endorsed, or expounded—new ways of appearing in society and who suggested new ways of organizing (or, for many reformers and investigators, "disorganizing") interpersonal relations. As we have seen, a first response to the problem of the mass idol was to emphasize the artificiality or falseness of the star, an idea heartily embraced by the film industry at the moment of the Hollywood scandals and a salient component of Valentino's deviant stardom. Many reformers, social scientists, and "objective" journalists typically portrayed any popular interest in the lives of film stars as a leisure activity with little or no ties to reality. While escapism had real social effects for them, stardom was not going to be counted as a legitimate source of knowledge or as a place to think about social transformations. Yet, as deCordova and others have shown, much of early fan culture operated on the assumption that behind the appearance of the star a greater reality was waiting to be glimpsed. What that reality ultimately was and who could glimpse it were the terms of a struggle that led to the professionalization of a class of communication experts.

The most significant and determining response to the American star culture of the 1920s was the objectification of star receptions by social scientists who sought to claim for themselves the sole privilege of adequately understanding the social processes of personality formation. As discussed in Chapter 2, the Payne Fund studies that were conducted in the latter half of the 1920s and into the early 1930s were an attempt to determine the effects of movies and movie attendance on children and young adults. While the studies were funded and initially organized by reformers seeking to gain scientific evidence for their claims about the detrimental effects of Hollywood films, the educators, sociologists, and psychologists who directed these studies all sought to employ methods of analysis that were impartial to any prejudiced or anticipated outcome. Both qualitative and quantitative methods were developed to measure the contributions that motion pictures made to the mental, emotional, and physical development of children and young adults. Many of these studies resulted in inconclusive findings, or, more accurately, they produced findings that did not support the idea (on which the reformers had counted) that motion pictures directly influenced child and adolescent behaviors. While limited and flawed, the experimental Payne Fund studies continue to be cited as an important founding moment in the history of mass communications studies.[41]

As I also mentioned at the end of Chapter 2, the published studies did not make the film celebrity a central component of their research, though many of them subtly registered a preoccupation with children's knowledge and opinions about stars. A child's inability to distinguish certain types of celebrities from others (movies stars from well-known politicians, for instance) or to properly evaluate the personalities of different kinds of celebrities (real criminals are bad; fictional criminals are bad, though they might be compelling, actors who play criminals might be either good or bad) was seen as an indicator of deviance. The "movie-made" child was more likely than a child with more limited film experience to see romance as the basis for important life choices. A movie-made child was more likely to understand personality as an expression of sexual passions, instincts, and emotions directed toward one's self and toward others. Rather than being a static product of rational choice and self-discipline, personality was developed through experiences and consumption and it was legible as a life history of pursuits, accomplishments, encounters, romances, conflicts, and friendships. Interestingly, the movie-made child shared the social scientists' understanding of personality as developmental, prone to deviance, and determined, in large part, by environment. Information about social settings, recreational activities, and personal relationships were just as important to movie audiences for determining and learning about Hollywood stars as they were to the social scientists of the Payne Fund studies in determining and learning about movie audiences. The assumptions, discourses, and sometimes even the methods of analysis of these two groups overlapped considerably; the difference was that, according to the scientific investigators of modern personality, film audiences' ideas about media personalities were often founded on false knowledge provided by mass-cultural products which often confused or even deceived consumers.

The archival discovery of what is thought to be a draft for the projected but never published volume of the Payne Fund studies, *Boys, Movies, and City Streets* has provided an occasion for historians to re-evaluate the importance and accomplishments of these early research studies on motion picture audiences. This newly found manuscript, what would have been Paul Cressey's contribution to the studies, has led media historians Garth Jowett, Ian Jarvie, and Kathryn Fuller to grant Cressey an honorary place in the history of communication research because of his apparent breakthrough in thinking about the social aspects of motion pictures. By studying movie attendance as only one of several interrelated social factors contributing to the experiences of children and adolescents,

Cressey attempted to understand how the movie house constituted a unique so-cial world (much like the taxi-dance hall) which provided opportunities and benefits to its patrons unavailable in other parts of their social lives.[42] In the surviving manuscript—now fittingly titled *The Community—A Social Setting for the Movies*—Cressey reported on and interpreted the interviews that he and oth-ers had conducted in an East Harlem tenement district of Manhattan in the early 1930s and which were part of a larger Boys' Clubs of America study on juvenile delinquency that was sponsored by the Bureau of Social Hygiene. Cressey found that, for many of the boys and young men who had participated in the inter-views, motion pictures provided them with an "informal education" that was lacking elsewhere in their lives.[43]

In the manuscript, Cressey discusses the appeal that film stars held for the young men of this depressed community and he says that, at different moments in their lives, many of these young men "aspired to be movie actors." Movie stars ap-parently provided "even boys of superior native endowment who read extensively in books" with models for emulation and admiration. As an example, Cressey notes how, for a particular "boy, who if anything might be regarded as superior in his community, there seems to be nothing incongruous in associating in the same galaxy of heroes such figures as Rudolph Valentino and Voltaire, and Buck Jones and Sabatini."[44] Cressey does not explain why he sees these names as "incongru-ous." The implication is that despite this young man's mental superiority, his ad-miration of film stars has overridden his ability to discriminate lasting cultural artifacts from the more transitory interests of modern consumer culture, much in the same manner that Mabel Normand was portrayed as incapable of making crucial distinctions between high and low culture, as well as between properly masculine and properly feminine pursuits. At another place in his study, Cressey discusses the intense interests in motion picture stars that exist among the young men of the neighborhood as a kind of "pseudo-knowledge:"

> [it] is certain that the typical boy of this community, when interviewed about his motion picture experiences, can give information concerning photoplays, actors, and actresses and concerning the private lives of actors and actresses which far out distances that which an average adult can furnish.
>
> With this great amount of information there has grown up among the boys on the street of this community a certain body of pseudo-information concerning ac-tors and actresses which in itself is but a reflection of the intense interest and intel-lectual significance of these actors and actresses and their photoplays in the lives of these young men. Much of this pseudo-knowledge is false and if publicly stated would be just grounds for libel suits.

Cressey cites several examples of this pseudo-information as it was reported to a "special investigator" and which includes such ideas as: "Fatty Arbuckle is so physically constructed that a normal sex life is impossible for him;" "Rudolph Valentino was not only a great Italian, but the greatest of all movie actors, and he died as a result of having too many 'affairs' with Hollywood beauties;" "many of the leading actors in the movies are inverts or have unnatural sex practices which make it impossible for them to continue marriage for any length of time;" and "most of the so-called 'bad men' in the movies are really good in private life and vice versa."[45]

Despite the fact that Cressey was largely sympathetic to the social and economic position of these young men and that he admired their creativity and intelligence, he saw their need for "pseudo-knowledge" about the stars as a need to educate themselves about issues and states of affairs with which they had no immediate experience or first-hand knowledge. Hollywood's products were, for him, a mediated form of schooling that answered to real social needs that were being fulfilled by rumor, innuendo, and gossip. Had these boys been able to set their minds to something that immediately concerned them and with which they had had more direct experience, they would not have lingered in the realm of mere opinion and conjecture. Alienation never has a use value. If Cressey's work marks an important moment in the consolidation of a scientific approach to the mass media, which I believe it does, then the distinguishing marks of that science were not going to be the specificity of its discourse that it, in fact, borrowed from the very cultures it studied. Nor was it going to be the processes of personality formation that it took as its objects of investigation.[46] What would set the science of motion pictures apart from mass reception were its truth-functionality and its ongoing project of correction.

NOTES

INTRODUCTION

1. Walter Benjamin, "The Work of Art in the Age of Its Technological Reproducibility: Second Version," *Walter Benjamin: Selected Writings, Vol. 3, 1935–1938*. Howard Eiland and Michael W. Jennings, eds. (Cambridge: Harvard University Press, 2002), 114.

2. Ibid., 113.

3. Ibid., 115. This is Benjamin's phrase for the initial political interest the masses took in motion pictures.

4. See Lea Jacobs, *The Decline of Sentiment: American Film in the 1920s* (Berkeley: University of California Press, 2008), particularly Chapter 5.

5. The 2005 Turner Classic Movies documentary, *Garbo*, directed by Christopher Bird and Kevin Brownlow, continues this normative project by making the actress' off-screen romance with John Gilbert the most sustained and determining factor in her popular success. The word "lesbian" is not heard on the soundtrack until sixty-eight minutes into the film, when Gore Vidal's mention of Garbo's "lesbian nature" initiates a six-minute sequence about her donning of trousers and other gender-bending traits. The sequence concludes with Garbo's great nephew pronouncing as "conjecture" all attributions of lesbianism to his famous aunt, while asserting that we have compelling and ample evidence of her several, deeply passionate romances with famous men. The next segment begins with Garbo's romance with conductor Leopold Stokowski, and the subjects of non-normative sexuality and gender identity are never broached again. On the visibility of Garbo as part of early 1930s lesbian culture, see Chapter 2 of Andrea Weiss' *Vampires and Violets: Lesbians in Film* (New York: Penguin, 1993).

6. Richard deCordova, *Picture Personalities: The Emergence of the Star System in America* (Urbana: University of Illinois Press, 1990); and Janet Staiger, "Seeing Stars," in *Stardom: Industry of Desire*, ed. Christine Gledhill (London Routledge, 1991), 3–16.

7. deCordova, *Picture Personalities*, 143.

8. One important exception here is the work of Lary May, who argues that certain stars in the 1910s facilitated the rise of consumerism and a popular acceptance of a corporate labor market. See especially his chapter on Douglas Fairbanks and Mary Pickford in *Screening Out the Past: The Birth of Mass Culture and the Motion Picture Industry* (Chicago: University of Chicago Press, 1983), 97–146. Daisuke Miyao's recent study of Sessue Hayakawa describes how the Hollywood star system in the 1910s and early 1920s negotiated an orientalist consumer market and an increasing xenophobic culture to normalize Hayakawa's racial identity by Americanizing it, a negotiation that would ultimately fail by the early 1920s. See *Sessue Hayakawa: Silent Cinema and Transnational Stardom* (Durham, N.C.: Duke University Press, 2007).

9. Richard Dyer, *Stars* (London: BFI Publishing, 1979); and *Heavenly Bodies: Film Stars and Society* (New York: St. Martin's Press, 1986).

10. Edgar Morin, *The Stars*, trans. Richard Howard (Minneapolis: University of Minnesota Press, 2005).

11. See Dyer, *Heavenly Bodies*, 19–66.

12. The value of such an approach has been demonstrated most recently by Adrienne L. McLean in *Being Rita Hayworth: Labor, Identity, and Hollywood Stardom* (New Brunswick, N.J.: Rutgers University Press, 2005).

13. Judith Mayne, *Cinema and Spectatorship* (London: Routledge, 1993), 126.

14. Joel Pfister, "Glamorizing the Psychological: The Politics of the Performances of Modern Psychological Identities," in *Inventing the Psychological: Toward a Cultural History of Emotional Life in America*, ed. Joel Pfister and Nancy Schnog (New Haven, Conn.: Yale University Press, 1997), 167–213.

15. Eve Kosofsky Sedgwick, *Epistemology of the Closet* (Berkeley: University of California Press, 1990), 85.

16. Here is an example of this view from an otherwise insightful work on the historical reception of films: "Homosexuality or bisexuality, of course, has long been a possible way of understanding one's self, but I believe that in the United States the notion that heterosexuality is only one of the possible sexual trajectories has just recently penetrated heterosexuals' self-imaging. It was possible to ignore this when non-heterosexuality was defined in hegemonic discourses as deviance. And many people still hold to that definition." From Janet Staiger, *Interpreting Films: Studies in the Historical Reception of American Cinema* (Princeton, N.J.: Princeton University Press, 1992), 75.

17. Alistair Cooke, *Douglas Fairbanks: The Making of a Screen Character* (New York: Museum of Modern Art, 1940); May, *Screening Out the Past*, 109–18; and Gaylyn Studlar, *This Mad Masquerade: Stardom and Masculinity in the Jazz Age* (New York: Columbia University Press, 1996), 10–89.

18. For an informative discussion of Hollywood's negotiation of popular criminals in the early 1930s, see Thomas Doherty's chapter, "Criminal Codes," in his book *Pre-Code*

Hollywood: Sex, Immorality, and Insurrection in American Cinema, 1930–1934 (New York: Columbia University Press, 1999), 137–70.

19. Gaylyn Studlar, "Valentino, 'Optic Intoxication,' and Dance Madness," in *Screening the Male: Masculinities in Hollywood Film*, ed. Steve Cohan and Ina Rae Hark (New York: Routledge, 1993): 23–45.

20. Richard Dyer, "Whiteness," *Screen* 29 (Autumn 1988): 44–65; and "The Colour of Virtue: Lillian Gish, Whiteness and Femininity," in *Women and Film*, ed. Pam Cook and Philip Dodd (Philadelphia: Temple University Press, 1993), 1–9. An important series of essays on the cultural significations of blackness in classical Hollywood cinema can be found in James Snead, *White Screens/Black Images*, ed. Colin MacCabe and Cornell West (New York: Routledge, 1994).

21. See Dyer's discussion of "negritude" in the reception of Paul Robeson, *Heavenly Bodies*, 67–139.

22. Jowett points out that Henry James Forman's *Movie Made Children*, a work that drew on the Payne Fund research but completely misrepresented its findings, was the more often cited study. See Jowett, *Film: The Democratic Art* (Boston: Little, Brown and Co., 1976), 220–29.

23. Unscrupulousness could be quickly telegraphed to a film audience by portraying a character's interest in the German philosopher, as when the dishonorable intentions of a dance instructor are made clear in the 1927 production of *The Satin Woman* (Gotham) by showing him reading a volume of Nietzsche after flirting with the young and impressionable Jean (Alice White). The Library of Congress holds an incomplete 35mm print of the title.

CHAPTER 1

1. David T. Courtwright, *Dark Paradise: Opiate Addiction in America before 1940* (Cambridge: Harvard University Press, 1982).

2. Of the three major scandals, only the Arbuckle trials and the murder of William Desmond Taylor continue to receive significant popular and scholarly attention. Two full-length books have been written about the Arbuckle case, and, as part of their coverage of the O. J. Simpson murder trial in 1995, news commentators and journalists made continual reference to this earlier celebrity scandal. There have also been numerous treatments of the Taylor murder as an "unsolved mystery," and there is even a monthly newsletter dedicated to the Taylor murder published on-line since April 1993. See David Y. Yallop, *The Day the Laughter Stopped: The True Story of Fatty Arbuckle* (New York: St. Martin's Press, 1976); and Andy Edmonds, *Frame-Up! The Untold Story of Roscoe "Fatty" Arbuckle* (New York: William Morrow, 1991). For book-length treatments of the Taylor affair as an entertaining Hollywood murder mystery, see Sidney D. Kirkpatrick, *A Cast of Killers* (New York: E. P. Dutton, 1986); and Robert Giroux, *A Deed of Death* (New York: Knopf, 1990). The factual bases of these works are critiqued in Bruce Long, *William Desmond Taylor: A Dossier* (New York: Scarecrow, 1991). The monthly newsletter *Taylorology* can be found on-line at www.taylorology.com. Issues 38 (Feb. 1996) and 39 (Mar. 1996) of *Taylorology* reproduce newspaper and magazine clippings relevant to the Reid

scandal. Besides a short chapter in Kenneth Anger's *Hollywood Babylon* and a sixteen-page article published in the 1960s, no substantial attention had been paid to Reid's biography or the scandal of his addiction since his mother wrote and published her sentimental remembrance in 1923 until the appearance of E. J. Fleming's biography of the star in 2007. Kenneth Anger, *Hollywood Babylon* (San Francisco: Straight Arrow Books, 1975); Dewitt Bodeen, "Wallace Reid Was an Idol in the Age of Innocence with Feet of Clay," *Films in Review* 17 (Apr. 1966): 205–20; Bertha Westbrook Reid, *Wallace Reid: His Life Story* (New York: Sorg Publishing Co., 1923); and E. J. Fleming, *Wallace Reid: The Life and Death of a Hollywood Idol* (Jefferson, N.C.: MacFarland and Co., 2007). Bodeen's article includes an extensive filmography for the actor and is reprinted in Dewitt Bodeen, *From Hollywood: The Careers of 15 Great American Stars* (South Brunswick, N.J.: A. S. Barnes, 1976), 91–115. Fleming's book-length biography is well researched and thorough, but the author sometimes is too preoccupied with halting rumors (such as Reid's alleged homosexuality, for example) and, thus, the book is not as useful as it might be in advancing our understanding of the historical reception context for the troubled star. Nevertheless, he has assembled a useful collection of primary material in his notes to the chapters. Fleming continues to maintain that Reid suffered from morphine and not heroin addiction. Anthony Slide's entry for Wallace Reid was dropped from the third revised edition of the *International Dictionary of Films and Filmmakers* (Detroit, Mich.: St. James Press) when it was published in 1997.

3. See, for example, Robert Sklar, *Movie-Made America: A Cultural History of the Movies* (New York: Viking Books, 1975), 82–85; and May, *Screening Out the Past*, 179.

4. Jowett, *Film*, 166–69; and Raymond Morely, *The Hays Office* (Indianapolis: Bobbs-Merrill Co., 1945), 52–56.

5. Team owners had hired Landis to be commissioner of baseball after sensational revelations of corruption and racketeering had shaken the public's faith in the country's national pastime[o]. For an analysis of the regulatory responses to the Black Sox scandal of 1919 and the Arbuckle scandal of 1921, see Sam Stoloff, "Fatty Arbuckle and the Black Sox: The Paranoid Style of American Popular Culture, 1919–1922," in *Headline Hollywood: A Century of Film Scandal*, ed. Adrienne L. McLean and David Cook (New Brunswick, N.J.: Rutgers University Press, 2001), 52–82.

6. Valentino had just been jailed and tried for bigamy in Los Angeles. While the case was ultimately dismissed, the star's marriage complications and his troubles with the law had drawn quite a lot of tabloid attention during May and June of 1922.

7. 29 June 1922, *Congressional Record*, 67th Congress, 2d sess., 9657.

8. "Griffith Sees Peril in Sincere Fanatics," *New York Times*, 16 Feb. 1922.

9. See Leslie Midkiff DeBauche, *Reel Patriotism: The Movies and the First World War* (Madison: University of Wisconsin Press, 1997).

10. deCordova, *Picture Personalities*.

11. May, *Screening Out the Past*, 189–90.

12. Eileen Bowser, *The Transformation of the Cinema, 1907–1915* (Berkeley: University of California Press, 1994), 108. In 1931, Hollywood business historian Benjamin Hampton credited the public with "the full and undisputed charge of [the star system's] creation during every moment of its history." Hampton believed that the early interests in the film

performer had caught the studios completely off-guard. As a film producer who worked in the industry through the early scandal era, Hampton would have a large stake in promoting this particular view of the star system. See his *A History of the Movies* (New York: Cocici, Friede Publishers, 1931), 83–100.

13. In early 1910, for example, Pathé announced in *Moving Picture World* its promotions of popular French actors: "In regard to the personalities of the moving picture stage, Pathes have a great opportunity to make public the identities of the artists who work for them, because Pathes are one of the greatest moving picture houses in the world. They have gone after talent, and the talent which works for them properly looks for its reward of publicity for its effort." Quoted in deCordova, *Picture Personalities*, 54.

14. See the two fan letters addressed to Florence Lawrence in deCordova, *Picture Personalities*, 56–57.

15. Ibid.

16. National Education Association, *Proceedings* 60 (1922): 254, as quoted in Jowett, *Film*, 172.

17. For example, see Dominick Dunne's mention of the Arbuckle scandal in "L. A. in the Age of O. J." in *Vanity Fair* (Feb. 1995): 46.

18. M. Elizabeth Kapitz, Letter to the Editor, *New York Times*, 21 May 1922, sec. 2, p. 6.

19. deCordova, *Picture Personalities*, 50–52. For a much more extensive discussion of the scandal and film career of Clara Smith Hamon than what follows, see my essay "Tempting Fate, or, the Secretary as Producer," in *Looking Past the Screen: Case Studies in American Film History and Method*, ed. Jon Lewis and Eric Smoodin (Durham, N.C.: Duke University Press, 2007), 117–50.

20. See "Clara Hamon Freed by Murder Jury," *New York Times*, 18 Mar. 1921, pp. 1–2.

21. "Fight Films Showing Clara Smith Hamon," *New York Times*, 25 Mar. 1921, p. 12. The trades reported her contract to be for $50,000 a year (*Moving Picture World*, 9 Apr. 1921, 573).

22. For a brief history of this film's production, see Kevin Brownlow, *Behind the Mask of Innocence: The Social Problem Films of the Silent Era* (New York: Alfred A. Knopf, 1990), 153–55. Brownlow incorrectly identifies Clara Smith Hamon as "shoot[ing] her husband," Jake Hamon.

23. Brownlow, *Behind the Mask*, 154

24. "California Movie Houses Bar Clara Smith Hamon Films," *New York Times*, 24 Mar. 1922, p. 19. The statement was issued by the Allied Amusement Industries of California. See also "Bumpy Road Awaiting Clara Hamon in Movies" and "Oppose Undesirable Films," *Moving Picture World*, 9 Apr. 1921, 573, 574; and "Screen Interests Protest Clara Hamon in Films," *Motion Picture News*, 9 Apr. 1921, 2442.

25. *The New York Times*, 25 Mar. 1921, p. 12.

26. New York State Governor Nathan L. Miller had just signed legislation establishing a motion picture censorship commission in his state, an event that was considered a major setback for the industry's anti-censorship efforts. See statements by Gabriel L. Hess, chairman of the censorship committee of NAMPI, *Moving Picture World*, 28 May 1921, 379.

27. *Moving Picture World,* 9 Apr. 1921, 573. *Fate*'s producers hardly claimed otherwise; in a public appeal for investors in the film, they claimed that no one had ever "entered motion pictures with an income assured and insured as is Clara Smith Hamon" (*Variety,* 29 Apr. 1921, 46).

28. "Half-Breed Guide Named by Stillman in Divorce Suit," *New York Times,* 12 Mar. 1921, p. 1.

29. "Frame-up Charged by Mrs. Stillman; Letters Revealed," *New York Times,* 7 May 1921, pp. 1, 3.

30. "Mrs. Leeds, Named in Stillman Suit, Century Show Girl," *New York Times,* 18 Mar. 1921, pp. 1, 3; "Notorious Stars as Stock Sale Lure," *Variety,* 8 July 1921, 30; and "Inside Stuff," *Variety,* 3 June 1921, 44.

31. "Rule on Beauvais Film," *New York Times,* 31 Dec. 1921, p. 5. Emphasis added.

32. *Variety,* 3 June 1921, 44.

33. Herbert Howe, "What Are Matinee Idols Made Of?" *Photoplay* 23, 5 (April 1923): 41, 104.

34. See, for example, the quotations from the industry publication, *Camera,* in "The Trouble with the Movie Face," *The Literary Digest,* 14 Jan. 1922, 28.

35. Mrs. Wallace Reid quoted in William Parker, "Mrs. Reid Denies Claim that Husband Is Member of National 'Dope' Ring," *Los Angeles Evening Herald,* 20 Dec. 1922, p. A14.

36. Mrs. Reid quoted in William Parker, "Reid Got 'Dope' Habit in N. Y., Says Wife," *Los Angeles Evening Herald,* 19 Dec. 1922, pp. A1, A14.

37. Thomas W. Bailey, "Wallace Reid Details Plans of Lasky Firm," *San Francisco Chronicle,* 27 July 1919, p. 4E.

38. Richard Koszarski, *An Evening's Entertainment: The Age of the Silent Feature Picture, 1915–1928* (Berkeley: University of California Press, 1994), 276–78. Kevin Brownlow refers to this accident as an "explanation [that] was so straightforward one wonders why it did not circulate at the time of his death." Actually, it did circulate widely and was a very important component of the public representation of Reid's addiction, though the explanatory work performed by the story of the train wreck was anything but straightforward (Brownlow, *Behind the Mask of Innocence,* 107).

39. Dorothy Davenport Reid, "Wife Pens Dramatic Story of Wallace Reid's Drug Ruin: Dope Curse Traced to Car Injury in 1919," *San Francisco Examiner,* 31 Dec. 1922, p. 6.

40. Danae Clark, *Negotiating Hollywood: The Cultural Politics of Actor's Labor* (Minneapolis: University of Minnesota Press, 1995).

41. Fleming maintains that the second series of articles were actually written by Davenport Reid's close friend, Adela Rogers St. John, a Hearst news correspondent. He also speculates that they were written at the direction of Will Hays and/or Jesse Lasky to protect the industry. See Fleming, *Wallace Reid,* 218.

42. Lynne Kirby, "Male Hysteria and Early Cinema," *Camera Obscura* 17 (May 1988): 113–31. See also Lynne Kirby, *Parallel Tracks: The Railroad and Silent Cinema* (Durham, N.C.: Duke University Press, 1997).

43. Bertha Westbrook Reid, *Wallace Reid,* 74.

44. "Reid Recovering," *Variety*, 27 Oct. 1922, 47.

45. Dorothy Davenport Reid, "Overpowering Mastery of Dope Demon Described," *The San Francisco Examiner*, 4 Jan. 1923, p. 10.

46. "Wally Reid in His Best Stunt Conquers 'Dope,'" *Rochester Herald*, 17 Dec. 1922, p. 1.

47. The man taken into custody was Claude Tynar (or Tyner) Waltman, a young writer who was identified in *Variety* as "Thomas H. Tyner, alias Claude Walton, alias, Bennie Walton." Mrs. Reid does not name Waltman but mentions this arrest in her revelations to the Hearst newspapers saying that "the boy's" claims were untrue or misinterpreted ("Had Dope for Star," *Variety*, 19 Nov. 1920, 39). Waltman apparently committed suicide a couple of weeks after Reid's death; he left a note saying "going to join my pal" (*Variety*, 8 Feb. 1923, 47). Waltman's arrest on heroin possession in 1920 is at odds with the general view that, during this period, heroin use was primarily an East Coast phenomenon, centered mainly around New York City and Philadelphia. Ironically, Mrs. Reid's insistence that her husband became addicted to drugs in New York City in 1921 suggests that heroin played a role in his drug habit since heroin had almost entirely eclipsed morphine in that city as the narcotic of addiction. Mrs. Reid also claimed that her husband on several occasions had received packages of drugs in the mail from New York City. See Dorothy Davenport Reid, "Wally Reid's Confirmed Use of Drugs Revealed," *San Francisco Examiner*, 3 Jan. 1923, p. 10. Mrs. Reid also lamented late-night parties at her husband's apartment in New York City; when Adele Whitely and Gladys Hall interviewed the star there one morning in the summer of 1921, they noted "several festive evidences" and mentioned that "Wally is weary" (*Motion Picture Magazine* 22 [Sept. 1921]: 22–23). On the prevalence of heroin use in New York and other East Coast cities, see Courtwright, *Dark Paradise*, 101–12. On the relation between crime and heroin addiction, see "Saving Youth from Heroin and Crime," *Literary Digest* 81 (24 May 1924): 32–33, and Lawrence Kolb, "Drug Addiction in Its Relation to Crime," *Mental Hygiene* 9 (1925): 74–89.

48. Courtwright, *Dark Paradise*, 87–101.

49. Ibid., 113–47. A psychopathic model of narcotic addiction emerged in the 1920s. As more and more addicts came from the ranks of the lower classes, drug addiction simultaneously came to be understood in terms of abnormal mental or emotional development. The foremost proponent of this theory was Lawrence Kolb, who studied and treated addicts for the U.S. Public Health Service; see "Types and Characteristics of Drug Addicts," *Mental Hygiene* 9 (1925): 303–13. See also Eugene T. Lies, "Constructive Play as a Preventative of Narcotic Addiction," in *Narcotic Education*, ed. H. S. Middlemiss (Washington, D.C.: H. S. Middlemiss, 1926), 130–36. For a brief comparison of the different public policy approaches taken to narcotic addiction in Great Britain and the United States during the 1920s, see Terry M. Parssinen, *Secret Passions, Secret Remedies: Narcotics Drugs in British Society 1820–1930* (Philadelphia: Institute for the Study of Human Issues, 1983), 201–21.

50. Samuel Hopkins Adams, "The Cruel Tragedy of 'Dope,'" *Collier's* 73 (23 Feb. 1924): 7–8, 32.

51. Louis Weadock, "Screen Idol Succumbs to Drug Curse," *San Francisco Examiner*, 19 Jan. 1923, pp. 1, 3.

52. At this time, Hearst was also busy exploiting Juanita Hansen, a film actress arrested for possession of narcotics in January 1923. Hansen had been a popular serial queen, though her stardom waned considerably after 1920. Although acquitted of the drug charge, she publicly confessed to having been a heroin addict in the past. Hearst arranged a speaking tour for the troubled actress and announced plans for an anti-narcotics film featuring Hansen. See "Juanita Hansen's Offers," *Variety*, 8 Feb. 1923, 47. Even before her arrest, though, the Hearst newspapers reported that Hansen's name was among those found on a patient list confiscated from a clinic in Oakland, California, whose doors had been shut for providing addicts with illegal narcotics ("Police Seize Records of Dope Hospital," *San Francisco Examiner*, 3 Jan. 1923, p. 3). Reportedly, Reid had also been a patient at the clinic ("'Sociologist' Arrested as Drug Seller," *San Francisco Examiner*, 2 Jan. 1923, p. 1). Hansen's addiction was far less disruptive for the industry than Reid's since her film career was effectively over at the time of the scandal.

53. *Human Wreckage* is a lost film. In 1983, Martin Sopocy included *Human Wreckage* in a filmography of extant works by Thomas H. Ince and erroneously reported that a print of the film existed at the Library of Congress; see Jean Mitry, "Thomas H. Ince: His Esthetic, His Films, His Legacy," trans. Martin Sopocy and Paul Attallah, *Cinema Journal* 22 (Winter 1983): 2–25. While there was a film entitled *Human Wreckage* at the Library of Congress, by 1975 that film had been correctly identified as *Sex Madness* (Cinema Service Corp., 1938), an exploitation feature about venereal disease copyrighted under the title *Human Wreckage*. Citing the scholarship of George Pratt, Sopocy also questioned Ince's actual involvement with the production of *Human Wreckage*, claiming "the extent of the connection is unclear" and that the film's "relation to the Ince canon remains one of the ambiguities of Ince studies." This ambiguity appears to be solely based on the relative lack of prominence given to Ince in the film's publicity. Yet Ince was mentioned in the press coverage as the producer of *Human Wreckage* less than three weeks after Reid's death, from the very moment that the proposed film was announced. See "Watchdogs of Law Aid Dope Film," *Los Angeles Daily Times*, 7 Feb. 1923, sec. 2, p. 7; and "Among 'Dope' Films, Which Will Be First?" *Variety*, 8 Feb. 1923, 46. Additionally, the Thomas H. Ince Corporation is listed as the producer on the copyright registration records for *Human Wreckage*. On the application for license from the Motion Picture Commission of New York State, the film's title is given as "'HUMAN WRECKAGE' (A Thomas Ince Production)." Ince was undoubtedly the film's primary producer and he was probably credited as such in the American release prints of *Human Wreckage*. The relative absence of Ince's name from trade advertising is better understood as evidence of his reticence about the overseas reception of *Human Wreckage*. For example, Ince's distribution agreement for Argentina required that his name be removed from all promotions of the film in that country. (Agreement between Argentine American Film Corporation and R-C Pictures, 23 Dec. 1924, Thomas Ince Collection, Container 41, Business Files for Foreign Distributors, Folder 2, Manuscript Division, Library of Congress, Washington, D.C.)

54. See the continuity script for "Human Wreckage" by G. Gardiner Sullivan in Thomas H. Ince Collection, container 29, Production File for *Human Weckage*, Folder 2,

Manuscript Division, Library of Congress, Washington, D.C. This script has the type-written title of "Dope" scratched out and the title "Human Wreckage" penciled in.

55. *Photoplay* 23 (May 1923): 84. Sullivan had been the scenarist on many of Ince's most important productions including *Civilization* (Triangle, 1916). For the script of *Human Wreckage*, Sullivan likely "borrowed" material from other writers. For example, in Ince's file for the film there is a seven-page treatment written by Will Lambert for a film about a district attorney who becomes addicted to narcotics while prosecuting a difficult drug case. This untitled story bears more than a few similarities to the Sullivan scripts for *Human Wreckage*. (Thomas H. Ince Collection, Container 29, Production File for *Human Wreckage* File, Folder 1, Manuscript Division, Library of Congress, Washington, D.C.) In 1917, Ince had also supervised the production of *Love or Justice* (New York Motion Picture Corp.), a film based on a Lambert Hillyer script about a lawyer who becomes a drug addict. Kevin Brownlow also reports that Albert Rogell complained of Ince stealing important material for *Human Wreckage* from his own anti-narcotics film, *The Greatest Menace* (J. G. Mayer, 1923). See Brownlow, *Behind the Mask*, 117–18. Another possible, if somewhat macabre, source for *Human Wreckage* may have been a manuscript authored by "Claud[e] Tyner Waltman," a drug dealer and a friend of Reid's who killed himself just weeks after the star's death (see note 38). Before committing suicide, Waltman gave Mrs. Reid a manuscript on "narcotics evil," a work for which he had been unable to find a publisher. Mrs. Reid claimed to have retained the manuscript in her possession after Waltman's death ("Youth Slays Self to Join Star in Death," *Los Angeles Examiner*, 4 Feb. 1923, pp. 1, 4).

56. Manuscript, Thomas Ince Collection, Container 29, Production File for *Human Wreckage*, Folder 3, Manuscript Division, Library of Congress, Washington, D.C.

57. *Motion Picture News*, 14 July 1923, 130–31.

58. "Reid's Death Warning to Public," *San Francisco Examiner*, 20 Jan. 1923, p. 3.

59. *Webb et al. v. United States* (1919). See Courtwright, *Dark Paradise*, 106–7.

60. The original script of *Human Wreckage* had proposed that a federal hospital for drug addicts be built on San Clemente island, but, as Kevin Brownlow has pointed out, the proposed site soon became a practice range for the U.S. Marine Corps (Brownlow, *Behind the Mask*, 115–16).

61. Indeed, as several statements made by Mrs. Reid attest, she very much supported the efforts of law enforcement to halt the illicit traffic in narcotics, and federal and state law enforcement agencies had lent their support to *Human Wreckage* from the very beginning of its production. However, Mrs. Reid denied early reports that she planned to avenge her husband's illness by exposing the "traffic in narcotics in both Los Angeles and the East" (*Rochester Times-Union*, 18 Dec. 1922, p. 25). Years later, she claimed that her husband had no contact whatsoever with the illegal drug trade since he was capable of "charm[ing] any doctor into giving him the tablets he wanted" (Bodeen, "Wallace Reid Was an Idol," 216). Of course, any physician who was so fooled into supplying Reid with non-diminishing doses of narcotics for any length of time would have faced federal prosecution under the Harrison Act if found out.

62. Brownlow, *Behind the Mask*, 109.

63. Theodor Adorno, *Minima Moralia: Reflections from Damaged Life*, trans. E.F.N. Jephcott (London: Verso, 1993), 17.

64. A striking example of this sort of reception is a Wallace Reid scrapbook begun by an unknown person(s) at the moment of the star's death. The first several pages contain newspaper clippings about Reid's illness and death. Moving backwards in time, subsequent pages are devoted to fan magazine material from earlier moments in Reid's stardom such as a rotogravure of Reid with Cecil B. DeMille taken from the June 1921 issue of *Motion Picture Magazine*. While the scrapbook clearly functions as a memorial, it also poses Reid's career as a type of case study, as a life whose defining moments are narcotic addiction and death. Scrapbook in the care of the author.

65. Reid, *Wallace Reid*, 103. Capitals in the original.

66. Charles A. "Buddy" Post, "Wally Reid, My Friend," *Motion Picture Magazine* 26 (Jan. 1924): 84.

67. Gladys Hall, "Will Wallace Reid's Son Succeed Him?" *Motion Picture Magazine* 36 (Jan. 1929): 50.

68. Wallace Reid Memorial subscription, Wallace Reid file, Paper Collections, George Eastman House, Rochester, N.Y.

69. Memorandum from A. L. Ferguson, 26 Sept. 1939, Wallace Reid Memorial Fund file, Box C-66, The Diocese of New York of the Episcopal Church, N.Y.

70. Frederick Lewis Allen, *Only Yesterday: An Informal History of the Nineteen Twenties* (New York: Harper and Row, 1931), 81. "Miss Scranton on the Boardwalk" refers to the annual Inter-City Beauty Contest held in Atlantic City, New Jersey, at which the first Miss America was crowned in September 1921. The press delighted in reporting that Samuel Gompers, president of the American Federation of Labor, was an enthusiastic member of the audience for the pageant in 1922. Morvich was a famous thoroughbred race horse who achieved an impressive record of eleven wins in eleven consecutive races before winning the Kentucky Derby in 1922, his final victorious start.

71. Milton Sills, "The Actor's Part," in *The Story of the Films*, ed. Joseph P. Kennedy (Chicago: A. W. Shaw Company, 1927), 189–92.

72. "The Lesson of Reid's Death," *Variety*, 25 Jan. 1923, 10.

73. See, for example, "Present Production Costs Contrasted with Low Figures of the Past," *New York Times*, 19 Dec. 1926, sec. 7, p. 9; and "A New Phase Opens in the Film Industry," *New York Times*, 3 July 1927, sec. 8, p. 3.

CHAPTER 2

1. *Chicago Daily News*, 30 July 1924, p. 1.

2. Paula Fass, "Making and Remaking an Event: The Leopold and Loeb Case in American Culture," *The Journal of American History* 80, no. 3 (Dec. 1993): 920.

3. As an example of the New Queer Cinema, *Swoon* would be the exception here in its attempt to foreground and embrace the nostalgia that often subtends the cultural memory of the case by using that nostalgia in a strategy of viewer seduction. This "historical fantasy" about Leopold and Loeb tended, I would argue, to increase anxieties about

human sexuality during the HIV hysteria of the Reagan and Bush eras. The political prudence and effectiveness of that effort is another question entirely.

4. D. A. Miller, "Anal *Rope*," in *Inside/Out: Lesbian Theories, Gay Theories*, ed. Diana Fuss (New York: Routledge, 1991), 131.

5. Estelle Freedman, "'Uncontrollable Desires': The Response to the Sexual Psychopath 1920–1960," *Journal of American History* 74, no. 1 (June 1987): 103–4.

6. Sociologist Janice Irvine has pointed out that Kinsey's research, in response to a perceived crisis in heterosexual relations and marriage, supported the radically new view that men and women were essentially the same. The similarity of the sexual responses of men and women, even at the level of biological organization and anatomical structure, surely made the construction of sexual difference through simple binaries increasingly difficult. See Irvine's article, "From Difference to Sameness: Gender Ideology in Sexual Science," *The Journal of Sex Research* 27, no. 1 (February 1990): 1–24.

7. Miller, "Anal *Rope*," 126. Emphasis in original.

8. Fass, "Making and Remaking an Event," 943.

9. Cultural critic Holly Potter's excellent discussion of the trial's publicity argues that Darrow's defense sought but failed to instantiate a new popular understanding of criminality by giving the "new psychology" such prominence in the testimony. I am maintaining that Darrow was only exploiting the emergent possibilities of media celebrity already in place (something that Potter also explores in terms of public relations) and that Hollywood star reception had already manifested the assumptions that identity was developmental and relational. From my point of view, this was not something that had to be forged; it was something that was subsequently lost. See Potter's master's thesis, "Leopold and Loeb: Texts and Contexts of an American Cause Célèbre" (Master's thesis, McGill University, Montreal, 1991).

10. John Logan, *Never the Sinner* (Woodstock, N.Y.: Overlook, 1999), 13–14.

11. In this regard, William Healy's *The Individual Delinquent* (Boston: Little, Brown, 1915) signals a significant shift in the scientific study of criminals by making the exhaustive case study of the criminal's childhood and early family relationships a central part of its methodology. Healy was head of the Juvenile Psychiatric Institute in Chicago and was one of the experts for the defense in the Leopold and Loeb trial.

12. Maureen McKernan, quoted in "The Crime and Trial of Loeb and Leopold," *The Journal of Abnormal Psychology and Social Psychology* 19, no. 3 (Oct.–Dec., 1924): 223.

13. See especially the testimony of Drs. Hugh T. Patrick and Harold Douglass Singer in "The Loeb-Leopold Murder of Franks in Chicago, May 21, 1924," *Journal of the American Institute of Criminal Law and Criminology* 24 (Nov. 1924): 380–87.

14. For coverage of their experiences with governesses, see "'Dream Life' Bared by Doctor to Save Leopold and Loeb," *Chicago Daily News*, 1 Aug. 1924, pp. 1 and 3.

15. *The Chicago Tribune*, 31 May 1924. Quoted in Hal Higdon, *Crime of the Century: The Leopold and Loeb Case* (New York: G.P. Putnam's Sons, 1975), 115.

16. See the defense speech of Benjamin J. Bachrach in Alvin V. Sellers, *The Loeb-Leopold Case* (Brunswick, Ga.: Classic Publishing, 1926), 230.

17. *New York Times*, 22 July 1924, p. 4.

18. John H. Wilmore cited cases of this in his argument that the remission of the death penalty in this case encouraged others to commit similar criminal acts. "The Loeb-Leopold Murder of Franks," 402.

19. For a discussion of the relation between stars and everyday people, see Dyer, *Stars*, 49–50.

20. Anita Loos, *Gentlemen Prefer Blondes* (New York: Grosset & Dunlap, 1925), 156.

21. "Flashes from Eastern Stars," *Motion Picture Classic* (Mar. 1925o): 52, quoted in Koszarski, 245.

22. Ted Le Berthon, "Absolutely Mr. Chaplin! Positively Mr. Freud! Psycho-analysis Comes to the Movies," *Moving Picture Classic* (Aug. 1924): 37.

23. Sigmund Freud, "Negation," in *General Psychological Theory*, trans. Joan Riviere (New York: Macmillan, 1963), 213–17.

24. Le Berthon, "Absolutely Mr. Chaplin!, Positively Mr. Freud!" 37.

25. Darrow quoted in Sellers, *The Loeb-Leopold Case*, 180.

26. Yallop, *The Day the Laughter Stopped*, 268.

27. "Topics of the Times," *New York Times*, 20 April 1922, p. 13.

28. According to Yallop, *The Day the Laughter Stopped*, 270. This was the position of National Committee of Better Films who issued a statement in January 1923 stating, "When, however, offensive incidents in the life of a screen star have been so widely published that an unsavory odor has been attached in the public mind to the actor's very personality, then such incidents become an element in the moral influence of a film and can no longer be overlooked." See "Cuts Out Arbuckle Films" *New York Times*, 12 Jan. 1923, p. 13. The National Committee for Better Films was affiliated with the National Board of Review (NBR). Once Hays had temporarily reinstated Arbuckle, the National Committee decided to go beyond the NBR's policy of evaluating only screen content to consider what was known about the performers who appeared in films. The National Committee wrote to the subscribers of their publication, the *Monthly Photoplay Guide*, explaining their decision to exclude all Arbuckle pictures from future lists of recommended films: "We believe the youth of the country is apt to accept as popular heroes those who are prominently identified as screen stars and the question naturally arises as to whether Mr. Arbuckle should again be presented on the screens of the country in a way that might imply approval of the affair in which he has acknowledged taking part and hence influence young people adversely." See the folder on Roscoe Arbuckle in Box 64, Records of the National Board of Review, New York Public Library.

29. Nathan G. Hale Jr., *The Rise and Crisis of Psychoanalysis in the United States: Freud and the Americas, 1917–1985* (New York: Oxford University Press, 1995), 76. See Hale's discussion of the Leopold and Loeb trial, 91–93.

30. Meyer Levin, *Compulsion* (New York: Pocket Books, 1957), 347.

31. White never studied with Freud and it is doubtful that they ever met. While White received all his medical training in the United States and had served as superintendent of St. Elizabeth's since 1904, Elizabeth Shepley Sergeant, in her 1927 vignette of White, found it necessary to combat the myth "that only those American doctors who came under the personal influence of Freud have accepted psychoanalytic technique" (see Elizabeth Shepley Sergeant and E. O. Hoppé, *Fire Under the Andes: A Group of North American Portraits*

[New York: Alfred Knopf, 1927]). White's cultural celebrity can be appreciated by noting that his portrait comes after a chapter devoted to the theatrical artistic designer Robert Edmond Jones and before one on Eugene O'Neill.

32. Quoted in Higdon, *Crime of the Century*, 140.

33. "The Loeb-Leopold Murder of Franks," 368.

34. White quoted in Higdon, *Crime of the Century*, 210.

35. Higdon, *Crime of the Century*, 159.

36. "Pretty girls by the dozen pouted and rolled their eyes at the doormen. They were either sweethearts of 'Dick' or 'Babe,' or they 'just wanted to see those dear boys,' they said. The gruesomeness of the crime seemed to have no effect upon the feeling of the giddy little flappers, who begged to get into the courtroom." Quoted in Maureen McKernan, ed., *The Amazing Crime and Trial of Leopold and Loeb* (Chicago: Plymouth Court Press, 1924), 71–72.

37. This "responsible" journalism was made easier by reporting on the court's own censorship of testimony: "He [Leopold] said Loeb was a close friend and that they had a habit of dining together as frequently as three times a week. For the second time [defense attorney] Mr. Bachrach reached unprintable matter and leaned over the three stenographers to whisper to them something for the record only." *New York Times*, 30 July 1924, p. 2.

38. Glueck quoted in Sellers, *The Loeb-Leopold Case*, 24.

39. See, for example, "Dr. Healy Whispers 'Incredible Pact' Between Boys" and "Court Bars Portion of Testimony from Press," *Chicago Herald and Examiner*, 8 Aug. 1912, p. 3.

40. Published in abbreviated form in McKernan, *The Amazing Crime*, 83–140.

41. White's testimony quoted in Higdon, *Crime of the Century*, 211. See also White's testimony in *The Chicago Daily News*, 1 Aug. 1924, pp. 1 and 3; and 2 Aug. 1924, pp. 1 and 3. White testified that Leopold and Loeb had established a "fused personality."

42. Sigmund Freud, "A Special Type of Object Choice Made by Men," in *Sexuality and the Psychology of Love*, trans. Joan Riviere (New York: Macmillan, 1963), 53.

43. Sigmund Freud, *Three Essays on the Theory of Sexuality*, trans. James Strachey (New York: Basic Books, 2000). See 1910 footnote on 10–11.

44. See footnote 6 of Sigmund Freud, "The Psychogenesis of a Case of Homosexuality in a Woman," in *Sexuality and the Psychology of Love*, trans. Barbara Low and R. Garber (New York: Macmillan, 1963), 145.

45. As Dr. White testified, "I cannot see how Babe would have entered into it all alone because he had no criminalistic tendencies in any sense as Dick did, and I don't think Dickie would have ever functioned to this extent all by himself. So these two boys, with their peculiarly inter-digitated personalities, came into this emotional compact with the Franks homicide as a result." Quoted in Higdon, *Crime of the Century*, 211.

46. Symposium comments taken from "The Loeb-Leopold Murder of Franks," 395.

47. "The Loeb-Leopold Murder of Franks," 362.

48. Freud, "The Psychogenesis of a Case of Homosexuality in a Woman," 147–48.

49. See, for example, the 1926 footage of the crowds in front of Campbell's Funeral Church contained in the short 1941 tribute film, *Rudolph Valentino* (Astor Films), included as part of the Flicker Alley DVD Collection, *Valentino: Rediscovering an Icon of Silent Film* (2007).

50. "Outsider Gets View of Trial," *Chicago Herald and Examiner,* 3 Aug. 1924, p. 3.

51. "Lorraine and 'Patches,' Once Rivals, Now Pals," *Chicago Herald and Examiner,* 8 Aug. 1924, p. 1.

52. It is not until *The Ego and the Id* that Freud will discuss the effects of the positive and negative Oedipus complexes as being simultaneously negotiated. Yet, as Kaja Silverman has pointed out, Freud seems to want to suggest that a particular resolution and identification will be relatively stronger for any particular individual and will result in a specific sexual disposition. See Silverman, *Male Subjectivity at the Margin* (New York: Routledge, 1992), 356–62.

53. Richard Dyer has noted that theorists of star-audience relations often suggest that women and adolescents have the most intense relationships to stars. Explaining that stars often embody the desires of marginalized groups, Dyer tentatively accepts the truth of this and adds gays to the list. Yet the empirical evidence of these groups' participation in intense fandom may, ultimately, only work to confirm the meaning of such pleasures for the same dominant ideology that marginalizes these groups. See Dyer, *Stars,* 37.

54. Herbert Blumer and Philip M. Hauser, *Movies, Delinquency, and Crime* (New York: Macmillan, 1933), 205.

55. Frank K. Shuttleworth and Mark A. May, *The Social Conduct and Attitudes of Movie Fans* (New York: Macmillan, 1933), 56–57.

CHAPTER 3

1. See, for example, Robert Oberfirst, *Rudolph Valentino: The Man Behind the Myth* (New York: The Citadel Press, 1962); Brad Steiger and Chaw Mank, *Valentino: An Intimate and Shocking Exposé* (New York: MacFadden Books, 1966); and Irving Shulman, *Valentino* (New York: Trident Press, 1967). Ken Russell also begins his screen biography of the star, *Valentino* (1970), with the spectacle of raucous crowds smashing through the plate glass windows of Campbell's Funeral Church. An entire book has been published recently on Valentino's death and funerary rites, once again posing the spectacle of the mass hysteria attending Valentino's funeral. See Allan R. Ellenberger, *The Valentino Mystique: The Death and Afterlife of the Silent Film Idol* (Jefferson, N.C.: McFarland, 2005).

2. Shulman, *Valentino,* 15.

3. The most important texts are Miriam Hansen, *Babel and Babylon: Spectatorship in the American Silent Cinema* (Cambridge: Harvard University Press, 1991), 245–94; and Gaylyn Studlar, *This Mad Masquerade: Stardom and Masculinity in the Jazz Age* (New York: Columbia University Press, 1996).

4. Michael Morris, *Madam Valentino: The Many Lives of Natacha Rambova* (New York: Abbeville Press, 1991).

5. Emily W. Leider, *Dark Lover: The Life and Death of Rudolph Valentino* (New York: Farrar, Straus, and Giroux, 2003), 126. Ivano's remarks come from an interview with Anthony Slide. To be fair, Leider continues by citing testimony from Ivano and others about Valentino's passivity in sexual relations with women; in other words, according to these witnesses, Valentino was a heterosexual bottom. Nevertheless, Leider continues to cite Ivano's testimony about Valentino's sexual normalcy and his potency throughout the

book, as when Ivano, seeking to dispel rumors of Rambova's lesbianism, claimed that during the time when he lived with the couple, Valentino had come to his room in the early morning hours with an erection, highly alarmed because Rambova had become unconscious during coitus. According to Ivano, Valentino believed "he had killed her" (140). Leider places Rambova's sexuality and friendship with lesbians such as Nazimova in a "bohemian enclave in Hollywood" where "an atmosphere of experimentation prevailed" (133–34). Here the author constructs a knowing and sophisticated Hollywood, one beyond the cruder categories of homo/heterosexual identities that subsequent biographers seek to impose. See her dismissal of David Bret's claim that Valentino had an affair with Jacques Hébertot in Paris in 1923. For Leider, such an attribution "fails to allow for the fantasy factor: Valentino exerted and continues to exert enormous power as an object of desire for both sexes. Lusting after him, imagining him as your lover, telling somebody that he was, isn't the same as bedding him" (271–72). Thus, Leider's more "sophisticated" reading of Valentino's sexuality still privileges testimony about his "real" heterosexuality over what will continue to be assumed to be only some understandable imaginings about homosexuality, imaginings that are entirely predictable since there are always going to be some people who want Valentino to have been gay. David Bret, *Valentino: A Dream of Desire* (London: Robson Books, 1998). Leider reads Valentino's close and affectionate relations with some men (actors Norman Kerry and André Daven) as based principally on narcissism, since these men bore a physical resemblance to the film star. What is most disturbing about Leider's biography is her explanations of the attacks on Valentino that followed the publication of Rambova's half-nude photos of the star in Nijinsky-like make-up and poses. Leider explains that the scandal caused by these photos resulted from their distorted and unsophisticated reception by a mass audience. "To many Americans, the photographs of him that highlighted his dance background disclosed effeminacy rather than primitive power and passion. Those who wanted to reduce him to a negative label couldn't be bothered with complexities. The idea that we all contain qualities that can be read as masculine or feminine, dominant or submissive, didn't enjoy wide currency. Neither did the notion that different cultures might define masculinity in different ways" (186). One might well ask what constitutes a negative label for Leider. She implies here that receptions of Valentino as "queer" or as a "fairy" were produced either by a bigoted or a degenerate audience, both incapable of culturally nuanced understandings of human sexuality and gender expression. Such explanations are excellent examples of how classism effectively works in the service of heteronormativity by marshalling representations of various pathological audiences. For an insightful consideration of how homophobia negotiates the historical archive, see Patricia White, "Black and White: Mercedes de Acosta's Glorious Enthusiasms," *Camera Obscura* 45 (2000): 227–64.

6. In reference to deviant gender expressions in *The Sheik*, Amy Lawrence writes, "The balance of savagery and gentlemanliness is what . . . allows an audience member to fine-tune a private orientalist fantasy to his or her heart's content." See "Rudolph Valentino: Italian American," in *Idols of Modernity: Movie Stars of the 1920s*, ed. Patrice Petro (New Brunswick, N.J.: Rutgers University Press, 2010), 95.

7. Anger, *Hollywood Babylon*, 107–14.

8. Morris, *Madam Valentino*, 264.

9. Judith Mayne, *Directed by Dorothy Arzner* (Bloomington: University of Indiana Press, 1994), 3.

10. See, for example, Patricia White, *Uninvited: Classical Hollywood Cinema and Lesbian Representability* (Bloomington: University of Indiana Press, 1999); and Lee Edelman, "Imagining the Homosexual: *Laura* and the Other Face of Gender," in *Homographesis: Essays in Gay Literary and Cultural Theory* (New York: Routledge, 1994): 192–241.

11. One of the more longstanding debates in the study of the American silent cinema has concerned the class composition of cinema audiences during the nickelodeon era. Manhattan has received the most sustained attention from film historians who continue to marshal city maps, census documents, telephone directories, photographs of theater fronts, and many other types of demographics in order to claim that this or that particular social class was the predominant audience for nickelodeon film exhibition in New York City. Much of this debate has recently been concerned with the proper place and interpretation of empirical evidence for attributing a particular social identity to an historical film audience. For a summary of these debates see the essays by Sumiko Hagashi, Robert Allen, and Ben Singer that are published as Dialogue, *Cinema Journal* 35, no. 3 (Summer 1996): 72–128. See also the collection of short essays on the state of film history edited and introduced by Simiko Higashi in "Film History, or the Baedeker Guide to the Film Historical Turn" *Cinema Journal* 44, no. 1 (Fall 2004): 94–143.

12. See, for example, Dyer, *Heavenly Bodies*; Richard Meyer, "Rock Hudson's Body," in *Inside/Out: Lesbian Theories, Gay Theories*, ed. Diana Fuss (New York: Routledge, 1991), 259–88; and Patricia White, "The Queer Career of Agnes Moorhead," in *Out in Culture: Gay, Lesbian, and Queer Essays on Popular Culture*, ed. Corey Creekmur and Alexander Doty (Durham, N.C.: Duke University Press, 1995), 91–114.

13. DeCordova, *Picture Personalities*, 143.

14. Morris, *Madam Valentino*, 110.

15. Gaylyn Studlar, "Valentino," 23–45; and Marjorie Garber, *Vested Interests: Cross-Dressing and Cultural Anxiety* (New York: Harper Collins, 1993).

16. Garber, *Vested Interests*, 356.

17. Ibid., 353–74. The important basic texts on femininity as masquerade are Joan Riviere, "Womanliness as Masquerade," *International Journal of Psycho-Analysis* 9 (1929): 303–13; and Jacques Lacan, "The Signification of the Phallus," in *Ecrits: A Selection*, trans. Alan Sheridan (New York: W. W. Norton, 1977), 281–91.

18. For a more radical view of masquerade and a critique of the binary construction of ontological gender see Judith Butler, *Gender Trouble: Feminism and the Subversion of Identity* (New York: Routledge, 1990); and D. N. Rodowick, *The Difficulty of Difference: Psychoanalysis, Sexual Difference, and Film Theory* (New York: Routledge, 1991).

19. The recent work of film historian Laura Horak has shown how the popular novelist and screenwriter Elinor Glyn shaped Valentino's star image during and after their collaboration on *Beyond the Rocks* (Famous Players-Lasky, 1922), with Glyn's interest in promoting European forms of sensuality contributing to Valentino's subsequent self-presentation. Ultimately, Horak's research suggests that these inscriptions of old world decadence helped contributed to emerging queer cultural forms in the United States to the extent that they failed to achieve credibility. Laura Horak, "'Would You Like to Sin

with Elinor Glyn?' Film as a Vehicle of Sensual Education" *Camera Obscura* 25, no. 74 (2010): 75–117.

20. Adela Rogers St. Johns, "What Kind of Men Attract Women the Most?" *Photoplay* 25 (Apr. 1924): 17.

21. In her work on the émigré film star Pola Negri, Diane Negra notes how the vamp figure innovated by Theda Bara "is too aware of her own commodity status" not to have disturbed conventional divisions between the gendered spheres of production and consumption (and, I would add, between reality and appearance). See her book, *Off-White Hollywood: American Culture and Ethnic Stardom* (London: Routledge, 2001), 55–83. It could be argued that Valentino is an inheritor of this part of the vamp's vanity and self-manufacture.

22. "Valentino Injunction," *Variety*, 6 Oct. 1922, 46; "Valentino Injunction Has Been Modified," *Variety*, 25 Jan. 1923, 47; and "Rodolph Not Allowed on Stage or Screen," *Variety*, 1 Feb. 1923, 46.

23. Advertisement for "An Immigrant Boy Who Became the Idol of America," *Photoplay* 23 (Jan. 1923): 35.

24. Ruth Waterbury, "Wedded and Parted, or, in Other Words, the Story of Natacha Rambova Valentino," *Photoplay* 23 (Dec. 1922): 118.

25. Press kit for *The Young Rajah* (Famous Players-Lasky, 1922), Copyright File, Division of Motion Pictures, Broadcast, and Recorded Sound, Library of Congress, Washington, D.C.

26. Waterbury, "Wedded and Parted," 118.

27. Gaylyn Studlar, "The Perils of Pleasure? Fan Magazine Discourse as Women's Commodified Culture in the 1920s," *Wide Angle* 13 (Jan. 1991): 6–33.

28. Waterbury, "Wedded and Parted," 58.

29. "An Open Letter from Valentino to the American Public," *Photoplay* 23 (Jan. 1923): 34.

30. See Chapter 1 of Alexander Doty, *Making Things Perfectly Queer: Interpreting Mass Culture* (Minneapolis: University of Minnesota Press, 1993), 1–16. See also Chris Straayer, *Deviant Eyes, Deviant Bodies: Sexual Re-Orientation in Film and Video* (New York: Columbia University Press, 1996).

31. Doty, *Making Things Perfectly Queer*, 15.

32. "The Vogue for Valentino," *Motion Picture Magazine* (Feb. 1923): 27.

33. Ibid., 28.

34. Ibid.

35. See Hansen, *Babel and Babylon*, 245–68.

36. Studlar, *This Mad Masquerade*, 172.

37. See Studlar, "Valentino." Studlar attempts to interpret Valentino's deviance in relation to the cultural reception of exotic dance in the 1910s and 1920s. The tango teas and Diaghilev's ballet become, for her, those sites at which ethnic otherness, effeminate masculinity, and decadence all merge into an attribution of deviant masculinity that is more or less definitive of "the woman-made man" who threatens white femininity, both sexually and racially. She also continues her claim about "the well-documented rejection of Valentino by American men," but in footnote 10 Studlar finds it necessary to claim that

she has "found no evidence of the rumors [about Valentino's sexual ambiguity] in any of my research."

38. See, for example, Chapter 2 of Stuart Ewen and Elizabeth Ewen, *Channels of Desire: Mass Images and the Shaping of American Consciousness* (Minneapolis: University of Minnesota Press, 1992), 23–51.

39. See, for example, Giorgio Bertellini's critique of this historical model and his excellent research on the complicated receptions of Valentino by Italian Americans living in New York City during the 1920s, particularly his discussion of the Italian-language newspapers that only turned their attention to the famous movie star at the moment of his death. "Duce/Divo: Masculinity, Racial Identity, and Politics Among Italian Americans in 1920s New York City," *Journal of Urban History* 31, no. 5 (July 2005): 685–726.

40. Hansen, *Babel and Babylon*, 263.

41. One way around the paucity of reception evidence is to consult the memories of people who had been part of a star's historical audience. In her study of women's reception of Hollywood stars during the 1940s and 1950s in Britain, Jackie Stacey used questionnaires sent to and returned by women who answered advertisements Stacey had placed in women's magazines. While such an approach faces several methodological difficulties, it does begin to get at the real diversity of historical reception. The possibility of producing such an investigation of the silent period is now impossible. See Jackie Stacey, *Star Gazing: Hollywood Cinema and Female Spectatorship* (London: Routledge, 1994).

42. For example, the massive Cecil B. DeMille archive established at Brigham Young University and the Hays Office files at the Academy of Motion Picture Arts and Sciences Library have both been made available to researchers within the last forty years.

43. Eve Kosofsky Sedgwick has pointed out how just the opposite could be true: "But to the extent that, as Freud argued and Foucault assumed, the distinctively sexual nature of human sexuality has to do precisely with its excess over or potential difference from the bare choreographies of procreation, 'sexuality' might be the very opposite of what we originally referred to as (chromosomal-based) sex: it could occupy, instead, even more than 'gender' the polar position of the relational, the social/symbolic, the constructed, the variable, the representation" (*Epistemology of the Closet*, 29).

44. George Chauncey, *Gay New York: Gender, Urban Culture, and the Making of the Gay Male World, 1890–1940* (New York: Basic Books, 1994), 54.

45. Ibid., 291–99.

46. George Chauncey, "Christian Brotherhood or Sexual Perversion? Homosexual Identities and the Construction of Boundaries in the World War One Era," *Journal of Social History* 19 (Winter 1985): 189–211.

47. Steiger and Mank, *Valentino*, 136.

48. Chauncey, *Gay New York*, 53–54.

49. Ibid., 33–41.

50. I am in no way attempting to idealize urban working-class milieus as somehow immune from homophobia. I am only pointing out that it was far easier for a man to wear flamboyant eye make-up in a cheap dance hall or on the street in the Bowery than it was for another a man to wear the same eye make-up in a boardroom or on the street in the Upper East Side.

51. Of course, today there are plenty of men who have regular and even exclusive sex with other men without self-identifying as homosexual. It is just more difficult for them to do so now, as is evidenced by the way these men were overlooked in those early HIV/AIDS interventions that were directed at gay men's sexual practices. The Center for Disease Control eventually switched its terminology from "gay men" to "men who have sex with other men."

52. Michel Foucault, *The History of Sexuality*, Vol. 1, trans. Robert Hurley (New York: Vintage Books, 1980), 101.

53. Nevertheless, Foucault does view the late nineteenth century as that moment when a single discourse on sexuality finally saturates of the social totality: "It can be said that [the end of the nineteenth century] was the moment when the deployment of 'sexuality,' elaborated in its more complex and intense forms, by and for the privileged classes, spread through the entire social body." See *History of Sexuality*, 121–22.

54. See Ellenberger, *The Valentino Mystique*, 43–60; Leider, *Dark Lover*, 379–87; Morris, *Madam Valentino*, 181–86; Oberfirst, *Rudolph Valentino*, 298–312; Shulman, *Valentino*, 317–19; Steiger and Mank, *Valentino*, 167–79; and Jack Scagnetti, *The Intimate Life of Rudolph Valentino* (Middle Village, N.Y.: Jonathan David Publishers, 1975), 106–19.

55. Morris, *Madam Valentino*, 181.

56. Garber, *Vested Interests*, 362.

57. *Chicago Sunday Tribune*, 28 July 1926, p. 10A.

58. For instance, see Herbert Howe's attack on Valentino that I discuss in Chapter 4.

59. See, for example, Ben Lindsey and Wainwright Evans, *The Revolt of Modern Youth* (New York: Boni and Liveright, 1925).

60. Other papers included the *New York Evening-Graphic*, the *Greenwich Village Weekly News*, and the *Broadway Tattler*. See Chauncey, *Gay New York*, 300, 321–24.

61. Sedgwick, *Between Men: English Literature and Male Homosocial Desire* (New York: Columbia University Press, 1985), 23. Emphasis in the original.

62. Walter Lippman, *Public Opinion* (New York: Macmillan, 1922). For an important analysis of Hollywood's participation in securing corporate forms of governance, see Mark Garrett Cooper, *Love Rules: Silent Hollywood and the Rise of the Managerial Class* (Minneapolis: University of Minnesota Press, 2003).

63. "Parlor pinks" was a term that referred to members of the petite bourgeoisie who were believed to hold either radical convictions or radical pretensions, depending on one's point of view.

64. As reported by Karsten Witte in "Fetisch-Messen: Notiz zu Kenneth Anger," *Frauen und Film* 38 (May 1985): 72–78. My translation.

65. Foucault's ideas about the practice of "effective history" can be found in "Neitzsche, Geneology, History," in *The Foucault Reader*, ed. Paul Rabinow (New York: Pantheon Books, 1984), 76–100.

66. Jennifer Terry, "Theorizing Deviant Historiography," *Differences* 3, no. 2 (1991): 56. Emphasis in original.

67. Also important here is Rancière's attempt to resurrect Jules Michelet's dream of the historian "delivering the voice of the poor" by making visible their place of silence.

Jacques Rancière, *The Names of History: On the Poetics of Knowledge*, trans. Hassan Melehy (Minneapolis: University of Minnesota Press, 1994).

68. For a good survey of effeminate male characters in silent film and a discussion of the sexism that authorized their ridicule, see Vito Russo, *The Celluloid Closet: Homosexuality and the Movies*, rev. ed. (New York: Harper and Row, 1985), 4–30.

69. See Chauncey, *Gay New York*, 301–29

70. David M. Lugowski, "Queering the (New) Deal: Lesbian and Gay Representation and the Depression-Era Cultural Politics of Hollywood's Production Code," *Cinema Journal* 38 (Winter 1999): 5.

71. Chauncey, *Gay New York*, 328.

72. See "The Motion Picture Code of 1930," in *The Movies in Our Midst: Documents in the Cultural History of Film in America*, ed. Gerald Mast (Chicago: University of Chicago Press, 1982), 321–33. On the relation between gender and state-sponsored representations of workers during the Depression, see Wendy Kozol, "Madonnas of the Field: Photography, Gender, and 1930s Farm Relief," *Genders* 2 (Summer 1988): 1–23.

73. On the PCA's role in creating textual ambiguity through its censorship activities, see Lea Jacobs, *The Wages of Sin: Censorship and the Fallen Woman Film, 1928–1942* (Berkeley: University of California Press, 1997).

74. See Robert K. Murray, *Red Scare: A Study in National Hysteria, 1919–1920* (Minneapolis: University of Minnesota Press, 1955).

75. Antonio Negri, "Keynes and the Capitalist Theory of the State," in *The Labor of Dionysus: A Critique of the State-Form*, Michael Hardt and Antonio Negri (Minneapolis: University of Minnesota Press, 1994), 26–27.

76. Hansen has analyzed Valentino's masochism in his performance style and film roles. See *Babel and Babylon*, 269–94.

77. All quotes in this paragraph are from "Valentino in New Roles," *Los Angeles Daily Times*, 8 Feb. 1923, sec. 2, pp. 1–2. See also, Inside Stuff on Pictures, *Variety*, 15 Feb. 1923, 46.

78. Steven J. Ross, *Working-Class Hollywood: Silent Film and the Shaping of Class in America* (Princeton, N.J.: Princeton University Press, 1998), 137. Quotations are from the shooting script of "Americanism," the original title of *Dangerous Hours*.

79. Program guide ([Spring 1999]: 3–4) for the Mary Pickford Theater, Library of Congress, Washington, D.C.

80. Brian Taves, Archival News, *Cinema Journal* 38 (Summer 1999): 112. Interestingly, Taves makes several factual errors in his short description of the extant films of Valentino. For example, he claims that *The Young Rajah* only survives as "a Czechoslovakian trailer," but the trailer for this film held by the Library of Congress is Italian (*Il Giovane Rajah*) with Italian intertitles, and it was generated from material held at the Cineteca Nazionale in Rome. Taves repeats this same mistake in his report in *Cinema Journal*. Flicker Alley and Turner Classic Movies have collaborated on a reconstruction of *The Young Rajah* from a very incomplete 16mm print and other materials. The reconstruction is part of the DVD release, *The Valentino Collection: Rediscovering and Icon of Silent Cinema* (Los Angeles: Flicker Alley, 2007).

81. Koszarski, *An Evening's Entertainment*, 301.

82. For a detailed account of these purchasing trips see Natacha Rambova, *Rudy: An Intimate Portrait of Rudolph Valentino by His Wife Natacha Rambova* (London: Hutchinson and Company, 1926), 73–127.

83. While the fan magazines stayed away from the more sensational aspects of these events which were relished by the newspapers and tabloids, Valentino's marriage complications were suggestively covered in photo spreads such as "The Wives of Rodolph " *Photoplay* 22 (November 1922): 68–69.

84. It should be noted that this description occurs in an intertitle at the end of the film when Rodrigo leaves Mary and Jack behind. In keeping with the ambiguity of love interests which structures the entire film, this description can just as easily be read as referring to Rodrigo's feelings for Jack.

85. See Gayle Rubin, "The Traffic in Women: Notes Toward a Political Economy of Sex," in *Toward an Anthropology of Women*, ed. Rayna Reiter (New York: Monthly Review Press, 1975), 157–210.

86. Sedgwick, *Between Men*, 25.

87. Hansen, *Babel and Babylon*, 269–81.

88. Julian Carter, "Normality, Whiteness, Authorship: Evolutionary Sexology and the Primitive Pervert," in *Science and Homosexualities*, ed. Vernon Rosario (New York: Routledge, 1997), 155–76.

89. Ibid., 165.

90. On the "indefinite nature" of primitive mentality see Lucien Lévy-Bruhl, *The "Soul" of the Primitive*, trans. Lillian Clare (New York: Macmillan, 1928). Arguing against the evolutionary essentialism of a primitive identity, Franz Boas nonetheless described primitive knowledge as more affective and more rooted in crude sense-impressions than the intellectual categories that define civilized European society (Franz Boas, *Mind of Primitive Man* [New York: Macmillan, 1911]).

91. Carter, "Normality, Whiteness," 165.

92. See also Julian B. Carter, *The Heart of Whiteness: Normal Sexuality and Race in America, 1880–1940* (Durham, N.C.: Duke University Press, 2007).

93. "In earlier years the mere physical and mechanical expansion of the industry was so swift that there was neither time nor mood to consider adequately the moral and educational responsibilities inherent in this new thing." Will H. Hays, "Supervision From Within," in Kennedy, *The Story of the Films*, 31.

94. The Library of Congress elected to show an incomplete 41-minute version of *Moran of Lady Letty* as part of their 1999 Valentino film series. At the screening on February 18, Brian Taves claimed that the screened print was the most complete version of the film in existence. There are, however, more complete versions currently available. For example, a nearly complete, 70-minute viewing print in 16mm exists at George Eastman House, Rochester, NY. Flicker Alley used a 67-minute 35mm print from a private European collection for their DVD release of *Moran of Lady Letty* as part of their 2007 *Valentino Collection*.

95. Because of Dalton's performance, *Moran* roughly corresponds to what Chris Straayer has termed the "trans-body" film that she contrasts with the "temporary transvestite film." In the temporary transvestite film, a character of one gender assumes the

clothes and manners of the opposite gender, allowing for a reading of any romantic exchanges involving that character as simultaneously homosexual and heterosexual. Such films usually depend, though, on a final casting-off of the assumed disguise so that the character's anatomical sex can assure gender certainty, heteronormalcy, and narrative closure. Trans-body films, on the other hand, "literalize in the image a gender inversion theory of homosexuality that collapses homosexuality with transexualism via the notion 'a women in a man's body' or vice versa. Because the trans-body plot is communicated through bodily gestures, poses, and actions, it is difficult to see the narratively implied heterosexuality in the visually implied homosexuality." Of course, *Moran* uses Valentino's seemingly inalienable effeminacy to re-establish a "visually implied heterosexuality" and thus we are faced with the possibility of multivalent homosexual/heterosexual reading within the trans-body film that is more radical (unresolvable) than those that typify the temporary transvestite film (Straayer, *Deviant Eyes,* 42–78).

96. Quoted in Shulman, *Valentino,* 180.

97. "Colorful News," *The New York Amsterdam News,* 1 Sept. 1926, pp. 1–2. See also the lengthy article by Kelly Miller comparing Eliot and Valentino that appeared in the paper's magazine section on the following week, "Harvard and Hollywood," *The New York Amsterdam News,* 8 Sept. 1926, sec. 3. In her defense of Valentino's value for the masses, Miller observed, "Eliot's life was consecrated to truth and service; in the lexicon of Valentino these terms did not exist."

98. "Actor Dies from Blows of Central Park Officer," *The New York Amsterdam News,* 1 Sept. 1926, p. 1.

99. Ibid.

CHAPTER 4

1. Quoted in Richard Grupenhoff, *The Black Valentino: The Stage and Screen Career of Lorenzo Tucker* (Metuchen, N.J.: Scarecrow Press, 1988), 66.

2. Valentino mentioned his own concerns about racial misrecognition in an interview early in his star career. Attempting to "transcribe a suggestion of the very charming Italian accent," the interviewer reported that Valentino claimed he was unable to sunbathe: "Now I cannot swim much at thees California beach, because I am very dark in complexion, an' the sun it burn me too black for pictures. I become like a neegroe." Gordon Gassaway, "The Erstwhile Landscape Gardener," *Motion Picture Magazine,* 20 (July 1921): 92.

3. Richard Dyer, "*The Son of the Sheik,*" in *Only Entertainment* (London: Routledge, 1992), 101. This article was originally written in 1982.

4. Additionally, there was growing popular interest in T. E. Lawrence and his participation in the Arab revolt against Turkey in 1917. Lawrence was almost always pictured donning Arab attire. In 1919 and 1920, news journalist Lowell Thomas helped promote the celebrity of the young British officer by touring with a film lecture about Lawrence's guerrilla activities in Palestine. Lowell Thomas, "The Matinée Idol of Arabia," *Asia and the Americas* 19 (Dec. 1919): 1205–13; and "The Modern Crusader." *The Picture Show* 2, no. 42 (21 Feb. 1920): 10.

5. Robert E. Park, "The City: Suggestions for the Investigation of Human Behavior in the Urban Environment," in *The City*, ed. Robert E. Park, Ernest W. Burgess, and Roderick D. McKenzie (Chicago: University of Chicago Press, 1970), 40–41.

6. Gaylyn Studlar, "Discourses of Gender and Ethnicity: The Construction and De(con)struction of Rudolph Valentino as Other," *Film Criticism* 13, no. 2 (1989): 23.

7. Studlar, *This Mad Masquerade*.

8. For satirical treatments of dance reformers' rhetoric, see Gregory Mason, "Satan in the Dance-hall," *The American Mercury* 2 (June 1924): 175–82; and " 'Trotting' to Perdition," *The Literary Digest* 80 (22 Mar. 1924): 30.

9. *New York Times*, 1 Mar. 1924, sec. 1, p. 5.

10. Paul Cressey, *The Taxi-Dance Hall* (Chicago: University of Chicago Press, 1932). Excerpts from this work were republished in *The Subcultures Reader*, ed. Ken Gelder and Sarah Thornton (New York: Routledge, 1997). This anthology places Chicago school sociology as an initial moment in the history of a critical tradition whose most recent manifestations are popular cultural studies and the work of the Birmingham Centre for Contemporary Cultural Studies. The University of Chicago Press republished Cressey's monograph in 2008.

11. All that remains of this projected work is a manuscript by Cressey at the Hoover Institute of War, Revolution, and Peace entitled "The Community—A Social Setting for the Motion Pictures." The manuscript has been published in Garth S. Jowett, Ian C. Jarvie, and Kathryn Fuller, *Children and the Movies: Media Influence and the Payne Fund Controversy* (New York: Cambridge University Press, 1996). The authors of *Children and the Movies* call Cressey "the unsung hero" of the Payne Studies and suggest that Cressey's "epiphany"—the idea that the social environment of the movie theater and the way that that environment was related to the larger context of young peoples' lives were more influential than the movies themselves—was a breakthrough insight that more fully connects the Payne Studies with current communication research and sociology. What I am arguing below is that Cressey's notions about how individuals make psychological adjustments to new urban social institutions were already a part of a popular understanding of mass culture and were inscribed in the address of mass cultural products like films and magazines, though Cressey was, perhaps, a privileged observer of this address and the experiences it entailed.

12. Cressey, *The Taxi-Dance Hall*, 51

13. Ibid.

14. Ibid., 90.

15. Ibid., 93–94

16. Richard Rodgers and Lorenz Hart, *The Rodgers and Hart Songbook: The Words and Music to Forty-Seven of Their Songs* (New York: Simon and Schuster, 1951). In 1931, Barbara Stanwyck and Ricardo Cortez starred in the romantic melodrama *Ten Cents a Dance* (Columbia) that was inspired by the Rodgers and Hart song, but the dangers faced by commercial dance-hall workers had already been the basis for the Joan Crawford film, *The Taxi Dancer* (MGM, 1927).

17. One such attack is the "Song of Hate" by Dick Dorgan in *Photoplay* 22, no. 1 (June 1922), reprinted and discussed by Hansen, *Babel and Babylon*, 258.

18. Herbert Howe, *Photoplay* 24, no. 4 (Sept. 1923): 58.

19. Letter from Vernette Akeley, *Photoplay* 22, no. 6 (Nov. 1922): 8, 10.

20. In an analysis of the historical development of photographic portraiture, Alan Trachtenberg compares the daguerreotype-based portraits from Matthew Brady's and Francis d'Avignon's *Gallery of Illustrious Americans* to the daguerreotypes made of South Carolina slaves that were commissioned by Harvard naturalist Louis Agassiz for anatomical study of racial characteristics. Trachtenberg attributes a paradoxical "presence-in-absence" to the stares of the slaves: "Without the public mask to mediate their encounter with the lens, the eyes of the enslaved African can only reveal the depth of their being—for, as naked, they are permitted no social persona. . . . Often we feel a similar effect in anonymous images found in old shops or studied in collections—an uncanny rapport with vibrant shadowy traces of persons on a silver-coated plate who continue to live in spite of stilted poses and stiffness." Alan Trachtenberg, *Reading American Photographs: Images as History, Matthew Brady to Walker Evans* (New York: Hill and Wang, 1989), 56. In the February 1923 edition of *Moving Picture Magazine*, Valentino was pronounced a "Phantom Rival in every virtuous domestic establishment" by an anonymous psychologist. "The Vogue of Valentino," *Moving Picture Magazine* (Feb. 1923): 27–29.

21. Walter Benjamin, "The Work of Art in the Age of Its Technological Reproducibility: Third Version," in *Walter Benjamin: Selected Writings*, vol. 4: 1938–1940, ed. Howard Eiland and Michael W. Jennings (Cambridge: Harvard University Press, 2002), 251–83. See especially note 15 on Raphael's *Sistine Madonna*.

22. Interestingly, Adorno attacks Benjamin's valorization of mass audiences by accusing him of a regression into superstition: "You have swept art out of the corners of taboo—but it is as though you feared a consequent inrush of barbarism (who could share your fear more than I?) and protected yourself by raising what you fear to a kind of inverse taboo." See his 2 August 1935 letter to Benjamin in *Aesthetics and Politics*, trans. Ron Taylor (London: Verso, 1980), 123. See also Carl Einstein, *Negerplastic* (Münich: K. Wolff, 1920).

23. Benjamin, "The Work of Art," 257–58.

24. Benjamin mentions specifically as examples "the split second of a stride" and "the movement of picking a cigarette lighter or a spoon." He also uses an anatomical observation to describe the coming together of art and science in cinematography: "Actually, if we think of a filmed action as neatly delineated within a particular situation—like a flexed muscle in a body—it is difficult to say which is more fascinating, its artistic value or its value for science." Benjamin, "The Work of Art," 265–66.

25. Béla Balázs, *Theory of the Film*, trans. Edith Bone (New York: Arno Press and The New York Times, 1972), 42.

26. For an extended analysis of the way in which an ethnographic gaze is imbricated with the historical development of the cinema, see Fatimah Tobing Rony, *The Third Eye: Race, Cinema, and Ethnographic Spectacle* (Durham, N.C.: Duke University Press, 1996).

27. *Stars of the Photoplay* (Chicago: Photoplay Magazine Publishing Company, 1924), n.p.

28. Sander L. Gilman, *Difference and Pathology* (Ithaca, N.Y.: Cornell University Press, 1985).

29. Frantz Fanon, *Black Skin, White Masks*, trans. Charles Lam Markmann (New York: Grove Press, 1968), 116. Emphasis in original.

30. Catherine A. Lutz and Jane L. Collins, *Reading National Geographic* (Chicago: University of Chicago Press, 1993), 24.

31. Another example of the juxtaposition of ethnography and popular amusement which is more contemporaneous with Valentino's stardom would be Flaherty's lyrical documentary of Inuit life, *Nanook of the North* (1922), considered one of the "Ten Best Pictures of 1922" by film critics for both major newspapers and motion picture magazines. This early ethnographic feature was consistently praised by these critics alongside fictional melodramas such as *Orphans of the Storm* (D. W. Griffith, Inc.), *The Prisoner of Zenda* (Metro), *Tol'able David* (Inspiration Pictures), and *Blood and Sand* (Famous Players-Lasky), all 1922 releases. See *Film Year Book 1922–1923* (New York: Wid's Films and Film Folks, 1923), 345–49.

32. A. M. Hassanein Bey, "Crossing the Untraversed Libyan Desert," *The National Geographic* 46, no. 3 (Sept. 1924): 237–38.

33. See Ella Shohat, "Gender and Culture of Empire: Toward a Feminist Ethnography of the Cinema," *Quarterly Review of Film and Video* 13, no. 1–3 (1991): 45–84; and Nick Browne, "American Film Theory in the Silent Period: Orientalism as an Ideological Form," *Wide Angle* 11, no. 4 (Oct. 1989): 23–31.

34. Benjamin, "The Work of Art," 253, 255.

35. *Photoplay* 22, no. 5 (Oct. 1922): 68.

36. For example, see Malek Alloula, *The Colonial Harem*, trans. Myna Godzich and Wlad Godzich (Minneapolis: University of Minnesota Press, 1986).

37. Ella Shohat and Robert Stam, *Unthinking Eurocentrism: Multiculturalism and the Media* (London: Routledge, 1994), 164. Lucy Fischer's article on Busby Berkeley is "The Image of Woman as Image: The Optical Politics of *Dames*," in *Sexual Stratagems: The World of Women in Film*, ed. Patricia Erens (New York: Horizon Press, 1979), 41–61.

38. Georges Bataille, *Inner Experience*, trans. Leslie Anne Boldt (Albany: State University of New York Press, 1988), 72.

39. Bataille's use of the bullfight as ritual violence is evident in his early pornographic novel, *Story of the Eye*, trans. Joachim Neugroschel (San Francisco: City Lights Books, 1987); and the short anthropological essay "The Sacred" in *Visions of Excess: Selected Writings, 1927–1939*, ed. Alan Stoekl, trans. Alan Stoekl, Carl R. Lovitt and Daniel M. Leslie Jr. (Minneapolis: University of Minnesota Press, 1985), 240–45. Edgar Morin characterizes the 1920s as the "glorious period" of star archetypes. "Before 1930 the star was not afraid to steep himself in death" (*The Stars*, 15).

40. For a discussion of the German reception of *Four Horsemen of the Apocalypse* as an anti-German film and the government's diplomatic attempts to halt the distribution of the film in Europe, see Thomas J. Saunders, "German Diplomacy and the War Film in the 1920s," in *Film and the First World War*, ed. Karel Dibbets and Bert Hogenkamp (Amsterdam: Amsterdam University Press, 1995), 213–22.

41. For an analysis of the rapid growth of a highly rationalized clerical and service work force during this period, see Harry Braverman, *Labor and Monopoly Capital: The Degradation of Work in the Twentieth Century* (New York: Monthly Review Press, 1974).

42. Kathy Peiss, *Cheap Amusements: Working Women and Leisure in Turn-of-the-Century New York* (Philadelphia: Temple University Press, 1986).

43. "Does Beauty Pay? Take a Look at These Two, Then Answer," *Cleveland Press*, 16, May 1922. Quoted in Hansen, *Babel and Babylon*, 245.

44. Hansen, *Babel and Babylon*, 260.

45. Quoted in Richard M. Ketchum, *Will Rogers: The Man and His Times* (New York: American Heritage Publishing, 1973), 202. Emphasis added.

46. Having avoided a potential scandal when Pickford divorced Owen Moore to marry Fairbanks in 1920, the couple became Hollywood's ideal couple and spokespersons. In the aftermath of the Arbuckle trials of 1920–1921 and the murder of director William Desmond Taylor in 1922, Fairbanks and Pickford threatened to leave the United States to make pictures elsewhere unless the press and public ceased spreading unfounded rumors about vice in the motion picture industry. See "Movies May Quit America If It Isn't Nice to Actors," *Syracuse Post-Standard*, 15 Feb. 1922.

47. Amy Lawrence has astutely described how Valentino's stardom and his labor were closely yoked to the production of himself as a photographic image in "Rudolph Valentino," 101–2.

CHAPTER 5

1. Friedrich Nietzsche, *Twilight of the Idols*, in *The Works of Friedrich Nietzsche, Vol. 11*, ed. Alexander Tille, trans. Thomas Common (New York: Macmillan, 1896), 166–67.

2. Randolph Bartlett, "Would You Have Ever Suspected It?" *Photoplay* 14, no. 3 (Aug. 1918): 43–44.

3. Pearl Gaddis, "The Dream That Came True," *Motion Picture Magazine* 12, no. 11 (Dec. 1916): 83. Scores of stars became producers during this period (1916–1920) with many owning their own companies. On the entry of women stars into the ranks of producers, see Karen Ward Mahar, *Women Filmmakers in Early Hollywood* (Baltimore, Md.: John Hopkins University Press, 2006), 154–78.

4. Gaddis, "The Dream That Came True," 84.

5. Shelley Stamp, "Lois Weber, Progressive Cinema, and the Fate of 'The Work-a-Day Girl' in *Shoes*," *Camera Obscura* 56 (2004): 141–69.

6. Ibid., 146.

7. Ibid., 164–65.

8. Bartlett, "Would You Have Ever Suspected It?" 45.

9. Walter Benjamin, "Unpacking My Library," in *Walter Benjamin: Selected Writings, Vol. 2, Part 2, 1938–1940*, ed. Howard Eiland and Michael W. Jennings (Cambridge: Harvard University Press, 2002), 491–92.

10. Anyone interested in this book collection can consult the list of 129 titles that were part of the probate records of Normand's estate at the time of her death in 1930. Like most personal libraries, Normand's was eclectic. According to the estate records, several contemporary writers were represented in Normand's book collection by multiple works: Aldous Huxley (six titles), Margaret Pedlar (six titles), Oscar Wilde (four titles), and Robert

Hichens (four titles). The library also contained several volumes of philosophy (such as Plato's *Republic*, Spinoza's *On the Improvement of the Understanding*, and Henri Bergson's *On Laughter*), erotic literature (such as Leopold von Sacher-Masoch's *Venus in Furs*, Arthur Schnitzler's *Hands Around*, Frank Wedekind's *Tragedies of Sex*, and T. R. Smith's 1927 collection of *Poetica Erotica*), autobiographies of stage performers (such as Sarah Bernhardt's *Memoirs of My Life*, Lillie Langtry's *The Days I Knew*, Constantine Stanislavsky's *My Life in Art*, and Marie Dressler's *The Life Story of an Ugly Duckling*), collections of poetry (such as *The Rubaiyat of Omar Khayyam*, individual volumes of poems by Elizabeth Barrett Browning and Rudyard Kipling, John A. Joyce's *Peculiar Poems*, and Frank Foxcroft's 1918 collection of *War Verse*), books on aesthetics and cultural criticism (such as Arthur Quiller-Couch's *On The Art of Reading*, Kenneth MacGowan and Robert E. Jones's *Continental Stage Craft*, and Gilbert Seldes's *The Seven Lively Arts*), as well as clothbound screenplays of films in which Normand had starred (such as J. G. Hawk's *Mickey* [scenario by Anita Loos] and Linton Wells's *Suzanna*). For the complete list of titles, see William Thomas Sherman, comp., *Mabel Normand: A Source Book to Her Life and Films*, rev. ed. (Seattle: William Thomas Sherman, 2000), 258–59.

11. Bartlett, "Would You Ever Have Suspected It?" 44.

12. Anne Morey, *Hollywood Outsiders: The Adaptation of the Film Industry, 1913–1934* (Minneapolis: University of Minnesota Press, 2003).

13. On the role that censorship practices played in depoliticizing the cinema during this period, see Lee Grieveson, "Not Harmless Entertainment: State Censorship and Cinema in the Transitional Era," in *American Cinema's Transitional Era: Audiences, Institutions, Practices*, ed. Charlie Kiel and Shelley Stamp (Berkeley: University of California Press, 2004), 265–84.

14. Studlar, "'Perils of Pleasure?" 15.

15. I agree with Richard deCordova that the early star system elaborated a process of perpetual revelation about the identity of the stars, but I am suggesting that it was not principally a truth-functional elaboration. While we can read the promotion of the early stars as the revelation of so many "secrets" about them, we can also read that same promotion as promising a continual flow of information about personalities that were under development within a modern media apparatus. Similarly, those semiotic and discursive processes of the star system identified by deCordova were never completely hidden or unremarked in early star discourse. I am offering this discussion of Mabel Normand's library in support the idea that the "will to knowledge" was only gradually imposed on the star system as a means of surveillance.

16. Grace Kingsley, "Tells of Visiting Taylor," *The Los Angeles Times*, 3 Feb. 1922, p. 2.

17. H. G. Salsinger, "Truth About Hollywood as Found by Reporter," *Detroit News*, 9 Feb. 1922, pp. 1, 3. For other newspaper clippings relating to this incident see the on-line newsletter *Taylorology* 6 (June 1993) at www.angelfire.com/az/Taylorology/.

18. Samuel Gayley Mortland, "The Ends of Literature," *Fresno Morning Republican*, 21 Feb. 1922, p. 4.

19. Betty Harper Fussell, *Mabel: Hollywood's First I-Don't-Care Girl* (New York: Limelight Editions, 1992), 110.

20. Ibid., 239.

21. Ibid., 110–11.

22. Once, after giving a presentation on Normand's library, I was approached by a well-known scholar who has published important and influential work on poststructuralist film theory, historiography, and film history. The scholar's first imploring question to me was, "Do you think Mabel Normand actually read Nietzsche and Freud?"

23. See the chapter on Louise Brooks in Amelie Hastie, *Cupboards of Curiosity: Women, Recollection, and Film History* (Durham, N.C.: Duke University Press, 2007), 104–54.

24. Less than two years after the Taylor murder, Normand was again involved in a highly publicized scandal when her chauffeur shot and seriously wounded wealthy socialite Courtland Dines, while Normand and Edna Purviance were guests at Dines's Los Angeles apartment.

25. Hastie, *Cupboards of Curiosity*, 130.

26. Ibid., 141–44.

27. Pierre Bourdieu, *Distinction: A Social Critique of Judgment*, trans. Richard Nice (Cambridge: Harvard University Press, 1984), 24–25.

28. In 1919, Mabel Normand had a peanut roaster installed in her dressing room. *Motion Picture Magazine* 17, no. 6 (July 1919): 86.

29. This has to do with the policing of authority through institutional certification and positioning. As film scholars we might easily read an essay by Freud and an article from the *Police Gazette* without ever having our discernment put into question, excepting, of course, those of us who teach in English departments where one still occasionally finds colleagues who look upon such mixing as intellectually unbecoming, if not unwholesome. No one has ever asked me if I have actually read Freud. My guess is that no one ever asked Normand if she actually read the *Police Gazette*.

30. These authors differed from the earlier authors of the Normand library in that they constitute what Michel Foucault has termed "founders of discursivity," writers who not only innovate or extend a discursive practice but ones who create the possibility of divergences or departures from the very discourses their authorships found. In other words, unlike traditional science and art, the works of Freud and Nietzsche make disruption and deviation a constitutive quality of the discursive field. See Paul Rabinow, ed., "What Is an Author?" in *The Foucault Reader*, trans. Josué V. Harari (New York: Pantheon, 1984), 101–20. The autumn before the Taylor murder scandal, Herbert Howe reported coming across copies of Nietzsche's *Thus Spake Zarathustra* and Freud's *The Interpretation of Dreams* among several other books lying on a reading table in Normand's private rooms at the Sennett studio. See his article from *Pantomime* (12 Oct. 1921) entitled, "The Diaries of Mabel Normand," reprinted in Sherman, *Mabel Normand*, 129.

31. While most fan magazines such as *Photoplay* and *Motion Picture Classic* were prepared weeks, if not months, before their appearance on the newsstand, *Movie Weekly* evidenced a much more timely relation to developments in the nation's newspaper during the 1920s, even as it followed the practice of other fan publications in refraining from di-

rectly mentioning most current Hollywood scandals. For example, the 23 September 1921, issue of *Movie Weekly* reported on Normand's return from a European trip, a return also reported in the nation's papers on 13 September. The report accompanies Normand's "own" account of her recent overseas experiences, and while much of the content of this piece may have been prepared far in advance of her arrival, the writing was obviously revised to seem as responsive to current headlines as possible. It seems clear that the advice Normand dispensed to young would-be screen actresses earlier that year in the pages of *Movie Weekly* was shaped to similar ends. More than most fan publications, *Movie Weekly* promoted itself as a sort of Hollywood tabloid. See, for example, Truman B. Handy's commissioned five-part weekly series on William Desmond Taylor's life that began in the 18 March 1921 issue.

32. Cari Beauchamp. *Without Lying Down: Frances Marion and the Powerful Women of Early Hollywood* (Berkeley: University of California Press, 1997). See also Amelie Hastie's discussion of Pickford's advice column in *Cupboards of Curiosity*, 158–64.

33. Sherman, *Mabel Normand*, 265.

34. Mabel Normand, "How to Get into the Movies, Part IV," *Movie Weekly*, 11 Mar. 1922, 11.

35. Mabel Normand, "How to Get into the Movies, Part VI," *Movie Weekly*, 25 Mar. 1922, 11.

36. *Cincinnati Commercial Tribune*, 24 Feb. 1922, p. 6.

37. Rob King, *The Fun Factory: The Keystone Film Company and the Emergence of Mass Culture* (Berkeley: University of California Press, 2009), 238–40.

38. Ibid. See in particular King's discussion of Mary Thurman on pages 237–39. Since King is providing a history of the studio he is rightly discussing reification as an effect of a production process that was seeking the expansion and control of a market. I am discussing here the necessary failure of those very processes at sites of reception.

39. For an important consideration of both the early twentieth-century artist model as laborer and her appearance within the terrain of queer receptions, see Cynthia Chris, "Audrey Munson on Film: Purity in an Age of Censorship," in *"Queen of the Artists' Studio": The Story of Audrey Munson,* ed. Andrea Geyer (New York, Art in General, 2007), 79–86.

40. For example, such was the impetus behind *Middletown*, the much discussed and influential sociological study of daily life in an "average" American town during the 1920s: "Like the automobile and the radio, the movies, by breaking up leisure time into an individual, family, or other small group affair, represent a counter movement to the trend toward organization so marked in clubs and other leisure-time pursuits." Robert S. Lynd and Helen Merrell Lynd, *Middletown: A Study in Modern American Culture* (New York: Harcourt, Brace, and World, 1929), 265.

41. See Jowett et al., *Children at the Movies*, 1–121.

42. Ibid., 84–88.

43. Cressey's manuscript is republished in Jowett et al., *Children at the Movies*, 133–216.

44. Ibid., 199–200.

45. Ibid., 180–91.

46. For in-depth discussions of the relations of the Payne Fund studies to audience regulation and the formation of both communication studies and film studies, see Grieveson, "Cinema Studies and the Conduct of Conduct"; and Mark Lynn Anderson, "Taking Liberties: The Payne Fund Studies and the Creation of the Media Expert," both in *Inventing Film Studies*, ed. Lee Grieveson and Haidee Wasson (Durham, N.C.: Duke University Press, 2008), 3–37 and 38–65, respectively.

BIBLIOGRAPHY

ARCHIVES

Chicago Historical Society, Chicago, Ill. The Hal Higdon research papers and the Nathan F. Leopold papers, 1924 to 1970.

International Museum of Photography and Film at the George Eastman House, Rochester, N.Y.

Manuscript Division, Library of Congress, Washington, D.C.

Margaret Herrick Library, Academy of Motion Picture Arts and Sciences, Los Angeles, Calif.

Motion Picture, Broadcasting, and Recorded Sound Division, Library of Congress, Washington, D.C.

BOOK AND JOURNAL SOURCES

Adorno, Theodor. "Letters to Benjamin." In *Aesthetics and Politics,* translated by Ron Taylor, 110–33. London: Verso, 1980.

———. *Minima Moralia: Reflections from Damaged Life.* Translated by E.F.N. Jephcott. London: Verso, 1993.

Allen, Frederick Lewis. *Only Yesterday: An Informal History of the Nineteen Twenties* New York: Harper and Row, 1931.

Alloula, Malek. *The Colonial Harem.* Translated by Myna Godzich and Wlad Godzich. Minneapolis: University of Minnesota Press, 1986.

Anderson, Mark Lynn. "Taking Liberties: The Payne Fund Studies and the Creation of the Media Expert." In *Inventing Film Studies,* edited by Lee Grieveson and Haidee Wasson, 38–65. Durham, N.C.: Duke University Press, 2008.

———. "Tempting Fate, or, the Secretary as Producer." In *Looking Past the Screen: Case Studies in American Film History and Method*, edited by Jon Lewis and Eric Smoodin, 117–50. Durham, N.C.: Duke University Press, 2007.

Anger, Kenneth. *Hollywood Babylon*. San Francisco: Straight Arrow Books, 1975.

Balázs, Béla. *Theory of the Film*. Translated by Edith Bone. New York: Arno Press and The New York Times, 1972.

Bataille, Georges. *Inner Experience*. Translated by Leslie Anne Boldt. Albany: State University of New York Press, 1988.

———. "The Sacred." In *Visions of Excess: Selected Writings, 1927–1939*, edited by Alan Stoekl; translated by Alan Stoekl, Carl R. Lovitt, and Daniel M. Leslie Jr., 240–45. Minneapolis: University of Minnesota Press, 1985.

———. *Story of the Eye*, translated by Joachim Neugroschel. San Francisco: City Lights Books, 1987.

Beauchamp, Cari. *Without Lying Down: Frances Marion and the Powerful Women of Early Hollywood*. Berkeley: University of California Press, 1997.

Benjamin, Walter. "Unpacking My Library." In *Walter Benjamin: Selected Writings. Vol. 2, Part 2, 1938–1940*, edited by Howard Eiland and Michael W. Jennings, 491–92. Cambridge: Harvard University Press, 2002.

———. "The Work of Art in the Age of Its Technological Reproducibility: Second Version." In *Walter Benjamin: Selected Writings. Vol. 3, 1935–1938*, edited by Howard Eiland and Michael W. Jennings, 101–33. Cambridge: Harvard University Press, 2002.

———. "The Work of Art in the Age of Its Technological Reproducibility: Third Version." In *Walter Benjamin: Selected Writings. Vol. 4, 1938–1940*, edited by Howard Eiland and Michael W. Jennings, 251–83. Cambridge: Harvard University Press, 2002.

Bertellini, Giorgio. "Duce/Divo: Masculinity, Racial Identity, and Politics Among Italian Americans in 1920s New York City." *Journal of Urban History* 31, no. 5 (July 2005): 685–726.

Blumer, Herbert, and Philip M. Hauser. *Movies, Delinquency, and Crime*. New York: Macmillan Co., 1933.

Boas, Franz. *Mind of Primitive Man*. New York: Macmillan Co., 1911.

Bodeen, Dewitt. *From Hollywood: The Careers of 15 Great American Stars*. South Brunswick, N.J.: A. S. Barnes, 1976.

———. "Wallace Reid Was an Idol in the Age of Innocence with Feet of Clay." *Films in Review* 17 (April 1966): 205–20.

Bourdieu, Pierre. *Distinction: A Social Critique of Judgment*, translated by Richard Nice. Cambridge: Harvard University Press, 1984.

Bowser, Eileen. *The Transformation of the Cinema, 1907–1915. Vol. 2. History of the American Cinema*. Berkeley: University of California Press, 1994.

Braverman, Harry. *Labor and Monopoly Capital: The Degradation of Work in the Twentieth Century*. New York: Monthly Review Press, 1974.

Bret, David. *Valentino: A Dream of Desire*. London: Robson Books, 1998.

Browne, Nick. "American Film Theory in the Silent Period: Orientalism as an Ideological Form." *Wide Angle* 11, no. 4 (October 1989): 23–31.

Brownlow, Kevin. *Behind the Mask of Innocence: The Social Problem Films of the Silent Era*. New York: Alfred A. Knopf, 1990.

Butler, Judith. *Gender Trouble: Feminism and the Subversion of Identity*. New York: Routledge, 1990.

Carter, Julian B. *The Heart of Whiteness: Normal Sexuality and Race in America, 1880–1940*. Durham, N.C.: Duke University Press, 2007.

———. "Normality, Whiteness, Authorship: Evolutionary Sexology and the Primitive Pervert." In *Science and Homosexualities*, edited by Vernon Rosario, 155–76. New York: Routledge, 1997.

Chauncey, George. "Christian Brotherhood or Sexual Perversion? Homosexual Identities and the Construction of Boundaries in the World War One Era." *Journal of Social History* 19 (Winter 1985): 189–211.

———. *Gay New York: Gender, Urban Culture, and the Making of the Gay Male World, 1890–1940*. New York: Basic Books, 1994.

Chris, Cynthia. "Audrey Munson on Film: Purity in an Age of Censorship." In *"Queen of the Artists' Studio": The Story of Audrey Munson*, Andrea Geyer, 79–86. New York: Art in General, 2007.

Clark, Danae. *Negotiating Hollywood: The Cultural Politics of Actor's Labor*. Minneapolis: University of Minnesota Press, 1995.

Cooke, Alistair. *Douglas Fairbanks: The Making of a Screen Character*. New York: Museum of Modern Art, 1940.

Cooper, Mark Garrett. *Love Rules: Silent Hollywood and the Rise of the Managerial Class*. Minneapolis: University of Minnesota Press, 2003.

Courtwright, David T. *Dark Paradise: Opiate Addiction in America Before 1940*. Cambridge: Harvard University Press, 1982.

Cressey, Paul. *The Taxi-Dance Hall*. Chicago: University of Chicago Press, 1932.

"The Crime and Trial of Loeb and Leopold." *The Journal of Abnormal Psychology and Social Psychology* 19, no. 3 (October–December, 1924): 223–29.

DeBauche, Leslie Midkiff. *Reel Patriotism: The Movies and the First World War*. Madison: University of Wisconsin Press, 1997.

deCordova, Richard. *Picture Personalities: The Emergence of the Star System in America*. Urbana: University of Illinois Press, 1990.

Doherty, Thomas. *Pre-Code Hollywood: Sex, Immorality, and Insurrection in American Cinema, 1930–1934*. New York: Columbia University Press, 1999.

Doty, Alexander. *Making Things Perfectly Queer: Interpreting Mass Culture*. Minneapolis: University of Minnesota Press, 1993.

Dyer, Richard. "The Colour of Virtue: Lillian Gish, Whiteness and Femininity." In *Women and Film*, edited by Pam Cook and Philip Dodd, 1–9. Philadelphia: Temple University Press, 1993.

———. *Heavenly Bodies: Film Stars and Society*. New York: St. Martins Press, 1986.

———. "The Son of the Sheik." In *Only Entertainment*, 99–102. London: Routledge, 1992.

———. *Stars*. London: BFI Publishing, 1979.

———. "Whiteness." *Screen* 29, no. 4 (Autumn 1988): 44–65.

Edelman, Lee. "Imagining the Homosexual: *Laura* and the Other Face of Gender." In *Homographesis: Essays in Gay Literary and Cultural Theory*, 192–41. New York: Routledge, 1994.

Edmonds, Andy. *Frame-Up! The Untold Story of Roscoe "Fatty" Arbuckle*. New York: William Morrow, 1991.

Einstein, Carl. *Negerplastic*. München: K. Wolff, 1920.

Ellenberger, Allan R. *The Valentino Mystique: The Death and Afterlife of the Silent Film Idol*. Jefferson, N.C.: McFarland, 2005.

Ewen, Stuart, and Elizabeth Ewen. *Channels of Desire: Mass Images and the Shaping of American Consciousness*. Minneapolis: University of Minnesota Press, 1992.

Fanon, Frantz. *Black Skin, White Masks*. Translated by Charles Lam Markmann. New York: Grove Press, 1968.

Fass, Paula. "Making and Remaking an Event: The Leopold and Loeb Case in American Culture." *The Journal of American History* 80, no. 3 (December 1993): 919–51.

Film Year Book 1922–1923. New York: Wid's Films and Film Folks, 1923.

Fischer, Lucy. "The Image of Woman as Image: The Optical Politics of *Dames*." In *Sexual Stratagems: The World of Women in Film*, edited by Patricia Erens, 41–61. New York: Horizon Press, 1979.

Fleming, E. J. *Wallace Reid: The Life and Death of a Hollywood Idol*. Jefferson, N.C.: MacFarland and Co., 2007.

Foucault, Michel. *The History of Sexuality*. Vol. 1. Translated by Robert Hurley. New York: Vintage Books, 1980.

———. "Neitzsche, Geneology, History," translated by Donald F. Bouchard and Sherry Simon. In *The Foucault Reader*, edited by Paul Rabinow, 76–100. New York: Pantheon Books, 1984.

———. "What Is an Author?" translated by Josué V. Harari. In *The Foucault Reader*, edited by Paul Rabinow, 101–20. New York: Pantheon, 1984.

Freedman, Estelle. "'Uncontrollable Desires': The Response to the Sexual Psychopath 1920–1960." *Journal of American History* 74, no. 1 (June 1987): 103–4.

Freud, Sigmund. "The Psychogenesis of a Case of Homosexuality in a Woman," translated by Barbara Low and R. Garber. In *Sexuality and the Psychology of Love*, 147–48. New York: Macmillan Co., 1963.

———. "A Special Type of Object Choice Made by Men," translated by Joan Riviere. In *Sexuality and the Psychology of Love*, 49–58. New York: Macmillan Co., 1963.

———. *Three Essays on the Theory of Sexuality*, translated by James Strachey. New York: Basic Books, 2000.

Fussell, Betty Harper. *Mabel: Hollywood's First I-Don't-Care Girl*. New York: Limelight Editions, 1992.

Garber, Marjorie. *Vested Interests: Cross-Dressing and Cultural Anxiety*. New York: HarperCollins, 1993.

Gelder, Ken, and Sarah Thorton, eds. *The Subcultures Reader*. New York: Routledge, 1997.

Gilman, Sander L. *Difference and Pathology*. Ithaca, N.Y.: Cornell University Press, 1985.

Giroux, Robert. *A Deed of Death*. New York: Knopf, 1990.

Grieveson, Lee. "Cinema Studies and the Conduct of Conduct." In *Inventing Film Studies*, edited by Lee Grieveson and Haidee Wasson, 3–37. Durham, N.C.: Duke University Press, 2008.

———. "Not Harmless Entertainment: State Censorship and Cinema in the Transitional Era." In *American Cinema's Transitional Era: Audiences, Institutions, Practice*s, edited by Charlie Kiel and Shelley Stamp, 265–84. Berkeley: University of California Press, 2004.

Grupenhoff, Richard. *The Black Valentino: The Stage and Screen Career of Lorenzo Tucker*. Metuchen, N.J.: Scarecrow Press, 1988.

Hale, Nathan G. Jr. *The Rise and Crisis of Psychoanalysis in the United States: Freud and the Americas, 1917–1985*. New York: Oxford University Press, 1995.

Hampton, Benjamin B. *A History of the Movies*. New York: Cocici, Friede Publishers, 1931.

Hansen, Miriam. *Babel and Babylon: Spectatorship in the American Silent Cinema*. Cambridge: Harvard University Press, 1991.

Hassanein Bey, A. M. "Crossing the Untraversed Libyan Desert." *The National Geographic* 46, no. 3 (September 1924): 237–38.

Hastie, Amelie. *Cupboards of Curiosity: Women, Recollection, and Film History*. Durham, N.C.: Duke University Press, 2007.

Healy, William. *The Individual Delinquent*. Boston: Little, Brown, 1915.

Higashi, Simiko, ed. "Film History, or the Baedeker Guide to the Film Historical Turn." *Cinema Journal* 44, no.1 (Fall 2004): 94–143.

Higdon, Hal. *Crime of the Century: The Leopold and Loeb Case*. New York: G. P. Putnam's Sons, 1975.

Horak, Laura. "'Would You Like to Sin with Elinor Glyn?': Film as a Vehicle of Sensual Education." *Camera Obscura* 74 (2010): 74–117.

Irvine, Janice. "From Difference to Sameness: Gender Ideology in Sexual Science." *The Journal of Sex Research* 27, no. 1 (February 1990): 1–24.

Jacobs, Lea. *The Decline of Sentiment: American Film in the 1920s*. Berkeley: University of California Press, 2008.

———. *The Wages of Sin: Censorship and the Fallen Woman Film, 1928–1942*. Berkeley: University of California Press, 1997.

Jowett, Garth. *Film: The Democratic Art*. Boston: Little, Brown and Co., 1976.

Jowett, Garth S., Ian C. Jarvie, and Kathryn Fuller. *Children and the Movies: Media Influence and the Payne Fund Controversy*. New York: Cambridge University Press, 1996.

Kennedy, Joseph P., ed. *The Story of the Films*. Chicago: A. W. Shaw Company, 1927.

Ketchum, Richard M. *Will Rogers: The Man and His Times*. New York: American Heritage Publishing, 1973.

King, Rob. *The Fun Factory: The Keystone Film Company and the Emergence of Mass Culture*. Berkeley: University of California Press, 2009.

Kirby, Lynne. "Male Hysteria and Early Cinema." *Camera Obscura* 17 (May 1988): 113–31.

———. *Parallel Tracks: The Railroad and Silent Cinema*. Durham, N.C.: Duke University Press, 1997.

Kirkpatrick, Sidney D. *A Cast of Killers*. New York: E. P. Dutton, 1986.

Kolb, Lawrence. "Types and Characteristics of Drug Addicts." *Mental Hygiene* 9 (1925): 303–13.

Koszarski, Richard. *An Evening's Entertainment: The Age of the Silent Feature Picture, 1915–1928. Vol. 3. History of the American Cinema*. Berkeley: University of California Press, 1994.

Kozol, Wendy. "Madonnas of the Field: Photography, Gender, and 1930s Farm Relief." *Genders* 2 (Summer 1988): 1–23.

Lacan, Jacques. "The Signification of the Phallus." In *Ecrits: A Selection*, translated by Alan Sheridan, 281–91. New York: W. W. Norton, 1977.

Lawrence, Amy. "Rudolph Valentino: Italian American." In *Idols of Modernity: Movie Stars of the 1920s*, edited by Patrice Petro. New Brunswick, N.J.: Rutgers University Press, 2010.

Leider, Emily W. *Dark Lover: The Life and Death of Rudolph Valentino*. New York: Farrar, Straus, and Giroux, 2003.

Levin, Meyer. *Compulsion*. New York: Pocket Books, 1957.

Lévy-Bruhl, Lucien. *The "Soul" of the Primitive*. Translated by Lilian Clare. New York: The Macmillan Co., 1928.

Lies, Eugene T. "Constructive Play as a Preventative of Narcotic Addiction." In *Narcotic Education*, edited by H. S. Middlemiss, 130–36. Washington, D.C.: H. S. Middlemiss, 1926.

Lindsey, Ben, and Wainwright Evans. *The Revolt of Modern Youth*. New York: Boni and Liveright, 1925.

Lippman, Walter. *Public Opinion*. New York: Macmillan Co., 1922.

"The Loeb–Leopold Murder of Franks in Chicago, May 21, 1924." *Journal of the American Institute of Criminal Law and Criminology* 24 (November 1924): 380–87.

Logan, Josh. *Never the Sinner*. Woodstock, N.Y.: Overlook, 1999.

Long, Bruce. *William Desmond Taylor: A Dossier*. New York: Scarecrow, 1991.

Loos, Anita. *Gentlemen Prefer Blondes*. New York: Grosset & Dunlap, 1925.

Lugowski, David M. "Queering the (New) Deal: Lesbian and Gay Representation and the Depression-Era Cultural Politics of Hollywood's Production Code." *Cinema Journal* 38 (Winter 1999): 3–35.

Lutz, Catherine A., and Jane L. Collins. *Reading National Geographic*. Chicago: University of Chicago Press, 1993.

Lynd, Robert S., and Helen Merrell Lynd. *Middletown: A Study in Modern American Culture*. New York: Harcourt, Brace, and World, 1929.

Mahar, Karen Ward. *Women Filmmakers in Early Hollywood*. Baltimore, Md.: Johns Hopkins University Press, 2006.

Mason, Gregory. "Satan in the Dance-hall." *The American Mercury* 2 (June 1924): 175–82.

May, Lary. *Screening Out the Past: The Birth of Mass Culture and the Motion Picture Industry*. Chicago: University of Chicago Press, 1983.

Mayne, Judith. *Cinema and Spectatorship*. London: Routledge, 1993.

———. *Directed by Dorothy Arzner*. Bloomington: University of Indiana Press, 1994.

McKernan, Maureen, ed. *The Amazing Crime and Trial of Leopold and Loeb*. Chicago: Plymouth Court Press, 1924.

McLean, Adrienne L. *Being Rita Hayworth: Labor, Identity, and Hollywood Stardom*. New Brunswick, N.J.: Rutgers University Press, 2005.

Meyer, Richard. "Rock Hudson's Body." In *Inside/Out: Lesbian Theories, Gay Theories*, edited by Diana Fuss, 259–88. New York: Routledge, 1991.

Miller, D. A. "Anal *Rope*." In *Inside/Out: Lesbian Theories, Gay Theories*, edited by Diana Fuss, 119–41. New York: Routledge, 1991.

Mitry, Jean. "Thomas H. Ince: His Esthetic, His Films, His Legacy," translated by Martin Sopocy and Paul Attallah. *Cinema Journal* 22 (Winter 1983): 2–25.

Miyao, Daisuke. *Sessue Hayakawa: Silent Cinema and Transnational Stardom*. Durham, N.C.: Duke University Press, 2007.

Morely, Raymond. *The Hays Office*. Indianapolis: Bobbs-Merrill Company, 1945.

Morey, Anne. *Hollywood Outsiders: The Adaptation of the Film Industry, 1913–1934*. Minneapolis: University of Minnesota Press, 2003.

Morin, Edgar. *The Stars*. Translated by Richard Howard. Minneapolis: University of Minnesota Press, 2005.

Morris, Michael. *Madam Valentino: The Many Lives of Natacha Rambova*. New York: Abbeville Press, 1991.

"The Motion Picture Code of 1930." In *The Movies in Our Midst: Documents in the Cultural History of Film in America*, edited by Gerald Mast, 321–33. Chicago: University of Chicago Press, 1982.

Murray, Robert K. *Red Scare: A Study in National Hysteria, 1919–1920*. Minneapolis: University of Minnesota Press, 1955.

Negra, Diane. *Off-White Hollywood: American Culture and Ethnic Stardom*. London: Routledge, 2001.

Negri, Antonio. "Keynes and the Capitalist Theory of the State." In *The Labor of Dionysus: A Critique of the State-Form*, Michael Hardt and Antonio Negri, 23–51. Minneapolis: University of Minnesota Press, 1994.

Nietzsche, Friedrich. *The Works of Friedrich Nietzsche*. Edited by Alexander Tille; translated by Thomas Common. New York: Macmillan Co., 1896.

Oberfirst, Robert. *Rudolph Valentino: The Man Behind the Myth*. New York: The Citadel Press, 1962.

Park, Robert E. "The City: Suggestions for the Investigation of Human Behavior in the Urban Environment." In *The City*, edited by Robert E. Park, Ernest W. Burgess, and Roderick D. McKenzie, 1–46. Chicago: University of Chicago Press, 1970.

Parssinen, Terry M. *Secret Passions, Secret Remedies: Narcotics Drugs in British Society 1820–1930*. Philadelphia: Institute for the Study of Human Issues, 1983.

Peiss, Kathy. *Cheap Amusements: Working Women and Leisure in Turn-of-the-Century New York*. Philadelphia: Temple University Press, 1986.

Pfister, Joel. "Glamorizing the Psychological: The Politics of the Performances of Modern Psychological Identities." In *Inventing the Psychological: Toward a Cultural History of*

Emotional Life in America, edited by Joel Pfister and Nancy Schnog, 167–213. New Haven, Conn.: Yale University Press: 1997.

Potter, Holly. "Leopold and Loeb: Texts and Contexts of an American Cause Célèbre." Master's thesis, McGill University, Montreal, 1991.

Rambova, Natacha. *Rudy: An Intimate Portrait of Rudolph Valentino by His Wife Natacha Rambova*. London: Hutchinson and Co., 1926.

Rancière, Jacques. "The Misadventures of Critical Thought." In *The Emancipated Spectator*, translated by Greg Eliot, 25–49. London: Verso, 2009

———. *The Names of History: On the Poetics of Knowledge*. Translated by Hassan Melehy. Minneapolis: University of Minnesota Press, 1994.

Reid, Bertha Westbrook. *Wallace Reid: His Life Story*. New York: Sorg Publishing Co., 1923.

Riviere, Joan. "Womanliness as Masquerade." *International Journal of Psycho-Analysis* 9 (1929): 303–13.

Rodgers, Richard, and Lorenz Hart. *The Rodgers and Hart Songbook: The Words and Music to Forty-Seven of Their Songs*. New York: Simon and Schuster, 1951.

Rodowick, D. N. *The Difficulty of Difference: Psychoanalysis, Sexual Difference, and Film Theory*. New York: Routledge, 1991.

Rony, Fatimah Tobing. *The Third Eye: Race, Cinema, and Ethnographic Spectacle*. Durham, N.C.: Duke University Press, 1996.

Ross, Steven J. *Working-Class Hollywood: Silent Film and the Shaping of Class in America*. Princeton, N.J.: Princeton University Press, 1998.

Rubin, Gayle. "The Traffic in Women: Notes Toward a Political Economy of Sex." In *Toward an Anthropology of Women*, edited by Rayna Reiter, 157–210. New York: Monthly Review Press, 1975.

Russo, Vito. *The Celluloid Closet: Homosexuality and the Movies*. Rev. ed. New York: Harper and Row, 1985.

Saunders, Thomas J. "German Diplomacy and the War Film in the 1920s." In *Film and the First World War*, edited by Karel Dibbets and Bert Hogenkamp, 213–22. Amsterdam: Amsterdam University Press, 1995.

Scagnetti, Jack. *The Intimate Life of Rudolph Valentino*. Middle Village, N.Y.: Johnathan David Publishers, 1975.

Sedgwick, Eve Kosofsky. *Between Men: English Literature and Male Homosocial Desire*. New York: Columbia University Press, 1985.

———. *Epistemology of the Closet*. Berkeley: University of California, 1990.

Sellers, Alvin V. *The Loeb-Leopold Case*. Brunswick, Ga.: Classic Publishing, 1926.

Sergeant, Elizabeth Shepley and E. O. Hoppé. *Fire Under the Andes: A Group of North American Portraits*. New York: Knopf 1927.

Sherman, William Thomas, comp. *Mabel Normand: A Source Book to Her Life and Films*. Rev. ed. Seattle: William Thomas Sherman, 2000.

Shohat, Ella. "Gender and Culture of Empire: Toward a Feminist Ethnography of the Cinema." *Quarterly Review of Film and Video* 13, no. 1–3 (1991): 45–84.

Shohat, Ella, and Robert Stam. *Unthinking Eurocentrism: Multiculturalism and the Media*. London: Routledge, 1994.

Shulman, Irving. *Valentino*. New York: Trident Press, 1967.

Shuttleworth, Frank K., and Mark A. May. *The Social Conduct and Attitudes of Movie Fans*. New York: Macmillan Co., 1933.

Silverman, Kaja. *Male Subjectivity at the Margins*. New York: Routledge, 1992.

Sklar, Robert. *Movie-Made America: A Cultural History of the Movies*. New York: Viking Books, 1975.

Snead, James. *White Screens/Black Images*. Edited by Colin MacCabe and Cornell West. New York: Routledge, 1994.

Stacey, Jackie. *Star Gazing: Hollywood Cinema and Female Spectatorship*. London: Routledge, 1994.

Staiger, Janet. *Interpreting Films: Studies in the Historical Reception of American Cinema*. Princeton, N.J.: Princeton University Press, 1992.

———. "Seeing Stars." In *Stardom: Industry of Desire*, edited by Christine Gledhill, 3–16. London: Routledge, 1991.

Stamp, Shelley. "Lois Weber, Progressive Cinema, and the Fate of 'The Work-a-Day Girl' in *Shoes*." *Camera Obscura* 56 (2004): 141–69.

Stars of the Photoplay. Chicago: Photoplay Magazine Publishing Company, 1924.

Steiger, Brad, and Chaw Mank. *Valentino: An Intimate and Shocking Exposé*. New York: MacFadden Books, 1966.

Stoloff, Sam. "Fatty Arbuckle and the Black Sox: The Paranoid Style of American Popular Culture, 1919–1922." In *Headline Hollywood: A Century of Film Scandal*, edited by Adrienne L. McLean and David Cook, 52–82. New Brunswick, N.J.: Rutgers University Press, 2001.

Straayer, Chris. *Deviant Eyes, Deviant Bodies: Sexual Re-Orientation in Film and Video*. New York: Columbia University Press, 1996.

Studlar, Gaylyn. "Discourses of Gender and Ethnicity: The Construction and De(con) struction of Rudolph Valentino as Other." *Film Criticism* 13, no. 2 (1989): 18–35.

———. "The Perils of Pleasure? Fan Magazine Discourse as Women's Commodified Culture in the 1920s." *Wide Angle* 13 (January 1991): 6–33.

———. *This Mad Masquerade: Stardom and Masculinity in the Jazz Age*. New York: Columbia University Press, 1996.

———. "Valentino, 'Optical Intoxication,' and Dance Madness." In *Screening the Male: Exploring Masculinities in Hollywood Film*, edited by Steve Cohan and Ina Rae Hark, 23–45. New York: Routledge, 1993.

Terry, Jennifer. "Theorizing Deviant Historiography." *Differences* 3, no. 2 (1991): 55–74.

Trachtenberg, Alan. *Reading American Photographs: Images as History, Matthew Brady to Walker Evans*. New York: Hill and Wang, 1989.

Vasey, Ruth. *The World According to Hollywood, 1918–1939*. Madison: University of Wisconsin Press, 1997.

Weiss, Andrea. *Vampires and Violets: Lesbians in Film*. New York: Penguin, 1993.

White, Patricia. "Black and White: Mercedes de Acosta's Glorious Enthusiasms." *Camera Obscura* 45 (2000): 227–64.

———. "The Queer Career of Agnes Moorhead." In *Out in Culture: Gay, Lesbian, and Queer Essays on Popular Culture*, edited by Corey Creekmur and Alexander Doty, 91–114. Durham, N.C.: Duke University Press, 1995.

———. *Uninvited: Classical Hollywood Cinema and Lesbian Representability.* Blooming-ton: University of Indiana Press, 1999.

Witte, Karsten. "Fetisch-Messen: Notiz zu Kenneth Anger." *Frauen und Film* 38 (May 1985): 72–78.

Yallop, David Y. *The Day the Laughter Stopped: The True Story of Fatty Arbuckle.* New York: St. Martin's Press, 1976.

INDEX

215

TEXT
10/12.5 Minion Pro

DISPLAY
Minion Pro

COMPOSITOR
Westchester Book Group

PRINTER AND BINDER
Sheridan Books, Inc.